CENTRE AND PERIPHERY
IN MODERN BRITISH POETRY

LIVERPOOL ENGLISH TEXTS AND STUDIES, 41

CENTRE AND PERIPHERY IN MODERN BRITISH POETRY

ANDREW DUNCAN

LIVERPOOL UNIVERSITY PRESS

First published 2005 by
Liverpool University Press
4 Cambridge Street
Liverpool L69 7ZU

British Library Cataloguing-in-Publication data
A British Library CIP record is available

ISBN 0-85323-744-1

Typeset in Garamond by
Koinonia, Bury, Lancashire
Printed and bound in the European Union by
Antony Rowe Ltd, Chippenham, Wilts

Contents

Acknowledgements

Acknowledgments are due to the following: the Society of Authors, as the literary representative of the Estate of Gordon Bottomley; the W. L. Lorimer Trust for permission to quote from 'Seeker, Reaper' by George Campbell Hay, now printed in his *Collected Poems*, published by Edinburgh University Press; Carcanet Press for poems by Sorley MacLean (from *From Wood to Ridge*, 1989), Michael Haslam (from *A Whole Bauble*, 1995), and Iain Crichton Smith (from *Selected Poems*, 1981); Peters Fraser & Dunlop for permission to quote from *When was Wales?*, by Gwyn A. Williams. I have been unable to trace copyright holders for Brian Higgins, J. Redwood Anderson, Meurig Walters and Phyllis Bentley. Every effort has been made to trace copyright holders for permission to reproduce material in this book, and the publishers will be pleased to be informed of any errors or omissions for rectification in any subsequent edition.

The sections on Denise Riley and Colin Simms appeared in different forms in *Angel Exhaust*, in 1995 and 1996 respectively.

Preface

Dropping the h-sound in 'have' is a sign of low prestige, dropping the glottal stop in 'what' (to replace it with a historic t) is a sign of high prestige – although these sounds are more closely related to each other than to any others. Both are laryngeals: h is the ghost sister of ʔ. They are degree zero phonemes, set outside the structure of oppositions that generates the other phonemes in the English kit, and since they are not clusters of distinctive features, and cannot be decomposed, it is not surprising that for many speakers neither is a phoneme. Few speakers are missing both of them. The Indo-European laryngeals are phantoms, conjured up by Kurylowicz to explain, as the trace of a sound which vanished around 3000 BC, the resemblance between Greek *osteon*, 'bone', and Russian *kost'*, 'bone'. For some systematists, they might be described as two realisations of the same archiphoneme, because they cannot stand in lexical opposition to each other: h occurs only as a syllable starter, the glottal stop only as a syllable terminal. Each bears a resemblance to a non-linguistic, merely muscular, act, that of breathing out or of closing the windpipe to end the sounding of a consonant at the end of a speech group. Everyone south of York can be socially placed rather accurately on the basis of a plot of the distribution of the laryngeals in their speech. We could posit a law of complementary distribution stating that 'where speaker X possesses the initial h-sound they do not possess the syllable-final glottal stop' – which in fact is untrue. The disposition of sounds illustrates a number of rules: the conservatism of school grammar, the conceptual innovation of the 'substandard', the failure of recording systems to catch something outside their code (and the consequent 'lack of history' of the popular), the excessive status/prestige reading-coding of accidental distinctions, the more consistent pursuit by colonial populations of trends 'governed' within the parent territory – familiar to students of British society. The glottal stop is the summa of the inarticulate – quite literally, since it has no articulatory features.

The hope of poets of speaking with degree zero of class background, of becoming accessible to all parts of social knowledge by losing social attitudes, of reaching the whole market by transcending the oppositions on which it is structured, places them in a position analogous to laryngeals, vulnerable and outside the carefully ordered central space. In this outside, the transcendent and the meaningless are adjacent, and interchange: as Roy Fisher and W. S. Graham were generally seen as meaningless in the 1960s, and are now accepted as transcendent, the work of J. H. Prynne is today regarded by some as meaningless, by others as sublime.

The different flavours of h and ? do not exist, and do exist because they are perceived, and are powerful, and are arbitrary at the level of the collective but unchangeable at the level of the individual. Vocal geometry is not social geometry: the different status (high and low) of these two sisters who married different men is merely social. The varying price of various features of poetic speech is arbitrary, but within the forcefield with which a society envelops its members, the structural oppositions that set the positional meaning of any feature are so 'available' that anyone will acquire them to the extent that they are not lacking in insight, or mis-anthropic, or very young. The composition of meaning out of stacks of polar oppositions is so complicated, in poetic taste, that it is elaborate and robust as well as arbitrary. Questions such as 'Why is a broad vocabulary better than a narrow one?' or 'Why do you find intelligence attractive?' can hardly be set within the terms of a system which is founded upon them, among others, as laws. The distribution of poetic responses and utterances is predictable if we choose our level of precision correctly, just as the distribution of laryngeals, and of responses valuing them, is predict-able. You can either experience the glottal stop as a sign of solidarity and equality, or as a sign of squalor and of the rules of good behaviour being breached, but the range of other responses is very limited and thinly populated. Each poem is composed of an array of stylistic gestures, and the value of these is familiar, public, and largely agreed. Taste, like the law, is based on precedents to which the new and 'meaningless' is linked by a system of classification. The attempt of poets to reach a vantage point above the system demands that they selectively delete the oppositions present in their speech, and of which the system is composed, guiding them towards discourse which is *either* the set common to all groups, minimal, de-articulated, empty of distinctive features, *or* a superset, con-taining more oppositions than any real idiolect or social place possesses, a maximum of lexicon, syntagmemes and experiences. The aim of this book is partly to outline the former, or regionalist, school, and to trace its differences from the latter, known as the small press experimental school.

The sociologist Elizabeth Bott demonstrated, in the 1950s, that different people in the same community, asked to produce a map of class structure, produced quite different maps.[1] The class system is a product of people's perceptions, organises their perception of each other, and yet is proved by these to be a dozen or so systems of intermittent reality, competing for the site at which they could be real; and this is the state of social rules in general. Writing about poetry – about how a poet perceives and how others perceive those perceptions – is an act converging on a position that does not exist; one tries to occupy a site in social space that is not there, because it is either 'above' or 'outside' the real positions that make up the local universe.

Because of this manifoldness, selective attention is a skill central to poetry, or indeed to verbalising. Eric Homberger, in his 1977 history of modern British and American poetry, remarks: 'Other schools, traditions, groups, movements, in an increasingly Balkanized context, have had to be ignored'.[2] This is the geography we all move in, a wonderful excuse for selective treatment, making the reader's choice difficult and apparently (since I obviously belong to one of these neo-Pictish hill tribes) invalidating anything that I say. Criticism failed to take in or on the explosion of British poetry in the 1960s; this book is part of a project, not all to be written by me, whose directing idea was to describe all of these 'other schools'.

It is hard to draw a satisfying border around the subject. A given design draws a perimeter around the book, leaving lots of strands which lead, in a tantalising way, outside that perimeter. Doubling the size of the book would capture more of these strands and make us less tantalised, but would make the perimeter longer and so at least double the number of strands which tantalisingly overflow it. There is no particular extent which is more satisfying than other possible extents. However, the author can reach a point of exhaustion and give up. I have not considered Irish poetry, nor poetry written in Welsh, nor more than one section of Scottish poetry. In selecting poets I have generally avoided those discussed in my other book, *The Failure of Conservatism in Modern British Poetry*,[3] and those discussed, in a satisfactory manner, by other critics. It may be as well to emphasise chronological limits: the present is the domain of being, whereas the past is the domain of knowledge, and hence of extended writing. A large part of the book already existed in 1995, and has benefited from prolonged reflection. The need for reflection, too, means that the poetry in the foreground of this study was written, mostly, between 1940 and 1980.

The use of sociology, or rather of the set of up-down valuations and of other stored collective meanings within which a poem must be written and read, makes it impossible to write about Ireland without adding a second volume. Selecting poets on the basis of their country builds the principle of nationalism into the foundations of the book. I think I have shot myself in the foot here, since this gives nationalistic English readers the perfect excuse not to read Scottish and Welsh writers, whereas one of my main intentions is to make these writers more popular. I was reading Section 2 of Bobi Jones' 1986 poem *The Nightmare of Arthur* (*Hunllef Arthur*), it got to some battles where Arthur was massacring the barbarians, and I pulled up short because these barbarians were Picts, and I immediately turned, not only against Arthur, but against Bobi Jones. Why? Because the Picts lived in Scotland and therefore were my blood relations. When one set of reading rules suddenly transmutes into another, you get the chance to compare the two, briefly making transient qualities visible and conscious. One of my internalised rules states that 'it has a higher prestige if you forgive the hereditary enemy and enjoy culture produced by English, French, or Catholic people'; it comes up on screen as I am breaking it. Momentarily, I admire myself for being detached. Then Jones goes on to say that the Caledonian Forest should be renamed from Coed Celyddon to Coed Coluddion ('Bowels Wood'), because of all the Picts being disembowelled by Arthur's heroes; and how the weapons of Kay's troops flash among the branches like red squirrels, and indeed they are stuffing every hole in the ground with corpses against the winter. Then I say 'This is obnoxious and ignoble and I don't want to read a poem where the Picts lose'. What this book is about (mine, not Jones's) is how, although the modern focus of identification and side-taking in poetry is the individual who writes it, some poets have widened this boundary by hoisting a *community* into the role of primary actor. Jones thinks that he can glorify Arthur as a Christian ruler, killing to promote his religion, when its rules say that killing is wrong; he also thinks that he can write a (300-page) poem not about the writer's personality and still have the reader identify with the flow of events. But what we see is the command to identify exposed, like pipes stacked on the pavement, with nothing running through them. The kit of shapes with which we, reading, construct identifications, zones of observation, contests, and rules for establishing the winner, mirrors sets of patterned oppositions and qualities used in daily life which, like the use-rules of laryngeals, mediate subjectivity but are collective, predictable, follow rules, and are governed by the intelligence. The rules of British society are not secret, but lack a notation.

The British Library receives all Welsh books, but does not catalogue most of them. There is a nasty political background to this. It is the reason why I went to Aberystwyth in 1997, to read some books. The publisher does not believe me when I say that the details of *Bychanfyd,* by J. R. Jones, are not available – the book is not in London or Cambridge copyright libraries. As evidence I can point to my poem, 'On the Beach at Aberystwyth', published in *Fire* magazine and written about that trip. Who will stand up and say that J. R. Jones did not exist?

Being able to stand back and observe the staging of the contest is perhaps the greatest luxury a reader is offered today; being so committed to one side that there is no possibility of joining the other switches off the intelligence because its function is complete; a writer can only be interesting by being undecided and highly alert. You can sell a romance about courtship, but not about marriage or about people who dislike the opposite sex. Detachment is the power-seeking quality of the professional classes who, as in Aristotle's magisterial summary of the skill of a rhetorician, 'to be able to argue both sides', work for the highest bidder and so permit him the choice of what is desirable. Middle-class children are punished by their parents for not being detached, and so falling from the path which leads to professional status. The employer gets value for money. If intelligence has values, it ceases to be a commodity, and so is unsaleable. If I wrote in a partisan way, the book would not be published; this is a non-prestige mode – a glottal stop. Prose – poetry too – which adopts prestige speech modes too assiduously gives off a certain smell. Emotional attachment can be achieved by everybody, it is not the prerogative of the upper middle classes, and this is why we say that detached observation of the play of forms is the highest pleasure.

Notes

1 Elizabeth Bott, *Family and Social Network* (London: Tavistock Publications, 1957).
2 Eric Homberger, *The Art of the Real* (London: Dent, 1977), p. ix.
3 Andrew Duncan, *The Failure of Conservatism in Modern British Poetry* (Cambridge: Salt Publishing, 2003).

Part 1
The Spatial Distribution of Cultural Assets

The State of Poetry

Crisis and Disaffection

The British industrial crisis of the early 1980s was especially severe and rapid in its onset; its political consequences were unusually deep because the central government was not saying that this was a disaster that it would do everything in its power to ameliorate, it was saying that any kind of intervention in favour of weak firms or large payrolls was immoral and corrupting, and that what hurt most was most virtuous. This broke the faith of entire sectors of society in government. The media correctly made the electorate aware that the Conservatives were losing elections in the North, Wales and Scotland, while winning in the South – putting strain on the notion of the United Kingdom, and on countrywide poetic links, while inducing *greater* centralisation as Westminster punished the disloyal periphery.

The graph of unemployment had been going up steadily since about 1967; the decline of Britain as a trading nation began in the nineteenth century; the number of people in employment now is not smaller than what it was in the early 1960s; the rustbelt of declining heavy-industrial regions stretches right across Europe to North Kazakhstan. None of these facts has the political importance of the contempt and hatred signalled by the Tory party for the working class outside the South-East, which made millions afraid of the government just as they became wholly dependent on it. The disintegration of the post-war social democratic consensus – however few of the victims are optimistic enough to have become 'radicalised', however many voters are content with the government and scared of change – discredited its theologians and frontmen, including the managers of the poetry world. Poetry is an art practised largely by those employed in education, which makes them state employees; a general revulsion against the clerks in the dole office is likely to be generalised to teachers. Poets frequently call on a collective, and if the notion of the collective has been identified with a sickness, with betrayal, with furious and uncalmable resentment, poetry mutates, imploding into domesticity or expanding into a revolutionary stance. The consensual identifying of the inhabitants of the South-East with evil, theft and lies wrote off London literature and made possible a new understanding of twentieth-century poetry.

Class and regional tensions have reduced to an improbable degree since I began writing this book; the rise of the new economy in regions beyond the Trent-Severn-Exe line has closed an entire period of politics and sensibility. Flushed with victory, we would nonetheless be unwise to ignore the connection between the collapse of Britain's historic export industries, an export economy dominated by arms sales, the need for American friendship to maintain this, and a strangely Republican foreign policy line being followed by Labour. The tensions in Labour policy formation between the wishes of the regions and the louder voices of the City of London (and of Washington and the WTO) have been soothed by a kind of political genius, but have clearly not disappeared into the museum.

The Mysterious Devastation of the Atlantic

It is the decline of the Atlantic trade which explains much of the regional economics of modern Britain. Regional poverty, the modern version of the East–West divide, explains both why there is so much resentment of the central region (the Midlands and the South-East), and why there are so many people looking for a more radical solution to the problems of Atlantic Britain. Sinn Fein, Plaid Cymru, the SNP, Militant Tendency, communists: in the North-West there is a striking concentration of voters who want to change not just current decisions but the rules of the political system. There has been a common decline of the Atlantic ports – Glasgow, Liverpool, Belfast, Swansea, Cardiff, and many others besides – following the decline of the Atlantic trade. Since this involved two ends (despatcher and receiver, who is also purchaser), the Celtic nature of the Western ports and their regions is only coincidental to their decline; they are Celtic because the Western half of the island, and archipelago, are Celtic, but the shift of trade is international.

However parlous the plight of the old industrial regions, central government has historically pumped resources from the taxpayer to these regions; the widespread belief that the prosperity of the South-East and Midlands core is due to money being sucked away from the North and West is harder to prove and is, I think, paranoid. The recession afflicted areas on the east side of the country (such as Tyneside) and in the centre, as well as others in the Midlands and South-East: boroughs such as Hackney and Tower Hamlets in London, for example. The geographers Kirby and Robinson point out that 'Greater London and surrounding towns constitute the country's most important manufacturing area: some 2.5 million workers are employed',[1] but clearly pressures on industry, and the exorbitant local cost of land and property, have made life difficult and insecure for the industrial workers of the South-East.

To explain the eighteenth- and nineteenth-century boom of the Atlantic ports, we have to recall the economic and political conditions which allowed, for a limited historical period, world trade to be dominated by Britain. The overseas markets to which British goods were shipped from the Atlantic ports included the USA, Canada, Australia, Latin America, South Africa, India and China. Isn't it true that they bought because they had no native industries yet; or because their financial sectors were run by British banks; or because they were colonies outright? Times change. The exports to these territories declined at a very uneven rate, and the composition of exports kept changing, while the volume at times even increased. There were no 'events' that one could dramatise or, for example, write a poem about; all the same, the curve is mostly one-way, and no-one expects Canada, Australia and the United States to become farming communities again, eager to buy British manufactured goods. American railways were once built of British steel... Meanwhile, the growth of markets in Europe was a solace at national level, but demanded port facilities in the east of the country, while manufacture could more conveniently take place close to those outward shores and to the European continent. The growth of the North Sea and Channel trade did not cause the decline of the Atlantic; rather, the latter is a secular and international curve. A decline in the new industries and new ports would do nothing to alleviate the recession in the West; on the contrary, a decline in tax revenues would bring mechanical pressure to bear on welfare expenditures and threaten the worst off. Transfer payments from the prosperous classes (and regions) of Britain to the less prosperous are no longer high in comparison with other developed countries, but the net flow has been very appreciable.

The main inheritor of British markets has been the USA, as the world's leading exporter of manufactures: I suppose I used to get angry about this, as a young man. But the logic of criminalising someone who does what you do – in this case export – is that you criminalise yourself. You can't ask someone who's undergoing unemployment, the worthlessness of their skills, destitution, despair, to be philosophical; but art has to depict situations from all angles of vision in order to reach any kind of truth.

The Atlantic was, from say 1700 up to 1950, a river on whose banks stood the Empire: when we look at the big empty docks on the West coast, the real meaning of what we see is decolonisation. Yet Britain could export to Latin America, Africa, and even the USA, if it produced the right goods. The source of economic potency is in design and manufacture, not in naval power. Nobody who lets the Japanese in would exclude us – if we produced the right goods at the right price. As for the future, no-one really expects British industry to generate new jobs; it can thrive only by such advances in overall productivity that net employment can scarcely increase.

The regionalist thesis is that regional poverty exists because people in the South-East have preferential access to the government and makers of financial policy and simply take the money away from the outlying regions. But the thesis can only apply in the domain left untouched by other theses about regional inequality: for example, that it is caused by climate and geology, so that it is the fertility of the soil, dictated by the chemistry of the rocks that weathered down to make it, which decides the wealth and population density of a province; or that it is natural communications and access to trade routes which allow business to thrive in one area, making another less attractive. Another factor, important in the distant past, was simply openness to immigration: more advanced populations swarmed in to accessible and attractive areas (principally in the South-East) and introduced more productive techniques, which made the affected provinces much richer.

The question of failures by the City, the owners of capital, and by the government, as the origins of the problems of regional industries, and so of entire regions, requires us to go outside the world of appearances, i.e. prices and profitability directing capital, to the invisible, system-founding contests of which prices are the result. Either price – both the expression and the basis of power relations – is inherent in a commodity, such as labour; or its setting is a cultural act. Scepticism about the 'black and white' of figures which show that industry is unprofitable is culturally expressed as the critique of the means of literature, the unnatural history of what seems natural. The centre is only invoked because the regions, and their business leaders, were unable to win their own struggles; but this incites the retort that commerce, finance and government collaborated to reduce the share of sales revenues that reached primary producers, and competed to deprive the latter of the voice in policy that would have allowed them a remedy. The head offices of firms are mostly in London; interestingly, it has been argued that this strengthened industry: 'the emergence of the large corporation in British industry did promote the growth of a more coherent, politically aware, industrial interest which had more influence than in the past and was closer to centres of power in London, where the head offices of these major companies were based'.[2] This allowed firms, from about 1890, to draw more capital from the financial markets, rather than relying on personal savings and retained profits, in time-hallowed fashion.

State intervention to relieve regional imbalances and help depressed areas began in 1928. Without it, regional poverty would presumably have been much worse than it is today. A glance at the map of depressed areas (first called Special Areas, then Development Areas, then Assisted Areas) will show that government assistance has been concentrated in the Celtic areas. Since 1928, there have been large flows of tax money into the regions where the greatest hostility to the state and to centralised power prevails. Political divisions about small government or big also have a regional basis; in the 1980s, political commentators voiced fears that the Conservative and Labour Parties might be migrating towards a regional basis, rather than an ideological, moral or policy basis. The balance between national and local government has been under attack, and has been changed by reforms whose results have been extensive and controversial.

British radicalism, in poetry as in politics, has drawn much of its personnel and ideas from the Highlands, or adjacent regions, and from Ireland. In those Atlantic provinces, the ideas of capitalism, of rule from Westminster, of loyalty to a shared British enterprise which was basically fair and successful, were rejected by entire communities. If everyone had a job who wanted one, the idea of rejection wouldn't be so emotive today. When someone speaks of the centre, we also have to understand by that word, sometimes, the central body of opinions – about the sanctity of property, the undesirability of state intervention, the benevolence of the corporation, the goodness of the great, the desirability of things as they are now – which upholds the social order. Even if only a minority seriously oppose these, outside the storms of youth and the rare accesses of rage, that minority has included a remarkable number of poets. If you maintain these opinions, you presumably do accept that they will bring disasters, as they have in the past, and as they are doing now. Property is a collective verbal fiction, from which individuals with the power of speech always have the possibility of withdrawing their consent. The linguistic field of the poetry I am describing contains the different effects of political opposition, phonetic diversity and cognitive economic bases as material traces in its verbal fabric. Their distribution map reflects diversity from the behavioural norms of the metropolitan regions, where the population of the island is thickly concentrated. More elusive is the reaction to stylistic devices which are excluded, or misused, because they are associated with loyalty to the central authorities, as innovations reach outlying regions in the wrapping of imports from the centre. The political failure of minority parties leaves their adherents at a certain distance away from reality, and puts stress on language; as negation in the symbolic domain has become the residual act of unsuccessful righteousness, poetry is drawn into gestures of defiance and pride. Part of the appeal of avant-garde forms may be the wish not to give countenance to the chains of legitimation and webs of validation of the prevailing social system. For the reader, what is not being said may add up to zero.

The metropolitan and social-democratic poetry system, represented by magazines such as the *London Magazine*, *Encounter* and *Poetry Review*, by Radio Three and the British Council, was in a poor position when attacked, because of its lack of gifted poets and its exclusion of any serious political poetry. More or less in coordination with the rise of the New Right, it was winning a bitter battle against the ultra-politicised and formally challenging poets of the British Poetry Revival, erased from the public scene by a new alliance of populism and conservatism, closely resembling the Tory alliance of the tabloids and the wealthy. Anti-Thatcherism meant, in poetic terms, vociferous rage against Morrison and Motion's *Contemporary British Poetry*. It was a natural metaphor, since almost anyone who could read could see that this anthology was an attempt, *à la* Thatcher, to redefine everything radical over the previous twenty years as lunacy, subversion and godless communism. This mapping, whereby traditional:radical in poetry translated right:left in politics, was carried out by most readers, but was not literally true, and presents difficulties for the analyst. The conservative victory meant, like so many other counter-revolutions, the decay of the system through its failure to co-opt the most gifted of its 'internal enemies'; its victory was too sweeping, and therefore all innovative poetry was consigned to the unreviewed and undistributed small press world, to thrive in calm hostility.

In poetry, the avant-garde was locked out *en masse*, rather than being taken in and fed in a kind of zoo.

A wide range of anti-Thatcherite critics have mistakenly equated the mainstream, as defined by this anthology (and sustained by dozens of other editors, of course), with the urban South-East and the 'cultural iron triangle' of London–Oxford–Cambridge. This immediately, by the logic of oppositions, defined anything from Newcastle, Cardiff or Glasgow as radical, even when textual examination could show it to be conservative and worn out. It also effaced most of the formally radical poets, the stars of the Poetry Revival as defined by Eric Mottram, because they lived within the 'cultural triangle'. This disastrous reduction of artistic relations to geographical ones paralleled a wilful ignorance of the fact that London had the country's largest concentrations of Labour voters and of the unemployed, and the most radical Labour groups in the country. Part of our effort now must be to rewrite the modern history of poetry in poetic terms.

It is time to record some concrete details. A partial mapping of contemporary poets follows, to set out what my generalisations are founded on.

- Metropolitan mainstream: James Fenton, Andrew Motion, Tony Harrison, Hugo Williams.
- Formally radical poetry created away from the South-East: W. S. Graham, Roy Fisher, Basil Bunting, Edwin Morgan, Glyn Jones, Joseph Macleod, Lynette Roberts, Ted Hughes, John Riley, Peter Redgrove, Colin Simms, David Black, Alexander Hutchison, Ken Smith, John James, R. F. Langley, David Barnett, David Chaloner, John Ash, Tony Jackson, Brian Marley, John Seed, Barry MacSweeney, Michael Haslam, Grace Lake, Peter Didsbury, Jeffrey Wainwright, Peter Finch, Frank Kuppner, Kelvin Corcoran, Ian Duhig, John Goodby, W. N. Herbert, Elisabeth Bletsoe, Nick Macias, Nic Laight, David Greenslade, Rob MacKenzie.
- Within the regional group we also find poets who are traditionalist and, sometimes, sub-literary: Emyr Humphreys, George Mackay Brown, R. S. Thomas, Derick Thomson, Iain Crichton Smith, Sorley MacLean, T. S. Law, Bobi Jones.
- Radical or counter-cultural poets from within the south-eastern region: Charles Madge, Francis Berry, Christopher Middleton, Asa Benveniste, J. H. Prynne, Tom Raworth, Andrew Crozier, Anthony Barnett, Allen Fisher, Iain Sinclair, John Welch, B. Catling, Ulli Freer, Kevin Nolan, Tom Lowenstein, Martin Thom, Denise Riley, Bill Griffiths, Gavin

Selerie, Nigel Wheale, Jeremy Reed, John Wilkinson, cris cheek, Tony Lopez, Maggie O'Sullivan, Adrian Clarke, Robert Sheppard, Michael Ayres, Simon Smith, D. S. Marriott, David Rushmer, Helen Macdonald, Robert Smith, Vittoria Vaughan.

The above classification is meant to be easily memorable, and so has not been subdivided. No claim is made that these distinctions apply to all the significant poets on the scene, or that the radical:traditional opposition is more than a schematic reading of a complex landscape. The number of poets listed comes from distaste at the selectivity and incompleteness that too many critics have shown in presenting a 'map' of the poetic scene.

Giving Away Power: The Question of Guilt

The linkage between white educated articulate man as poet and white educated articulate man as civil servant or manager is bizarre, thoroughly unacceptable to all the poets, and accepted by the harmonic logic of analogy shared by almost everyone else. Illiterates have low status, low income, and restricted economic possibilities; higher literacy correlates with wealth and status, and to miss this you would really have to be hard of hearing. The contemporary poet is grimly trying to become nativised, to merge with a community. He says 'I'm one of you'; and the reader replies '*You're* one of *me*?' The project is not succeeding. The secret wish is to become the Other, to shed at the same time guilt and moral restraint, to go bush: me native, you anthropologist.

Guilt at speaking about how society works comes from epistemological challenges posed by the colonies struggling for liberation, by the working classes, by women, by the young, by ethnic minorities within the metropolis, by the 'peripheral' nationalities of Ireland, Scotland and Wales. The strain on public utterance comes from its linkage to governmental action, itself under pressure because it was expanding so fast in the post-war decades; the more people expected of the government, the more they would fight to control its policy.

The flight to the margins comes from a durable and unbearable condition of anxiety about being in charge. It is more frightening than the earlier radical ambition of seizing power and solving the functional problems. The possibility of fundamental change was a quality of the system, and profound pessimism about the system includes acceptance of its unreformability.

Guilt and grievance management are important parts of poetics. The sensation of guilt pervades the cultural atmosphere. In the perception of the collective, it is attributed to those who are or were in charge, and therefore to writers as soon as they claim either to know what the rules are, or how people should behave. Writing a philosophical poem makes you more analogous to the mighty, therefore more guilty, than if you write a rock song. Intellectual poetry is beset by a structural analogy of ultra-literacy: as it pursues literacy along its own axis, as it sheds sympathetic circularity and the egocentricity of the here and now, it resembles the discourse of the most powerful and authoritative, and is structurally obliged to be politically critical, to break down the status system and favour the unsung and excluded. The poets become ghosts within their own poems; the gesture is like postgraduate students of the elite faculties of philosophy handing out pamphlets at the gates of the Renault works. The poem finds its place on a spectrum that ranges from flaccid and indifferent, but full of solidarity and reassurance, to edgy, intellectually demanding, original in its way of seeing the world, but also tallying with the discourse of the upper middle class and of formal situations. The ellipsis is a figure that can signal either solidarity in low status or socially exclusive expecta-tions of shared knowledge and astuteness; it changes flavour from poem to poem, or even from hour to hour, being merely a telltale where the charges of malevolence or trust generated by the situation as a whole find an outlet.

Writing poetry that is youthful, empty-headed and drained of content may be an attempt to avoid the guilt gathering in the air. Another tactic is to attribute guilt to a group that is intellectually and politically distinct from yourself, with advocacy of the wronged group. Another is to make a gesture of giving away power, which assumes or pretends that you had administrative control of it in the first place: the poem as a ritual on the lawns of Government House where the colonial governor, resplendent in plumes and sword, gives away control of the poem and the claim to be able to think.

One of the catchphrases of the day is *radical subversion*, claimed for almost everyone. Yet the political system I grew up with has proved remarkably stable, or indifferent: property prices have almost ceaselessly gone up, the middle class expands apparently without limits, the power of liquid capital is much greater and much less challenged today than twenty-five years ago. This subversion which leaves the system it attacks untouched is none. Whatever phrase we use of it would have 'ineffectual' as its qualifying word. We might venture on: the hypocritical denial of an inferior status. Or: a rigged verbal contest which is roundly lost by the rigger. It is not even clear that modern poetry has managed to subvert its enfieffed and stultified predecessor; the poets of the 1950s seem to have succumbed to mortality rather than to any daring revolt of the critics. However, where so many people claim to be doing something, that something draws our attention: radical subversion of authority is the final goal of modern poetry, a consummation we would recognise, not from ever having experienced it, but because so many thousands of experiences have supplied fakes, spoofs and imitations of it, degrading and revealing the goal all at once.

The more of the world the poet pulls into the text, the more likely it becomes that a reversal of power will take place and the more organised voices from the world will prove the poet weaker and take over, repeating what was already said. As H. P. Lovecraft says, 'Call not that up which ye cannot put down'. Wherever the contested point of this struggle is becomes the area of maximum attention, the unsteady and even shattering pivot of the poem.

The Cultural Politics of Littleness

Recent British poetry shows a split between 'raising and belonging' poets, whose work is an expression of belonging to a 'community' and tries to raise its self-esteem or public image, and personal poets who have developed an individual style and are, variously, expressive of personal feelings, socially critical and radical, or intellectual. The former trend may exist more in the propaganda of its publishers and promoters than on the page, but could be identified in anthologies such as *The Urgency of Identity*, *Sixty Women Poets*, *Ladder to the Next Floor* and *Poetry with an Edge*. It can be said to represent that portion of the New Left which abandoned, or never held, advanced theoretical positions and, concomitantly, entered the state service at the local level and helped to sustain society, rather than remaining critical and exilic. These two stances, made solid only by an act of intellectual fiction, and occupying parts of a sociocultural space which contains many others, are diametric opposites (each one slights the assets which the other holds), contending for the space which is not filled by official or by amateur poetry; the shape of their extension into the stylistic, historical and sociological planes is the subject of the present work.

From the point of view of many theorists, Labour is a capitalist party and the Conservatives a socialist one. Such theorists make much of the non-partisan nature of major policies of British central government. The Tories, during the 1950s, did little to reverse the revolutionary shifts made by Labour in 1945–51, and Labour, elected to power in May 1997, have not wished to reverse the radical changes made by the Conservatives to trade union law, or to renationalise privatised industries. Frustrations with this common approach have been expressed through minority parties or through declining to vote; a decline in the popularity of both major parties at once comes and goes, but was at centre stage in the 1970s, when all governments were discredited by a price revolution. A system allows the major parties to scoop up all the spoils, and they stand opposed to forces, inchoate, marginal or frustrated, which reject that system. Parties that believe in the small scale would include the Liberals and Social Democrats, their successors the Liberal Democrat party, Plaid Cymru, and the Scottish Nationalists. The typical action of government, faced with a problem, is to appoint an administrative body to deal with it, working in an office, paid for by taxation, accountable to a central ministry, and staffed by professionally qualified workers, who increasingly are also graduates. The thesis of community politics is that the problem would be better solved by initiatives within the community, where the citizen supplies effort (or gifts of resources) rather than taxes, where the workers have no difficulty in communicating with the people being helped, and where they are accountable to the people all around them. The community develops pride and self-confidence, and the weaker members of society acquire skills and cohesion to solve their own problems, rather than becoming dependent.

Catchphrases such as 'grass roots', 'the community' and 'small is beautiful' bring to everyone's mind a set of arguments against state intervention and against firms employing more than half a dozen people. Small-scale gestures in poetry may be an expression of a political philosophy, as vehicles for a burden, in the sense of an integrated set of political theses and allegories. The growth of local government has meant an increase in the ranks of the middle class, also tilting the numerical balance of that class away from commerce and towards the state service: it directs higher education by absorbing so many of its products; it is caught up with the increase in specialisation, in educational levels, and in the numbers of professionals, which has been going on for at least 150 years; it goes along with great increases in the functions of government, and in taxation. If someone uses the catchphrase 'bureaucracy', this in practice means that they think government should do less, or at least spend less. No-one boasts of the increase in government employees; it is in fact a non-partisan truth that 'there should be fewer of them', and both Labour and Conservatives have laid claim to being communitarian parties on many occasions; the gap between communitarian rhetoric and professional-administrative practice is subtle and can be displaced onto non-voluntary factors, such as *force majeure*.

The split between Labour and Conservative is also evasive in this area; in so far as the Conservatives are a pro-capitalist party, their model has the town being filled with office blocks filled with graduate, white-collar professionals, following a rational-administrative set of rules, and working for a headquarters far away. These buildings belong to corporations, and they fulfil people's needs in exchange for cash. The household is still held incapable of fulfilling people's real needs, this time on the basis of local advantages of production rather than of socialism. However, in ceremonial speech the party claims to be on the side of small businesses.

There is a Green communitarianism, not compulsory for environmentalists. A belief in self-sufficiency asks to reduce trade; but trade is the basis of city life, and of large societies; smaller social units would not want to receive government from a higher unit, and in fact the reward of having power over your own life restored would compensate for the impoverishment caused by dismantling the world specialisation of labour and production. The deep attachment to the land which is the motive for looking after it properly is easier for 'local people', whose psychological radius is narrow but intense. It is an effective point that corporate managers and owners, government ministers and civil servants, ignore the local effects of their decisions only because they are physically far removed from the site (of an aluminium smelter or power station, for instance) over which they have power. Although Green thinking certainly includes world treaties adhered to by governments (over greenhouse gas emissions, CFC emissions, whale hunting and so on), exponents who do not want a strong local political power to emerge at the expense of big corporations and central government are very rare. One version of self-reliance would abolish food imports: no more hard wheat from the Canadian prairies, back to rye and barley bread from local grains used to cloudy skies. The calories spent on transport and storage are unnecessary to the core task of supplying food calories to a human mouth. The dislike of the wide radius is put on stage in the protest over the building of motorways; the thoroughfares are a public good, benefiting their future users, but the Greens think, consensually, that people ought to stay where they are, that long-distance trade is a bad thing, and that businesses that want to grow ought to be ashamed of themselves.

There is a feminist version of communitarianism, which starts from the position that men will behave badly so far as it is in their power, and that reductions of their power will reduce the scope and reach of their badness. High office, capital wealth, modern weapons and high technology are seen as instruments of male domination; they incite competition, make the means by which struggles for domination are carried out terribly destructive, and fund the domination of women, largely deprived of these instruments. Large organisations are conducive to male power, as opposed to matricentric ones (such as a primary school might be). Feminism is happier with the design of a thousand leaders of small communities, if only to disperse and de-concentrate the tumescent power now held by heads of state. The distaste of feminism, from its origins around 1970, for leaders makes it quite dissimilar to political parties, trade unions, and so on; its approach to changing society problematises the behaviour complex of party politics, side-taking, ideological position, polarisation, antagonism and winning. It also differs from other communitarian movements by its acceptance of Britain's largely urban nature, and its lack of reliance on place.

A third devolutionary current is the small nations model, which wants to dissolve the British state but is quite happy for Scottish and Welsh states to replace it. Whereas there are quite a number of Central Belt Socialists in Scotland who are in favour of a high-spending state based in Edinburgh, the equivalent position in Wales may not in fact exist: Labour voters do not want an independent Wales, and nationalists are anti-state, wishing to devolve its functions to parish level. Saunders Lewis's writings of the 1930s are oddly like the deep-Green vision of autarkic communes, although what he had in mind was probably feudalism.

Regional Intellectual History

Existing intellectual histories deal only with the thoughts of an elite of trained thinkers, giving them more space the more they fulfil a set of criteria of value which are clearly not shared by the majority of the population. Using such books as a guide to the ideas governing poems can only lead to shock and bewilderment, as poets have used quite different (and 'lower'?) sets of ideas. Histories explaining geographical variation in the distribution of ideas, or at what rate they permeate millions of people (rather than a few dozen professionals) are hard to come by. It has been claimed that the most technical and remote philosophy is practised preferentially in the universities, and particularly in the most prestigious universities, and that philosophy more oriented towards questions of how to lead life, how to be good, how to love, is pursued by lesser thinkers in proportion to the low and peripheral status of their appointment or their place of learning. The codeword 'mentality' is used to indicate that a historian is writing about the thought of ordinary people rather than of professional philosophers.

Such a thesis is advanced in Beveridge and Turnbull's *The Eclipse of Scottish Culture, or Inferiorism and the Intellectuals*,[3] which tries to write an intellectual history of modern Scotland, testing the hypothesis that there is a separate thought of the North, rather than simply a few million people who either form a public for English philosophers, or are so poorly informed that they can barely be said to think at all. Looking at a variety of Scottish thinkers (chiefly John Anderson, Alasdair MacIntyre and R. D. Laing), they draw a picture which is consistent, and which can there-fore point to a generator within society, rather than within 'thought' itself; and which links thought to morality, reducing the separation between the social being and the philosophising one. This inclination can be called communitarian. It makes the philosopher less powerful, less autonomous, less of a deity outside the picture which he constructs; but also less isolated and more useful. It is very close, as the authors admit, to the intellectual and moral attitudes of the Scottish clergy, and so to the previous dispensa-tion. If the principle of the most prestigious modern thought is to ignore the links of the mind to morality and to social networks, this may not be simply a correct tendency but rather part of a deliberate strategy to achieve maximum separation from the clergy, in order to seize the authority and state patronage that they once possessed or still do. The autonomy of books, and of the most highly educated minority, may not be purely desirable.

It is hard to find anything that could pass for an intellectual history of Wales. In fact, the absence of any Welsh intellectuals (more accurately, the need of someone who wants to act in that way to leave or renounce Wales) is the most significant point to grasp. The weakness of the secular intellectuals as a stratum has allowed a much greater development of religious opinion, of which one indicator among many is that all signi-ficant modern Welsh poets have been Christians. The attempt to provide a global solution to all the problems of life corresponds to a small number of educated people, and a lack of specialisation among them. Two examples of Welsh nationalist self-consciousness are *The Taliesin Tradition*, by Emyr Humphreys, and *Diwedd prydeindod*, by Gwynfor Evans. Both are strongly communal in approach, and the way they are written suggests that an inability to abstract and to count or measure follows from a strong identification with the group. The theme of the separation of different parts (or modes, or stable functional states) reminds us of what Bourdieu claims of the middle class in general, namely that it has a more detached attitude to social roles, and is more content to accept that any form of behaviour does not express 'the whole man', but is partial and stylised to achieve a single partial goal.

We can attempt to link this to the belief of many cultural spokesmen in the sixties that specialisation was unnecessary, and that, once they had grasped the key of wisdom (biochemical, sexual, Trotskyite, religious, etc.), they could solemnly pronounce on all subjects without bothering with detailed study. The relics of this moment are a violent dislike of gurus, and a violent craving for someone who possesses such a key, often experienced by the same person and even in the same moment. The connection is difficult to draw for lack of separation: every extremely vivid vision of the whole leads to intense scrutiny of details, to confirm the glimpsed pattern, and every intense scrutiny of details leads to new visions of the whole. We can trace this dialectic more palpably within individual lives: the partial vision is terrifying, because it suggests that our individual lives are cut off from everything grand and sublime except a tiny specialism which we conquer by sacrificing our entire lives to it; but as consumers we seek differentiation at every point, and this is built into all the practices around consumption. The role played by the personality in art is dictated by this opposition; the personality is our niche in the market, because it is unique and so differentiated. Yet the art must be impersonal to allow someone else to possess it. Each poet acts as a guru and empurpled bishop as soon as they become euphoric, and before they sober up. The counter-cultural hope for a deeper sense of community, mediated by new communications media and given right of way by the destruction of the boundaries holding up the nuclear family and private property, was followed by a new reliance on the corporation, or rather on a topology of thousands of corporations each satisfying a precise need in a narrow way, a set of social exchanges characterised by depersonalisation and lack of affect.

Local and Spiral Intelligentsia

Social anthropology gives us the useful concept of the *spiralist*, someone who moves horizontally across the country in order to rise in his or her profession. Spiralists are the opposite of, in popular parlance, 'genuine locals'. Local politics in Britain are often blurred by arguments about people who lack local roots because they are spiralists and have not lived in the place for long enough. They are felt to be lacking in respect and to be the carriers of dangerous new ideas. Evidence of these concerns is found less in poetry than in the coded messages in the biographies on book jackets. If someone gives profuse details about where they were born, grew up, and live ('I have three sets of roots...'), and nothing about their stylistic choices or philosophy of art, that indicates anxiety about accusations of 'rootlessness'; someone who gives the space to what they think about poetry probably does, then, think about poetry. Their jacket-bio is more likely to list the institutions they have been attached to than a town. Someone who believes in the new is not able, simultaneously, to claim that they are deeply rooted in a place and community. The audience, or writers, of raising and belonging poetry can partly be defined as 'writing and thinking people who are not associated with a university', whereas intellectual poetry is so associated.

The modern cheapness of information places a national and international culture in the hands of all. The logical unit of study is not the region, which is neither closed nor entire, but the system of taste, which generates oppositions and divisions which structure people's identifications, revolts and side-taking. Within a given region, strong local identification as a rule for choosing what to read is not a property of the reading public as a whole, but of a certain fraction. Although only a minority of the users of bookshops or libraries, they are significant either as activists, publishing poetry and shaping taste, or as poets. However deeply they burrow into the buried local culture (and this is especially rewarding and deep in the case of Wales and Scotland), however consistent they are in their psychological direction over decades, we are bound to suspect that the behavioural rules of those localisms are just like those of similar localisms all over the former Commonwealth, so that the opposition localism:metropolitanism is a constant in Wales, New South Wales, English-speaking South Africa, Ontario and so on, and that the discourse in which localists speak of their localism was not locally invented. If we return to the sixth-form classroom where teenagers are undertaking practical criticism of a few modern poems, we can see that the pupils are unstable: the learning process offers them the possibility of social advancement and perhaps of originating culture, but also drops them into a realm of consuming and of being culture which is highly competitive, and where they have none of the assets for which people strive, and so have initially the lowest status. The more they value the culture on offer, the more they subscribe to the superiority enjoyed over themselves by all university students of English literature all around the world. The more aware they are, the more they know that what they know may have been known by hundreds of others, in equal excitement, before them. In order to achieve originality (a value valued by the system as a corollary of finding most of its own verbal productions so boring) one must penetrate far more deeply into the system and internalise the knowledge which it offers, and of which it consists. Of course, one can say no. The pupil has local roots in a neighbourhood which are at odds with the essentially national or international knowledge being offered by the books; the pupils fail to understand the texts unless they can be translated into the terms of their personal emotional experience, fail in the terms of the academic system if they do not translate their own personal experience into the terminology and operations of thought acceptable to it. This experience sets up three terms: local and concrete, local and academic, non-local glamorous and literary. People who have been through this remaking experience, and whose ideas about literature were shaped by it, are bound to conceive literary taste through those three terms, whatever more powerful conceptual sets, and whatever new information, they add to them later. Poetry which arrives as literature, but which also claims the asset of localism, will exert a strong attraction on a certain proportion of however many thousand pupils have gone through this sixth-form mill. Because certain educational structures – broadly conceived to include set poets, the essay as a genre, practical criticism, certain prejudices of poetic taste, ideas about how a lesson is organised and so on – have been reproduced in secondary education around the English-speaking world, certain structures of reading and receiving a poem are also globally widespread, and we would not be wholly wrong if we imagined them to produce similar poems by and for the alumni of those classes.

Remoteness is an advantage in a poet chosen as object of possession, because it splits off the novice's emotional loyalties and inner feelings from the petty and everyday reality of school discipline and of still-childish dependence; one seventeen-year-old will choose Neruda, Brecht, Claudel or Charles Olson as a hero-figure precisely because these figures are separable from the schoolteachers. Other novices outflank the school system in the other direction by an extended localism, in which they seek out poets of regional odour, who are also not found in the respectable anthologies.

Some pupils fail in terms of the rules governing the courses, which, with their freight of poetic practices and know-how, fail in the eyes of a certain proportion of pupils, who selectively or globally reject the system. From this turbulence of contradictions and oscillations emerges the distribution of tastes whereby one set of individuals are localists and one set are oriented to national, or international, poets. For someone to emerge as a Welsh-thinking reader who reads only poetry written in Wales, consistently rejecting poetry from England and being offended or humiliated when a good poem is written in England, it is not enough that they were born in Wales, they must also have gone through a moment of marrying a taste, when they chose to be a regionalist.

Because the space of the poem is different from a literal physical space, stress on physical space competes with the poem, threatens it with shallowness and dependence. If we imagine all the children of a certain age in a town, we can see that some did not take to reading at all, but remained obstinately stuck in the here and now, unarguably local; the localists are in fact part of a spectrum of positions, where the extreme is occupied by those who never read at all, then successively come those who read but insist on it being as close to their daily life as possible, then those who read and accept books from far away. The other extreme position in this series might be those who deny any reference to the outside world within the text, severing any connection between the text and literal places, real people, or real life. The book plays every role from dead space to totality. Anyone in any position is liable to be outflanked by someone else who then tries to deny them the (positional) assets they believed themselves to possess. Competition and name-calling are part of the social complex around books, and it is very hard to avoid being accused, simultaneously, of conservatism and inauthenticity.

The boundary between school and university is an initial spiral path; you go to school where you live (unless it is a private school), but in Britain teenagers generally choose a university away from their home town, because leaving home is symbolically important and living at home would mean missing much of the student experience. The dissolution of a school year-group at the end of the second sixth-form year, when everyone disperses so that you can't stay 'there' even if you stay in town, is significant for a poet's tone of address. The poet is pitchforked into a new daily society (since almost all modern British poets are university graduates, another 'rule') and so there is a rift flanked by two societies, the home town and schoolfriends and then the university and new friends. A nineteen-year-old may well be faced, six times a year, by abrupt shifts from one place to another which are also shifts of emotional positions and social roles. The role of ideas and book-learning in British life is conditioned by this geographical and social arrangement. The way in which the new student takes them up depends on their reaction to the split, as contempt for ideas may reflect loyalty to the old community and enthusiasm for them may reflect enthusiasm for the new society. Some poetry expects you to be pitched wholeheartedly into the literary space and what it offers, other productions seem to assume that poetry doesn't really work and that we aren't really at home there.

Because secondary education has the role of a qualifying round for higher education, the two are differentiated, such that elements of linguistic style that are a vice in one sector appear as a virtue in the other, and vice versa; the difference of 'level' implies variation of lexical discrimination, of originality of content, of reflexivity, of the ratio of memorisation to doubt. The split may be shifted, so that sixth forms belong with higher education, and the real split occurs when the typical child is sixteen – and when, of course, a very high proportion of children leave full-time education altogether. There are, probably, systematic differences between poets who teach in schools and poets who teach at university level, and if we can disengage the differences in the linguistic regimes of the classroom environment at these two levels, we may be able to characterise poetic differences as projections of them. Because the stage at which someone leaves full-time education is strongly correlated with their socio-economic status, these fine differences of style may also carry a cachet of ease and superiority, which is attractive in itself – a term from a different game than acquiring knowledge. This split (secondary:higher) is correlated with the splits local inhabitant:spiralist and regionalist:metropolitan, and it reflects the pushing of literacy along its own axis, so that different sectors of the middle class, and different styles of poetry, are separated by the totality with which they accept the printed medium, and the set of data and procedures to which it gives access. At the moment when language is symbolic power, to use Bourdieu's term, fine gradations in the amount of it that an individual possesses, as legitimised and accepted by the listeners, acquire great importance.

The poetry of maximum prestige is known as modernism, by a fiction which gives it an aura of provenance. In reality, events in nightclubs around 1913 have almost no bearing on contemporary poetry, and the features of what is called 'modernist' poetry correlate much better with well-recorded features of middle-class speech than with the poems of T. S. Eliot, Ezra Pound or Edith Sitwell. Even the fact that a minority are desperate to acquire these traits, and regard them as 'superior', while the majority neither desire them nor look up to them, parallels the features of educated speech. They are consensual only within range of the more exalted English departments. This poetry rewards those who possess the qualities valued in higher education, while withholding rewards from those who lack these qualities (and cannot decode the verse), so it can be equated with the upper middle class; the raising and belonging sort of poetry rewards the qualities valued by schoolteachers, so can be equated with the lower middle class. The fraction of the (non-technical) middle class that identifies with schoolteaching, or with social work, has to be outgoing and non-selective, it has to value its human charges; originality would be a fault threatening comprehension, and refinement of language appears as narcissism. The number of schoolteachers far outnumbers the number of teachers in higher education, although this ratio keeps shifting; so it is predictable that there should be much poetry, of the raising and belonging sort, which has no pretensions to style, but in which the patient sticking to human subjects who are unattractive, and who are boring to read about, plays a central role. Higher education expects a selected audience (most children will never get into those classrooms) and promotes differentiation by punishing failure to specialise. It is hierarchically higher; both students, as future graduates, and teachers are of higher status than their equivalents in schools. Since the whole school system values literacy, those who possess and display higher literacy are admired by school-teachers; as poets, they possess both higher prestige and a smaller reader-ship. And they attract resentment; modernist poetry does not enjoy prestige (although it has a highly educated audience) partly because of class resentment from beneath, but also because of the amazing factional in-fighting within the super-literate group engaged with that poetry: the position, implied by the whole geometry of our social space, of being Poetic plus Superliterate is so prestigious that no-one will concede it to anyone else, so that the opinions in circulation are too heated and dissonant for any narrative of reputation to escape into the wider world. The satisfying superiority of the modernist–small press scene in creativity and originality is a muffled report, because only a narrow spectrum of the public values those qualities, and a much broader spectrum values loyalty and diligence.

The Regionalist Poetic Ideology

The traces of this spiral split in poetry are subtle and sometimes dubious. The stylistic carrier of devolutionary ideas would include avoidance of experiment, associated with metropolitan artists and audiences; avoidance of the literary register, as opposed to the colloquial, and so of anything specific to literature; avoidance of ideas (other than attacks on govern-ment and cities); avoidance of introspection and self-expression, since individuals in a community are like each other, and personal feelings are deviant; avoidance of stylistic originality, which sounds too much like competitiveness and the attempt to split the community; avoidance of thought, felt to belong to an educated minority, and so to be a threat to communal unity; avoidance of specialised knowledge, felt to inhere in an inorganic, instrumental mode of scientific perception. Writing in an unoriginal and old-fashioned way is badged as use of local resources. Reliance on traditionalist techniques may be an attempt to form an alliance with a non-literary readership, to whom these forms are familiar, instead of with a literary group of fellow-writers, scattered over different regions and countries and therefore 'non-local'. It is clear that most British poetry belongs to this mould. Anyone else is rebellious and at risk.

The attempts to shed outsider status and become accepted as part of the community follow a few well-known and convergent paths: centring poems on continuity, ancestry, culture and identity, on landscape, family, objects, ethnicity, roots, religion, and so on. I shall refer to this complex as the regionalist ideology. It seems unfair to label this school Blood and Soil, since they may not be wholly aligned with the peasant poets lined up by Will Vesper for Nazi anthologies (the *Jahresernte* series); but a handy mnemonic might be Blood Sod Spades God. Apart from ancestry (and heritage), the earth is the other fetish of authenticity, boiled down from centuries of peasant greed. Where attempts to empathise with other people and even with animals fail, geology comes on stage as a kind of heat death of the mind, an unimaginably late stage of decay. Where 'up in the air' is the hated state, being 'down to earth' regards stones as the perfect subject, and identifies the poet-patriarch with a stone, perhaps in the form of a standing stone, crag or mountain.

Jeremy Hooker's exegesis, in *The Presence of the Past*, of the Anglo-Welsh Second Flowering (and presumably also of his own poetry, written in Wales) is remarkable in contemporary British literature for articulating a whole theory that justifies a poetic practice, and relates it to history, politics, sociology and ethics.[4] The poet is to achieve authenticity by describing a particular place and by tracing its history. Partly this is a reaction against general schemes of history, found wanting, and against the poetry that they inspired: Hooker wants poetry to be true, and it is true by being precisely located. Another part is the resentment of poetry in the third person: following the poem 'Ars Poetica' by Anthony Conran, Hooker wants poetry to relate to its human subjects as I to you, not as the speaking self to someone referred to in the third person. (Somewhere behind this must lie Martin Buber's theories about Ich–Du relationships.) The people of the selected place are to be described faithfully, and accountably. The poem is to be filled up with information about places, people and work.

Its brilliance allows us to overlook for the moment the possible gaps between Hooker's exegesis and the ideas of the several poets concerned. In fact, his theory is the clearest statement yet of the regionalist ideology. Where it falls short is in the aesthetic drive. All its imperatives are ethical; it's quite possible to write poetry which has all the virtues Hooker recommends and which is artistically dead. Although I've pointed to theological precepts behind Hooker's thesis, I also think that his recommendations induce the virtues of a good administrator: adapted to local conditions, careful to get facts right, keen to conciliate local opinion, selfless and impersonal, obeying ethical imperatives. In line with these, it is more about avoiding failure than about achieving success. It doesn't leave much room for subjectivity. The image of the parish as the horizon of all action, and therefore all thought, and therefore all knowledge, reminds us that the parish or vestry was formerly the unit of local government, and notably of primary education and poor relief.

The talk around literature has focused a great deal in the past thirty years on the incredibility of literature, on the shattering of the literary text by the return to autonomy, and secession, of the (virtual) human figures inside it. A certain feminism holds that all accounts of female motivation written by men are false; we cannot grasp the communitarian ethos unless we accept, if only transiently, that all accounts of a human's awareness written by someone else are false. If our knowledge of what is inside other people's heads is conjectural, surely we should welcome conjecture. Regionalist poetry resists the temptation to explain people's motivation and state of mind.

The opposite policy extends a quality of middle-class speech, which is to describe things exophorically, by classification in a series (also a lexical series) which composes examples from a wide geographical range, passing over direct affective reactions. The ideologies of Marx and Freud seem to be an overfulfilment of these rules, and sum up what regionalism objects to. Both are mediated largely through print, so that mastery of them is confined to the most educated, or the most curious. They both deny the accuracy of the awareness of the average citizen: his or her understanding of business and sexuality, topics of central place in his or her existence, is tossed aside, and the expert (even a seventeen-year-old with access to a public library) knows more about them than the social actor himself or herself. We can reverse this triumph of study over living to observe that the attractions of reading are maximised by this access to hidden truths, and that there is a set of valuations of the power of the knowledge hidden in books, serially distributed, of which the belief that Marx and Freud are true is the maximum term, the extreme pole. This extreme quality may associate it with adolescence, or with a dominant social group, which has no need to qualify its ideas. This pole may be shared with other salvation religions. I mention these two because very few people today believe in them, and so the resentment felt by communitarians about (several generations of) past metropolitans is justified, and the position which is against abstraction, modernity, a general science of man, book learning, experts and so on has this genuine basis. I shall call these systems apocalyptic knowledge, since they involve access to a revelation (*apocalypsis*) of what is hidden to the uninitiated, and from the humans who are the objects, rather than subjects, of knowledge. The serial scale also affects someone's belief in the powers of the writer, and people who put a high value on these powers evidently spend more time reading (or writing). The writer's account of people's awareness, as the main content of history, competes with their own accounts; the dramatic needs of literature seem to rely on a contradiction between the awareness of the individual agent and the real course of past and future events around and over them. We can imagine three positions here: writing only autobiography, which reports on first-person conscious awareness of the workings of the self; belief in apocalyptic knowledge; and rejection of the possibility of knowledge, and of the usefulness of writing.

Much literary behaviour is only explicable by positing a residual glitter of salvation cults within poetry. The anxiety that other people know something vital that you don't is bound to be relieved by the theory (fantasy?) that you know something that they don't. The last version, when all veils have been torn away, is that education allows you to join the middle class, to earn a good salary, and to enjoy prestige and respect.

What may be at stake in the contest over apocalyptic knowledge is the ability of literati to serve the community in functions more exalted than those of clerk, book-keeper, gossip, child-minder, archivist, quizmaster and antiquary. The central problem of the raising and belonging school is that it denies the ability of the book to contain any information that the reader does not already possess. Living poets are not elemental Marxians or Freudians; although in 1968 it was assumed that those two bearded figures had mapped the landscape of class, power and sexuality, their prestige even at that time derived from a collective interest in these areas of knowledge which had mighty energies behind it and easily survived the realisation that both Marx and Freud had ignored the facts in favour of egocentric totality. Thirty years of flowering of those ideas have produced an equipment of knowledge and ideas which we do right to envy and chase after.

The critiques discussed seem to posit two opposed models of how the intelligent person conducts his or her life. The poles set *distance* versus *sympathetic circularity*, where distance is connected with morphological comparison, the rich set of related but different experiences, and the rich vocabulary that describes them, of mobile individuals, belonging to a middle class whose habit of seeking alliances over a wide area rather than within the neighbourhood is reflected by mastery of a non-local pronunciation, the prestige accent. Sympathetic circularity, the quality of communication in physically close groups, in room, household or neighbourhood, supplies the contents of consciousness by direct assimilation, annihilating distance and rational inquiry. Its contents are transient, not analysable, with a quality known as warmth or intimacy; the space for reflexivity is created by main force, the throwing out (by dissimilation and dissociation) of the messages sent by other people, as much as by the habit of solitude permitted by prosperity and luxury in allocating personal space, and by immersing oneself in reading. An irritated wish, sharpened and selectively eroded by formal discrimination, for new experience, implies the throwing out of both people and poems lacking originality and definition.

The poles set *specialisation* versus *all-round life-knowledge*. The latter is necessarily familiar, circular, vague and repetitive. It is bound to social authority, which is the only thing that makes you believe it, but it also implies a human relationship, it does not stand up on its own. The former is useless because it does not tell you how to live; useful as an exchangeable ware in a specialised situation which devises people whose needs are specialised enough to include it. Being refined enough to have the knowledge implies being refined enough to know that the amount of knowledge you haven't got is so vast that your prized fragment can't be especially important. The poles set *critical self-consciousness* against *traditionalism*. One refuses to say anything that is not original, the other refuses to say anything that is new. Tradition refers to behaviour patterns that we acquired early in life by direct imitation of our parents (chiefly), whereas critical perception comes at a later stage of life. We are able to describe it in words, because we had become conscious by the time we learnt it; we could consciously decide whether to adopt it as a behavioural stratagem, and comparative analysis was the method that swayed this decision. As a whole way of life, it cannot be explained, and so cannot legitimately be attacked or rejected. Even where it is referred to in print, it is fundamentally unavailable to the comparative, analytical, critical mode of perception that print implies. The problem with talking about 'the Welsh way of life' (or perhaps 'the working-class way of life') is that this mass of implicit knowledge is different in organisation from the knowledge that governs writing; this mismatch degrades what is said, which lacks a grip on its subject matter. But the surface anatomy of imitation, adaptation and reinforcement is visible whenever we spend a few hours watching a child with its parents.

The project of R. D. Laing and Aaron Esterson seems to have come close to defining the action of assimilation, a massive short-range force operating in the household which teaches the child social structure, which reproduces class differences, and which underlies the sympathetic circularity discussed by Bernstein in relation to speech styles.[5] Here we come closer than anywhere else to an exophoric, analytical definition of the inarticulate, infantile and immersing. We may well ask whether this line of investigation reflects a quite different set of priorities from that of linguistic philosophers; and whether it was humility that led the Scottish psychiatrists to study the mind by observing live subjects in interaction, as opposed to figments in argument, and so to make unexpected discoveries. Alasdair MacIntyre has based his philosophy on the notion that human beings are decisive in causing each other's happiness or unhappiness by exerting this force of sympathy and assimilation, and therefore that, while emotional states are governed by other people to whom we are attached, action must be governed by a sense of these consequences.[6] Beveridge and Turnbull ask whether the retreat of English academic philosophy away from ethics, and the study of other people's minds, and from the thought of happiness, is due to narcissism and willed sequestration from life.[7]

Criticism has been heard recently inside the Church of England about the horizontal split between the upper clergy and the lower. The former, we hear, are selected as the material of the future high command when in their teens; they are more academically successful and went to prestigious schools and universities; they knew each other, and the prelates, at an early age, and were socially acceptable to the rest of this elite group; they were selected to be teachers at theological colleges, or academic chaplains, or assistants to bishops, and their experience of parish work, and so of the lives of people from other social classes, is restricted; they are masters of writing, of public speaking, and of foreign ideas in theology; their opinions about supernatural religion, the rigid nature of moral injunctions, and the literal truth of the Bible, are liberal, and the arguments they use are too abstruse for the parish clergy to follow. They are more left-wing than the parish clergy, and more optimistic about the poor and dispossessed. The parish clergy tend to have fewer academic qualifications, and to have gone to less prestigious schools, as a result of coming from less well-off families. They do not linger in the theological college, but trudge off to immerse themselves in pastoral work, under the daily drift of social disasters. Because they spend more time with the deserving, and less time with other clergy, they are less sensitive to the nuances of opinion among the clerisy, less able to manipulate them, and their arguments, while robust, appear less developed and less refined. Because they are not daily under the eye of their superiors, they are less likely to shine and be promoted; deprived of the experience of life in the upper echelons of the Church, they are less well qualified to rule Church affairs and so fill in this gap. They spend their time with ordinary people, and not with professional theologians, and seem naive and positivistic to the latter. They distrust the poor and believe in authority as a bulwark against immorality; they are more inclined to see misery as the result of bad behaviour within the ranks of the poor. Whereas the lower clergy listen to the upper clergy, the upper clergy listen to the upper clergy. The broad outlines of this critique are strikingly similar to the outlines of poetic sociology, itself horizontally split.

The rhetoric of the community seems to neglect the existence of another association in which many people bind themselves together for mutual benefit, that is, the corporation. It is argued that the corporation has too much power, since in almost any part of the country you can find more people who don't work for one than who do; the excessive economic and political power of the corporations – doubted by no-one – points to the advantages of joining one and buying its products, and so to the disadvantages of relying on the community. What we call community looks like a residuary thing, a lop-sided area devoid of assets and left over when the corporation, the state and the household have staked their big claims. When you associate yourself in a firm, its hierarchical and formal structure guarantees that the other people associated with it must behave in precise and directed ways, whereas nothing seems to guarantee this in a community. You are well advised to give your best energies to the waged job, then, and this is what most people do. The corporation is disastrous for society because it rejects such a wide band of people, who are therefore unable to acquire the shiny goods which their fellows inside corporate walls turn out; but this rejection and selection make for the superiority of the corporation, and consequently persuade governments to do what it wants. The doctrine that corporations do not benefit their employees is something that, after mass redundancies, no-one believes, but it was already untrue in the 1960s. The sharing of benefits between shareholders, employees and consumers is an area of immense fascination and daily shifts, but is not, outside a neo-colonial territory with a corrupt government, one-sided. The inclusiveness of the community minimises the benefits it offers to any individual. One has to ask what the common object of the 'community' is, to match the corporation's ownership of machines, organisational rules and technical expertise, and the answer is simply place. This exposes the fact that the presence of places in a poem may include a political message, and also forces us to investigate how humans translate physical space into psychological space, or simply what place is.

The *Helikia* as Living Unit of Culture

The basic categories or units of study on which this work is based are the Individual and the Period, leaving a lingering wish to confound and transcend these. The Nation is the *a priori* category within which the book is confined. Can we replace them and test how well another system of analysis would do? Are they sacrosanct myths? Do their borders coincide with discontinuities of distribution in the underlying reality, the text mass, before a categoric grid is imposed on it? We are faced with the biography (for dead poets) or the interview (for living poets) as the replacement for the critical essay, which is read largely by the professionals who also write it. Other categories that could have been chosen are Place, Sex, or Class. The Genre or Style is a rival hero of the story. Perhaps more interesting would be a morphological analysis, which would start with individual poems, or perhaps individual lines, and build up a map of the significant poetry of the period by painstakingly collecting primary data and trying to build and test subsuming descriptions. Such collections – by no means established by work published to date – have to co-exist with causal hypotheses about the influence on poetry of regional origin, class origin, family structure, genetically given temperament, sexuality, social roles, political convictions, philosophical tenets, and so on. In order to gain a theoretical understanding of how poetry comes about, we must first have an adequate theory of how behaviour is governed. My category of choice is the *helikia*, a group of poets of like age, who go through life – and presumably through several literary periods – in some kind of association, exerting gravitational attractions or repulsions on each other. Patterns emerge from comparing all the poets born around 1945, or all the poets born around 1956; shared impulses may shape the linguistic area into which the poet ventures, or alternatively unique childhood experiences, roots of character, may be tempered by shared cultural imperatives later on. Perhaps we can observe several separate helikias for a given generation, the result of active dissimilation or of multiple centres of attraction.

Where do we look for originality? Is it in sociologically defined groups, from remote regions, uneducated poets, women, cultural minorities? Or is it from poets who have discarded the mass of conventional procedures and launched into the terrifyingly empty space of the unmapped? The interest in morphological originality defines the future as the periphery; and the *Textmilieu* that interests us is found in the area of the microsocial: not the isolated and destined individual, but small groups as linguistic matrices, the coterie, *nemus*, or *Hain*, forming an experimental polygon where new language can originate by play, without immediately being wiped out by indifference or conventional rules of what is poetic. When a dozen or so talented poets are living in close proximity, their contact has a furiously stimulating effect on each one; they unconsciously assimilate to each other, consciously compete by differing. This is how real style comes about. Milieu is human, not topographical. Social pressures to do anything else but write poetry are so intense that only direct social stimulation can make poetry psychologically real enough for the poet to live it. Part-time poets never get really skilled; they fail at every serious problem. The new is always pathological until it has become recognisable.

Little magazines are the pond where helikias can thrive and splash around; and poetic groups supply the listeners, without whom the individual poet could not learn to speak. An important organ of the helikia would be the artistic objective; we would expect to find that individuals used a variant on a shared style. The unstated Sublime of social language, breathing in an eternal present, never laborious or artificial, corresponds to the motion of live argument, debate in which neither side expects to retain their prepared position, as the source of true theory and formal insight. This allows the break from nature, i.e. from repetition.

Two more figures complete this stage set. First, the mass of conventional poetry; the suggestion is that such poets have never interacted with other people in questions of poetry, protecting their creative processes, which remain dull and indistinguishable from those of thousands of other people. Poets are mostly conservative and conventional; without the pressure of close contact with other intelligent, vocal and unconventional poets, they do not break through into poetic awareness. Such a group is most likely found in a large population centre, although it may form in a rural setting, as with the poets around Dymock in 1914. The second is a certain image of the self as adaptive, its original constitution holding two tenacious appetites to find stimulation and to win other people's approval; so that the impulses of poetry may not come from a 'deep self' (resembling the intact archaic stocks of dialect, in Romantic imagining) but from outside, from the atmosphere of a room filled with potent and excitable people. Each significant dialogue creates a shell self, equipped for that dialogue and able to compete with other shell selves or self-shells. One of these animated partial selves becomes the new poetic style.

The units of poetic morphology are simultaneously international and as small as a classroom. At the same time as participating in the intense mutual exchange of the magazine, the poet is typically entangled in the rich verbal worlds of American, French or Classical English past poetry. Each text is the product of a hundred others. We need a map of where the poet's head is, not merely his feet. Sound always carries around with it, by hysteresis, the topology of its immediate past; mathematicians have been occupied perfecting equations to work out from sound alone how many holes there were in a struck surface. This resembles, or continues, our ability to shape and mark sound by rapid reshaping of our vocal tract. The project is to fit the text back into the place it sounded from; in intense linguistic creativity and suggestibility, the poet is surrounded by a mnemonic acoustic swarm of voices, multiple shell selves; the voices do not come from the self alone, do not compose a single predictable line, but rather a decentralised polyphony in idealised exchange with a hundred allied voices. No-one speaks from isolation, even if milieu is illusory in a rush, *Rausch*, of flying voices. Words arrive saturated in context; a kind of animistic acoustic polyphony.

An Open Elite? or Narcissism, Exclusion, Insecurity

Speech carries at least two streams of information: one about the status of the participants, one about facts in the outside world. Halliday remarks: 'The essential characteristic of social structure as we know it is that it is hierarchical; and linguistic variation is what expresses its hierarchical character, whether in terms of age, generation, sex, provenance, or any other of its manifestations, including caste and class.'[8] Poetry differs from less organised speech by more careful patterning of stress and juncture; perhaps it differs also by more precise and patterned usage of meta-statements about prestige and status. One writes poetry in order (among other things) to be liked by other people, to impress, to justify oneself, to attract attention, to contradict accounts of oneself given by other people; poetry is in this way the isolation and perfection of an ordinary speech pattern, which becomes at one end eulogy, the rhythmic recording of the actual status structure; at the other, paranoia, where insecurity at not being liked, listened to, esteemed and so on causes rage and alarm.

A researcher, trying to analyse status within a social group whose layout is unfamiliar, might start by measuring attention. Someone whom others ignore is of low status. In the plurality of status valuations, the degree of commitment of low-status individuals to the system that gives them a low rating is in question: an index of the strength of their 'alternative', or 'virtual', status systems is the amount of attention given to them by real people. Art is one of a series of attention-seizing behaviours. The overt status of a poet as person can clash with the value and appeal of his or her poetry as a set of information: the rejected poet is likely to claim that the reader errs, not on aesthetic grounds ('my poem is boring'), but in applying status rules wrongly or narrowly ('you are socially prejudiced'), and to retaliate by invalidating the reader, creating a fragmentation of symbolic space which makes it hard for the poet to find the mediations that give his or her speech a firm external substance and an internal structure and differentiation.

Dislike has a topology. The virulent hostility between the mainstream and the avant-garde derives from competing systems of esteem. The avant-garde poet knows very well that he has no chance of being published in a magazine such as *Ambit* or *Poetry Review*, and (more palpably) no chance of being admired and appreciated by their audience. It's like an animal that feels insecure away from its home run. Conversely, a mainstream poet knows that he has no chance of being printed in an avant-garde magazine, or of being admired by the people who write, edit and read it. Loyalty, alliance and dread of rejection are also rules of speech. Somehow a poem or person with high value in one cultural group has low value in another, in a topography governed by opposite rules, that we value the *cultural assets* that we ourselves possess, and that we desire the *information* that we do *not* possess. Recognising the legitimacy of what denies you is a mark of sanity. Is sanity possible when what exerts authority is vindictive, petty, numb, partisan, suffering from avarice of the soul, and hence *illegitimate*?

Speech is self-presentation, in a public sounding chamber which constantly shows selves up as stupid, lazy, intelligent, talented, and so on. It is loaded with personal information that makes us vulnerable, arousing our defences. Poetry is enhanced speech, and is related to arts such as dance and clothes design, and is governed by self-presentation and the fear of being laughed at. Poetry is about loving the sound of your own voice. If the central thing is to admire the poet, this is closely akin to narcissism; it is projective and sympathetic, we acquire the poet's identity to the extent that we feel more proud, the more brilliant he is as an artist. The charm is something fickle and irrational and ego-driven, like admiring an actor or a pop star. Poetry has either to be seductive or banal. One enjoys poetry because one esteems the poet and therefore identifies with them; one esteems the poet because one enjoys their poetry and identifies with it. Where does one find the beginning in a loop?

The consensus among editors or event organisers or reviewers is that poets are a narcissistic lot. There's no sense in disapproving of what's normal. Grace is saved as the artist finds an external equivalent for self-love, becoming self-critical in a way that causes us to love what they love and halfway give up. Both reader's and poet's ego float into the limelight, buoyed up by some kind of hot stare.

To describe the emotional flows between groups in the Balkanised geography, we have to use words such as 'feelings of inadequacy', 'symbols of power', 'envy', 'imitation', 'appropriation', 'invalidation', 'fears of conspiracy', 'hostile silence', 'aggressive self-assertion', 'lack of trust', 'contest over assets', 'claims to ancestry', 'polarisation'. The meanings of words shift as you move around the country because the value placed on individuals also shifts. The word 'paranoia' springs to mind as I look at this list, because the practical agency that makes the landscape so fractured is the individual fearing low status, who goes on to invalidate the whole social process, because it means other people talking about him, and their talk contains his low status. Most people who want to be poets are turned down by the literary world; they may come to share this verdict, but during the years of denial they may also reject the whole literary process and be constantly imagining new shiny literary worlds in which they would be fêted and loved. These are the nuclei of political alternatives.

The largest national poetry competition has attracted 35,000 entries, from perhaps 18,000 people; it is hard to believe that all of them are gifted poets, although they all thought they could win prizes over the others; the literary managers carry out the rejection of hope as an elementary, daily function. They carry it out; but the poetry audience is largely composed of rejected poets. In the Balkanised realm, there is no legitimate form of legitimation: all sources of legitimation are subject to furious and almost consensual attack from other sources; rewards are scarce, and those who refuse to be reconciled without them are many. The insecure destroy the legitimacy of a common verbal order which at some (perhaps very near) moment, could legitimise them and end their insecurity. Most unsuccessful poets are wholly conventional, but the furious energy of response to being rejected may in fact give the unhappy poet the courage, self-criticism and drive to make the rejecters, who were right, wrong. Rejection of literary and social norms in vindictive rage may also be the clean slate, the empty space, which lets a new style soar away.

Something expands from egoism to identification to faction politics. I would like to propose that when people say identity, they mean self-esteem. If someone entitles a book *The Urgency of Identity*, it makes no sense, but *The Bursting Need for Self-Esteem* is immediately understandable. This would explain why the nineteenth century could do without the idea of identity; why the phenomenon is quite indefinable, why it shifts from second to second and according to who its owner is talking to, why it is 'internal' and yet seems wholly under the control of outside agencies, why it holds inexhaustible interest for the owner and none for anyone else, why it is invisible and cannot be observed, why it grows and grows the more its owner talks. I suspect that the subject is an artful way of sticking to the culture of magazines (where people talk endlessly about their identities, their sex lives, their diets, their clothes, their living-rooms, favourite restaurants and so on) while pretending that one is moving in the realm of ideas.

Perhaps the qualities of modern poetry, above all its unpopularity, are connected to the signalling of hierarchical or horizontal status. Painting or music leave your finite, fallen, social being behind at the outset; the realm of the artistic work, created from nothing and in an empty white space, doesn't reproduce the social order. Poetry can tap this free plenitude of ready-made and socially valid signals, but at the cost of losing its autonomy and right to make new rules. These status messages are picked up rather quickly by listeners belonging to the same society; poetry is then more like clothes and less like painting or music. If tribal affiliations are the content of the first page of your book, what are you going to put on the second page? Such poetry is appallingly repetitive; 'I'm me I'm me I'm me' on an endless loop. The marketing of British poets by their social affiliations turns up the volume of status markers so that it drowns out all other channels, and grants paranoia institutional standing. It points you towards poets who are basically similar to you, while what we want from art is to become somebody else for a brief but controlled span of time. The 'gravity map' of the break points between the inward pull of group loyalty and the outward pull of innovation and exoticism, their mutual determination and expiry, stresses the landscape underlying poetry.

We can wrap up these observations as tentative rules:

- Where the writer is impersonating a community, all individuality of style is effaced.
- Where the poet wants to sound like everybody else, all sense of occasion is lost for the reader, and the poem fails to seize one's attention.

- The styleless poem usually resembles the poem of the 1950s, or of the Georgian books; the styleless poet always looks at artistic poets as vain and morally inferior.

Some believe that poetry is an uncoded area, a borderless zone outside the geometry of power, where individuals have no fixed status and there is no linguistic hierarchy; a strand of poetry sets out to get rid of social status, taking this destruction as its stylistic message. The success of poets will depend partly on their ability to catch and sustain this moment. Literature also is both arbitrary and real, and exposing its methods is a common metaphor for exposing society.

Notes

1 D. A. Kirby and H. Robinson, *Geography of Britain* (Slough: University Tutorial, 1981), p. 230.
2 P. J. Cain and A. G. Hopkins, *British Imperialism: Crisis and Deconstruction 1914–90* (London: Longman, 1993), II, p. 20, referring to the period 1914–39.
3 Craig Beveridge and Ronald Turnbull, *The Eclipse of Scottish Culture, or Inferiorism and the Intellectuals* (Edinburgh: Polygon, 1989).
4 See Jeremy Hooker, *The Presence of the Past* (Bridgend: Poetry Wales Press, 1987).
5 See Basil Bernstein, *Class, Codes, and Control* (London: Routledge & Kegan Paul, 1971).
6 See Alasdair MacIntyre, *Whose Justice? Which Rationality?* (London: Duckworth, 1988).
7 Beveridge and Turnbull, *The Eclipse of Scottish Culture*, passim.
8 M. A. K. Halliday, *Language as Social Semiotic* (London: Edward Arnold, 1978), p. 184.

The Structure of Space

Radiation and Marginalisation

The possibility of misreading a line or a poem has directed us to sets of verbal analogies to the poem's parts, stacked and stored as history, sociology and literary comparison, as a field that dis-ambiguates them. The correlating has hitherto brought puzzlement and self-doubt: the pictures resemble each other but cannot be made to overlay satisfactorily. Making analogies does not give a perfectly clear picture, and any analogy is structured by two fiats: it is allowed to operate within a certain stretch of time and a certain area of the earth, but is held to cease to operate beyond a boundary. The extent and profile of the playing-field are both set by fiat.

Whatever the sociology and ideology of 'modern Britain' are, they are surely not geographically homogeneous; a book of poems does not just belong to one square mile, but how wide an approximation, in political reading, is permitted? I have written a chapter on the North of England which is open to attack, since the North is neither internally homogeneous nor sharply divided from its neighbours. We obtain different results if we divide Britain into two, ten, or thirty cultural regions. If you want to find out about the culture of a region, what books can you go to? There is a gap between the excessive detail and narrow relevance of a biography, and the excessive levelling and generalisation of a national history.

We can still throw out the geographical analysis in favour of class analysis, with its important implications for speech organisation, cognitive practices, access to prestige codes, political values, and attitudes to literacy and education, refusing to equate the social experience of agricultural, fishing, industrial and commercial areas, or, as palpably, of men and women. We might merge 'British culture', historically, in a much larger unit of Protestant Europe, and demonstrate shared figures, themes, genre rules and periodic changes across this whole cultural realm. It is impossible, while studying literature, to feel that one is studying the right aspect of it, preferable to all others; our present scheme is to study regional cultures. This will prevent certain misreadings, while leaving others intact.

What is the right size of unit for the study of literary history? We cannot call regional literary cultures into being just because we wish to curate them and to sell precious information about them. We should locate poetic variation where it actually exists. The conditions for a successful history of a literary topic are that it should cover everything to do with its theme, and that the parts of the work should be relevant to, and supportive of, each other, following a boundary within which all parts are intensely related to each other. For modern poetry, three combinations are plausible: English and American poetry together; English and Commonwealth poetry together; and English poetry taken as part of European poetry. The line being followed here is of viewing southern English poetry separately from that of Scotland, Wales and the English North. This suffers from the influences that cross this boundary, and because the degree of relevance of the parts actually included to each other is much less than total, or 1, and might be as low as 0.5.

A defensible unit of study would be one from within which most of the reading matter of the reading public within it is drawn. This favours Britain, since readers read more British books than anything else; and lets us off studying Manchester (for example), since clearly people in Manchester who read books read most of their books by authors from outside Manchester. The geographical and sociological scale within which we are open-minded, or outside which we start to be egocentric and uninterested, is at stake. Regionalists have a smaller radius than metropolitans. Wales and Scotland are natural units of study because they are recognised as units in the available source material, because a certain low proportion of the electorate in them votes for nationalist parties, and because a high proportion of writers active in them have also found them meaningful, even emotionally laden, entities. They also had developed literary cultures in the Middle Ages (and to some extent afterwards). None of this applies to the North of England.

Analysis by choice of reading material is a wish rather than a feasible method, since figures for this reading choice are not available. It exhibits a split that may be useful as well as disruptive: different people in a given area show quite different reading patterns. It may be highly significant that one person in Glasgow reads only Scottish books, rejecting anything English. In fact, such a diet makes someone highly aware of the problems besetting Scottish writers, and the most ardent followers of the national art are those most aware of its limitations, and the most political about the factors that bring about the limits. Resort to American culture may be a way of expressing distaste for English culture, and there is a specific Scottish way of consuming American culture in this complex of emotions, which cannot be equated with being pro-American.

The History of Space

Cyril Fox (in *The Personality of Britain*[1]) defined the role of the South-East as the mediator of Continental influences, always ahead in time of other British regions, always the wealthiest area and the source of authority. Barry Cunliffe (in *Greeks, Romans, and Barbarians*[2]) provides a general explanatory model for cultural radiation and trade in prehistoric Europe. He suggests, on the basis of wide finds of Mycenaean wares in Northern Europe, that the outlines of the system already existed in the Bronze Age. This defines the whole of Europe outside the Mediterranean as a periphery where relations with the core region are crucial to economic growth and in particular to the acquisition of social power: chiefs are legitimated by their access to prestige trade goods. These trade goods are then what we find in real graves; so we come out of the model and test its value. One can take exception to Cunliffe's suggestion that control of long-distance trade goods was the cause of chiefs' authority, rather than a consequence of it. Core areas (such as Rome) can buy peace on the frontier by establishing alliances through largesse; barbarian chiefs can make sub-chiefs happy by gifts; the system is stabilised because there are penalties for engaging in conflict. The underlying cause of the dominance of the South at this date is higher productivity; we can explain this in two ways, as increased specialisation (leading to far higher skill levels of technicians) and increased density of population (technicians progress again by interacting, competing and discussing). Urbanisation summarises these developments, but is only the peak of processes in rural society that were its forerunners. If productivity is the result of knowledge, it is then also the result of information.

Cunliffe argues that, just before the Roman invasion, '[c]entral southern and eastern Britain constituted a core zone, characterized by a well-developed system of coinage, by urban settlement, and by the consumption of quantities of imported Roman luxury goods'.[3] Around this core was a zone related to it but less developed; the third zone was the Beyond: 'Beyond, to the north and west of the Exe-Severn-Trent line, the tribes show little sign of having developed significantly from the simple economic systems already in force in the Early and Middle Iron Age [...] These areas were the source of most of the non-ferrous metals produced in Britain and probably provided the majority of the slaves exported from the country'.[4] This describes a *colonial* economy. Invasion and slave shipments are both examples of the Barbaricum exporting manpower. The borders drawn by the early Roman commanders were based on socio-economic patterns already existing; and based on a profit and loss reckoning that the periphery was too poor (and too savage) to be worth conquering. At this stage, the core:periphery opposition is partly also the agricultural:pastoral opposition, based on soil, topography and weather conditions. It is hard to distinguish between the influence of relative distance, which meant that civilisation coming from the south-east reached southern and eastern Britain more richly, and the influence of soil, disfavouring upland Britain. Roman rule brought intensive economic development, which also attracted military incursions from the Beyond, partially cancelling out its positive effects.

The study of the pre-Roman cultures of Europe is tangled up with the Indo-European theory and attempts to reconstruct a cohesive Ur-Indo-European culture. The search for such a culture, sited in South Russia or Central Asia, dismissed out of hand influences reaching Europe from the south-east and the zones of primary agriculture. These Near Eastern cultures were in the main Semitic; the wish to exclude from study Semitic influence on prehistoric Europe matches the political attitude of most of the Indo-European scholars, which was German nationalist. If we look at the Baldur myth in the pagan religion of the Scandinavians, we note striking resemblances to the corn and crop myths of the Near Eastern cultures; these cause us to look for influence, and this is likely, since agriculture came from the Near East and is likely to have brought its myths with it. So the cultures of Northern Europe, as they existed before the waves of Roman and Christian influence, are likely to have contained a broad mass of Near Eastern material, and thus to have incorporated elements from the centre of world civilisation. If we could retrieve Northern European culture from 500 BC, we would probably find it reflecting radiation from the centre; the academic literature does not test this hypothesis, because it was looking only for Indo-European survivals. Generalising, the culture of the periphery at time n is an adaptation of the culture of the centre of a time before *n*, or (n-m), where *m* is proportional to the distance *d* between the place and the centre.

Cunliffe suggests that the control of imported goods by chiefs in client relations with the sources of prestige goods in the Mediterranean gave such chiefs the edge in status competitions and in buying loyalty, two paths to political power within their tribes. The outlands were induced to valorise their resources, as slaves and minerals, in order to acquire the prestige goods, which thus promoted organised labour at the same time as aristocratic eminence, both adding up to greater class stratification. The cultural possibility of conservative peripheral nationalism and rejection of central cultural codes was already there in 2000 BC, and has occurred, probably, in waves ever since. But a chief who possessed certain imported assets had an incentive to prize them: almost all influential cultural agents stood within a chain where they excelled one neighbour by greater command of native peripheral assets, and the other neighbour by greater access to central and imported assets, so their interests were to conserve the system, since by devaluing it they would lose out to one side or the other. Extremists and rebels follow patterns immanent within the ancient system, by totalising either peripheral values or central ones.

The elaborate descriptions of gifts, as we have them in Welsh and Gaelic poems even into the eighteenth century, shed light on the political importance of object gifts back in the Bronze Age. We can sum up the cultural programme as *pay and display*. Christopher Hawkes developed, for British prehistory, the theory of 'cumulative Celticity'.[5] There was no single invasion by a homogeneous group bearing a stable and inflexible culture, which replaced what was there already. Instead the 'Celticity' of the tribes whom Caesar found in possession was the outcome of thousands of years of development, and several waves of cultural import. New sets of prestige weapons and equipment (chariots, horse tack and so on) are interpreted as competitive purchase and consumption of innovation by existing elites, rather than as 'invasions' where new peoples arrive and old ones vanish.

Surplus was poured, not into investment, but into feasting and other forms of extravagant display, of which art was the beneficiary. The need for chiefs to compete with other chiefs within the same geographical horizon leads to the wish to excel and so, mechanically, to artistic progress, and even, for crafts such as jewellery-making, technical progress. But it leads also to shared models, and the need for public acceptance of your display gesture militates for conservatism of form. Medieval Celtic society was the inheritor of forms pushed by furious creative thought in the past towards a natural climax, not easily excelled within the limits of oral composition or a certain empirical metallurgy, but which, once reached, embodied prestige and the heart's desire in the eyes of later smiths and bards and chiefs. The poems could be memorised and the ornaments worn and flaunted. Other elements of civilisation – law, formal courtesy, cookery, textiles, laws of hospitality, graces of speech – may have been equally classical and conservative. For such form-series, or more cogently *limits* to serial mutability of form, the word 'classical' is the appropriate one. They expressed, quite literally, links to the founding ancestors of the aristocracy.

The principle underlying the sumptuary system is a set of discriminations in which each term is $(n+1)$, where n is the object or ceremony, etc., with which it is competing. This implies a shared code, whereby the qualified audience recognise that object o really is superior to object n; and an occasion of exhibition, where this excellence can be taken in and resonate. Another principle is that the prestige object stands in an iconic relationship to the owning individual's qualities and station; which implies that restrained display is appropriate for those of lesser status.

The system of centre and periphery, with a collectively imagined cultural relief siting regions on a scale of higher and lower, brings a number of typical accompaniments: revanchism, being out of date, denial, regionalist ancestor-worship, admiration, envy and emulation, and the desire to possess the assets of the centre. Any culture creator we come across is either central or peripheral.

I propose a number of rules controlling reception of culture by societies and by individuals.

1. There is an oblique relation between daily work and cultural forms. Art is partly prestructured, partly free.
2. Several cultures can be expressions of the same base. They may be in competition with each other.
3. Consumers of art are opportunistic; they will eagerly consume what is available even if their everyday lives do not relate to it. Christianity spread over the whole of Europe despite its origin in a part of the Near East, and nourishment in the Eastern Mediterranean cities, which were economically quite different from Europe. Art provides the training necessary for it to be understood. This may be part of the human faculty for understanding other humans, a survival necessity; it's not enough to understand yourself. Materialism about economics cannot

unwrite the deeper materialisms of our monkey nature, expert at imitating, and at interpreting other people's states of mind from their behaviour.

4. Because of the conservative weight of familiarity with art, and the conservatism of artists with acquired skills, culture tends to lag behind socio-economic changes, and so acquire an autonomy that may be quite limited in time and space. The more prestigious the style module, the more conservative it is, and the less it records variation in events, as opposed to the timeless and elevated. The fewer the literates in any society, the less they record of their own society, rather than of copies of the shiny imports.

5. Art has a finite cost and is subject to cost laws like other commodities. A region has to support specialists in order to develop a culture of its own. There is a limited window of opportunity here, because a neighbouring region may well export culture that saturates the local market. The regional church and nobility could protect the specialists while they were still groping around for forms, could not produce a commodity to sell, and needed sustenance during their research. Some regions of Europe successively developed both art forms and a sociological stratum of qualified artists, lifting themselves into autonomy; and many regions never did, perhaps because the imported version was too appealing and too available.

6. A cultural object or institution cannot be reduced to a set of influences. We always allow for the system effects of the unique mix at each point. In some sense, each European country does have its own culture, however obvious to an outsider the borrowings are. Regions are not sealed vessels, they are also customers of metropolitan culture, and this culture also belongs to them and structures their ideology and practice. Culture is subject to mediations, and undergoes a constant process of adaptation. If a village musician in Campania plays a tune from a Neapolitan opera on a piano-accordion, the music reflects the limits of the instrument and the skills of the musician, and these qualify the 'pure idea' that the composer contributes. The rules of adaptation are of the highest interest.

7. The continuity of regional culture is not mystic or soaked into the ground, but fragile and limited by its concrete means of transmission. Children can only acquire what their parents teach them. We are wrong to think that the *Mabinogion* is part of the culture of modern Wales; it is antiquarian only. There was a breach of continuity in

Welsh culture in the sixteenth century. Texts that no-one reads are not part of any culture, not even a regional one. Culture has to reflect social structure to be meaningful, and this structure is probably the set of discriminations and rules of conduct internalised by children.

8. When we speak of 'social structure' we mean a probabilistic pattern, with much scatter and noise as well as certain regularities. The spread of Welsh votes over different parties qualifies the doctrine of geographical determination of behaviour, but confirms it within a defined range, since the pattern in Wales is different from anywhere else. Besides, nobody in Birmingham votes for Plaid Cymru. The 'rules' for behaving are limiting conditions within heterogeneous scatters of material: you can't predict where an apple will fall, but you can draw a circle outside which no apple will come to rest, and you can observe that the fallen apples lie in clusters. Behaviour traits also cluster in groups, so that someone who votes Conservative may enjoy poetry, but is unlikely to enjoy contemporary poetry. Fluids make their way across the cultural 'landscape' in watercourses, rather than at random. Identifying influence represents a victory for reason.

9. Prestige culture is not only much better recorded, but also much more clearly understood, than other cultural systems. Anyone educated has a feel for the Franco-Italian currents in British culture, which were mediated through the South-East and through the clergy and gentry, and which are significant because we talk about them, but other currents that may have flowed from Spain and North Africa into Wales and Ireland, or from Scandinavia into the north-east, or from Ireland into Cumbria, Galloway and the Hebrides, are overlooked, unrecognised, and forgotten or denounced as eccentric when they are brought up. The cognitive economics of folk culture, in its ardent mobility, importation and adaptation, are quite different from those of the literary style system. Peripheral cultures get overlooked, either because of the oral nature of their transmission and the fragmentation of the record, or because the curation and handing-down process was interrupted, as the language or the social stratum concerned had disappeared. The 'great tradition' has a privileged control of its own past, while the various 'little traditions' can either leave no trace, or be a puzzle. Kent is not the only part of Britain with a sea-coast.

10. We are trying to identify sets of rules generative of behaviours, internally coherent, and because collective able to mediate the deceptive gap between 'individual' and 'society', and to find a history of

subjectivity. The problem of commonality between art and politics is that all written accounts of the latter reproduce literary structures that do not truly represent the action rules being followed by the actors. Speeches and memoirs of politicians are ostentatious literary acts rather than unmediated records of political thought. Proposed structures should also be detectable in visual art, in theatre, probably in history-writing, possibly in music. The eighteenth-century historian of music, Charles Burney, said, splendidly, of his subject that 'Tis a chaos to which God knows whether I shall have life leisure or abilities to give order. I find it connected with Religion, Philosophy, History, Poetry, Painting, public exhibitions and private life.'

11. Speech is an act of consumption, marshalling and engrossing resources from a stock that is both common and restricted, on display and difficult to master. The vicarious experience we call identification is also an act of consumption; poetry is structured by both, and both are structured by a social geometry of assets, ranking, denial and indulgence, which also governs the construction and consumption of material goods.

Possible Regional Components of Style

The burden of a regional literature would be the political history of the regions, where national events have different values from in London, or in the flattening, all-round perspective of the nation. This is a literary history, and so we can only assess the value of the new perspective from the point of view of what reading pleasure it affords us: a kinky new angle that is interesting for about five minutes, or a new world of stories that seems significant to us and immerses us. How narrow were the notions of narratability in the eighteenth century, extended by so many multiple angles since then: not only the lower classes, and business, and domestic life, but also most of the nations of Europe outside Greece and Rome, were seen as unliterary, un-narratable. We have to beware both the fantasy of infinite narratability and the squeamish reaction that provincial subjects cannot be refined.

The mysteries of politics may be found in the process of comparing the version recorded in 'high cultural' texts, such as monastic or royal chronicles, with the barer version recorded in the traditions of families; it must mainly throw up errors of retrieval and misdirected identifications. Poetry tends buoyantly to offer us childish ideas about social relations and goodness as if they were more, rather than less, authentic and persuasive than adult accounts of these relations.

Local political culture turns serial events into a synchronic structure. The picture of events encoded in these political strategies is always blurred and reduced. We can see that French people have a different mentality from ours, embodying their history in however transmuted and battered form; we can see that people in Ulster have a different set of traditions from us on the mainland; it is possible that regions embody their histories through family memory, through the ideals and unbreakable injunctions offered to the child, captured by a behaviour camera and then retrieved to animate the political and social imagination in adult life. Poetry would then be a window on a core process of the personality and would offer us a cinema of differentiation and of the political imagination, flowing value onto the colourless fragments of unmediated reality. This regional memory has been especially cited and described by the Austrian historian Friedrich Heer, offering us notably (in *Der Kampf um die österreichische Identität*[6]) the theory that Hitler's apocalyptic and terror-ridden view of history derived from the massacres of Protestants in his native region of Upper Austria in the early seventeenth century, some 250 years before he was born. It replaces the pre-modern ideas of 'national character' and 'race'. It also follows a traditionally Austrian way of looking at history. As historians progressively identify smaller units of study, they uncover new stories and new and unsuspected patterns. In the phase of object choices formative of the personality, political traditions can only be a fraction of what is flowing into the child's head, and aren't the most interesting objects flittering and curving around. If the process of the family comes into camera range, it certainly doesn't seem that what happens is regionally bound; actually, feminism is the area of thought invoked by most of these retrievals. In fact, most of the poetry about local tradition, continuity and so on seems to be based on a rigid and inhibited version of family process, in which you deify your parents and grandparents, reassure yourself perhaps about your own gifts as a mother or father, but prevent yourself from thinking about, dramatising, or questioning anything. I don't see family process being displayed within the controlled and articulated space of the poem, but rather poetry being engulfed and confined by part of family process.

We can draw up, as a hypothetical model, three stages of the acquisition of Spectral Identity and the internalisation of personality models.

1. In the first stage, the young child is subject to imprinting, acquiring formative initial models; affabulates freely on a poverty of models; repeats and imitates before understanding; is susceptible to hints and traces within cultural forms.
2. In the second stage, in adolescence, there is intransigence, polarisation; seeking collective action to enable successful aggression; being more extreme than elders in the ideals of the elders; rejection of the actual state of society; investment in the potential or unreal states; ideals are involved in the choice of a mate, and the objects of competition with peers.
3. In the third stage, in maturity, one accepts the gap between ideal and reality; there is a greater ability to grasp other people's worldviews; less ability to form or modify internalised ideals. Culture is formulated in pithy and utterable form as part of the socialisation of the young, in their first phase.

If socialisation is a highly redundant topology, in which multiple pathways lead between all points, and individuals can reach multiple end points, this explains how a society can reproduce itself in conflicting, partial, forms; and culture, as extended social memory, whose internal structure is redundant or endlessly varied, has a symbolic anatomy which allows this indeterminacy.

Perhaps, then, cultural productions contain concealed imperatives. They respond when politicians want to revive a state of society of which, in the extinction of living memory, books and buildings are the only maps or relics – as is the case for Wales and Scotland now, and was for Ireland until 1921. One of the touchiest aspects of social behaviour is handling of conflict: socialisation must teach, to some extent, the quelling of anger as a function of self-awareness, but because patterns of violence are also culturally influenced it seems that other, perhaps covert or unacknow-ledged, streaks of acculturation encourage aggression and demonstrate effective ways of using it. If a child is told not to be violent but occa-sionally sees its father using violence within the home, hears overt praise for good fighters, overt praise for acts of successful violence against 'other' communities (e.g. against Protestants within the city), the lesson learnt may be that violence is manly and admirable. In areas where the govern-ment asserted its authority, in early modern times, by military action, the very success of the redcoats may have implanted a positive stereotype of ultimate force. The evaluation of physical force is one of the differences among the provinces of Britain.

Complacencies of the Terroir: Of Geography and Mutability

Colin Simms writes, about a cliff on St Kilda:

> Nearly, according to Hudson,
> called into extinction; Rare Race into museum collections,
> brighten with atlantic bar – cloud patterns roundelay of their depressions
> with something of the grey silver sea-spray's refractive sheen in this light,
>   actinic near to icelandic
> Not the little rusty Jenny wren of the mainland; nor even those of Shetland,
>   or Clear Island [...]
>
> (from 'St Kilda – Wren', in Eyes Own Ideas)

The poetry public has been affected by a topographical vision, whereby poetry varies every few square miles, like the wren varieties which Colin Simms writes about so accurately, and every habitat has its specific and locally perfect kind of poet. This is a seductive metaphor, but it produces a burden of expectations. Animals that are relatively large and mobile do not show small-scale variations, and may be indistinguishable, except by DNA analysis, over the whole island; for poets, the idea that the geography of the island is a guide to their distribution and behaviour patterns may be a lying piece of positivism, an administrator's dream of order and predictability. I would question the idea that social behaviour differs sufficiently in different parts of England to generate different kinds of poetry *ipso facto*.

The fantasy of continuous spatial variation is a beguiling one. It bears an odd resemblance to the continuous fine nuances of a speaking voice, for example, or of a well-written poem. Perhaps it is chiefly a transfer from the well-established and prestigious discourse of science; we are used to seeing maps showing geographical variation, and we tacitly accept that the things being measured vary coherently and obediently enough over space to make the mapping satisfying. Continuous fine variation does apply to English dialects, although with a big exception for cities, which tend to flatten variation out; if we see poetry as springing from the voice, it might be locally constant, and we would then expect there to be a specific Leicestershire poetry, as opposed to various people from Leicestershire writing poems in modes common to the whole country, and probably a couple of generations out of date. So much in European culture has sprung from the variability of the European landscape, the natural obstacles that prevented a single state and a single culture from taking unitary power, except for the Romans, and allowed a polycentric landscape of competing local cultures and languages to flourish, spontaneously generating many varieties, so that the decline of one country or style quickly led to the rise of another. The European Union spends its money encouraging the weak minority languages: no-one wants homogeneity, and, if I wanted to be original, I would certainly write in favour of homogeneity. The underlying model for this is, I suspect, the local advantages theory of trade, whereby the diversity of local products, firmly founded on the distinctive *terroir* and on local methods and preferences, is the engine for trade, and for rather voluptuous possibilities in wine, food and textiles, for example. It's trade the EU is all about. The restaurateur or shopkeeper longs for heterogeneity.

Only two of the poetry magazines are devoted to English dialect writing. Dialect writing was wiped out, even in Scotland, by the irrevocable progress and triumph of the South-East Midland variant in the fifteenth and sixteenth centuries. It is true that several other magazines – *Chapman*, *Lallans*, *Cencrastus*, for example – are devoted, partly or wholly, to poetry in Scots. The story of English dialects is not one of violent levelling of the ancient, authentic and structurally rich, but of constant innovation by indulgence of the linguistic appetites. Two of these are the appetites for innovation, out of boredom with the old words, and for upward mobility, pleased by appropriating words with upper-class, French, urban or learned auras. Dialect studies can be a source of the shifting, magpie-eyed, eclectic, display-minded, eddying, imitative, improvised, myriad, unauthorised, appropriative and fashion-based, as a way of showing why poetry pleases.

The belief in locality, as an adequate classification and evocation of poets, is based on a fear of morphology. The most widespread of representations of locality is the postcard. Despite its obvious aesthetic and ideological limitations, such as being static, frozen, repetitive, conventional, incapable of forming new symbolic statements, usually selecting something antique or natural, this is the readiest and most easily understood model for the regional poem. The concept of the postcard view has nothing indigenous about it, it is uniform in every continent, and based ultimately on technological convenience: we see the world in chunks, six inches by four, devoid of process, of conceptual thought, of causal relations, and, mostly, of humans. There is a Tourist Board view of the writer. Such an approach greatly prefers writers on landscape, whose poems could then be attached to landscape photographs, for mutual corroboration; and could promote the region as a commodity, consumed by its inhabitants as well as by tourists. It was hard for such poems to have a more than referential relationship to the region; they could not develop autonomy, or criticise social relations in that region. Often, as they wrapped themselves around an aesthetic object (such as a beauty spot or an old stately home), they ceased altogether to be aesthetic objects, reduced to an instrumental value.

With the growth of cities, local advantage ceases to be identical with the qualities of the *terroir*, and becomes dependent on human skill; products come to be differentiated and elaborated, and so does poetry. Urban land may be expensive, but it is not the land that generates the wealth, but human intelligence. In the virtual space of the city, the generation of value is not dependent on square feet, the composition of the soil and so on, but on human culture, which makes wealth from nothing, or out of itself. Space becomes convoluted in the same way that the foliage of a large tree, shaped as a light-catching organ, is multiplied and set at angles to catch every drop of light. So wealth moves away from origin and becomes more the result of process.

> Here the east-west flow upturns   past
> and (hope) again   at the edge of self
>   you know there's overturn
> any of us can feed on if we sound the continental shelf
> circulating the world, undulating it around a pulse with out
> spirit and rowlock, spirit in rhythm with him
> wavelength waves, bends water centering worlds
> white-side up   turbine out of the tunnel
> rowing-cruise rorquals bow heads acknowledge
> how the drift shapes nature at the ocean's edge.
>   (from 'Overturn', in *Eyes Own Ideas*)

This poem is specific to a place, and relies on close observation; it is nature poetry, but its poetic impact derives from conscious shaping, from intellectual work with language.

Each writer's work contains a virtual space, through which human figures pass; meanwhile the writer lives within a real space, passing through it as a human figure. Perhaps the verbal imagination makes a mnemonic use of real spaces or social constellations as templates for the acoustic-semantic organisation of the text. We are all familiar with an acoustic geography, whereby accent evokes the variation of local conditions, as the whole island is, with two Celtic exceptions, using the same sound system, an abstract but readily grasped matrix of which every local accent can be heard as a variation. Print cuts out this audible locality, inviting us to replace it in poetry by an intellectual, morphological serial variation based on stylistic nuancing and formal improvisation.

The new cannot be a literal transcript of speech patterns. Alienation is consciousness. The urge to verbalise comes from loss of what you had, at the moment of departure when it is becoming merely verbal; a child uprooted from one environment and put into another may become a writer because the mismatch of inside and outside forces a mass of material into consciousness. Migration is perhaps the basis of conscious sociological understanding. Unemployment may provoke political insight. It is psychologically impossible to describe what is there every day; everyday life has barely found its way into good poetry, which is why the project of depicting regional life in poetry is wholly unrealised.

Notes

1 Cyril Fox, *The Personality of Britain* (Cardiff: National Museum of Wales, 1932).
2 Barry Cunliffe, *Greeks, Romans, and Barbarians* (London: Batsford, 1988).
3 Cunliffe, *Greeks, Romans, and Barbarians*, p. 154.
4 Cunliffe, *Greeks, Romans, and Barbarians*, p. 157.
5 Christopher Hawkes, 'Cumulative Celticity in Pre-Roman Britain', *Etudes Celtiques*, Vol. XIII (1973), pp. 607–27.
6 Friedrich Heer, *Der Kampf um die österreichische Identität* (Vienna: Böhlau, 1981).

3

Centre and Periphery

Centres

The centre is impossible to find or define, since it is a paranoid fantasy of being controlled by a hostile and malevolent agency. How can you connect the government in Westminster, the electors who vote it in, the boards of multinationals, the shareholders of same, the City of London, the reviewers of poetry for the quality press, university teachers of English literature, the poets who are favoured by the reviewers, the Arts Council, the people who make television and radio programmes, the Americans who make cinema and much of what is shown on British television? Surely these are separate groups of people, with different interests and different sources of influence – even if each group is closed to outsiders, more or less. The embittered and pressured regionalist poet may wrap them all up together to explain why he (or she), his poetry, his whole region, have been cheated of their natural rights; but if a poet chooses politics as a theme, then the quality of his or her political analysis will be a restriction on the ultimate quality of the poetry. There is the possibility for someone of political acumen to link some of these maps of power together to make a really gripping kind of political poetry.

One of the weapons of the current promotional campaigns, deployed notably by Martin Booth and Neil Astley, seems to be hostility to people who studied at Oxford or Cambridge. I disagree with this; a few hours spent with one of those biographical reference books that list the site of someone's education have convinced me that some 40 of the modern poets I regard as good attended one or other of these old universities. It might have taken me a lot longer to count the bad poets who went there too, and so far the analysis of the promotional campaigners is good. But to understand the hostility, we have to consider the homogeneity with which Britain and the world regards those universities as the best; and how clearly the assets of culture, broad horizons, literary knowledge, command of language, which all poets covet, are present in ample quantities at them. The counter-values to education have been set as sensuousness, authenticity, emotional undividedness, communal loyalty. But lack of education is not an index of literary skill, nor is high-quality education an index of literary inauthenticity. The faction that advances the critique is perfectly happy to accept the value of the educational assets which they themselves, and their poetic clients, possess; but while someone at percentile 47 is pleased to regard those at percentile 46 as 'ignorant, innocent, in need of my help and guidance' and people at percentile 48 as 'stuck up, over-abstract, over-refined, arrogant, not local enough', people at percentile 48 feel just the same way about people at percentiles 47 and 49, and indeed people at percentile 86 feel the same way about those at percentiles 85 and 87. This solution satisfies everybody, but you can't write poetry criticism in such egocentric terms. Oxbridge has been picked as the villain figure only because a majority of the poetry audience are graduates (or students), and susceptible to resentments against the prestige universities: an attack on all universities would be equally revealing of the factors conditioning poetry, but unfortunately lacks adherents, because the poetry audience is not disposed to disparage the assets which it possesses itself. The system is composed of discontinuities, and each alliance minimises some while turning others into curtain walls.

The restrictions on a poet are, credibly, the artistic conservatism of the poetry-buying audience (or of the audience that *doesn't* buy poetry) and the insensitivity of the editors and reviewers to the new. A web of similarities suggests that the cultural managers are faithful to the audience's distaste for the new and difficult. Perhaps the past actions of past cultural managers, over 50 or 100 years, account for the pessimism of the audience about the new; but the notion that the mass audience is not following its own volition but is subject to control rays from a secret central transmitter is blatantly paranoid. The paranoiac has problems with the question of agency, of which the belief that those aren't your real feelings and desires but substitute ones inserted into your head by the subterfuge of your enemies certainly sounds like one. The public acceptance of the words 'clique' and 'coterie' is an index of paranoid thinking becoming mainstream. For the paranoiac, a group of friends talking to each other is sinister, because what they are doing is exchanging information in which he is undervalued or even left out. The paranoiac demands that other people's speech acts be controlled, and is outraged that this demand is denied. Thinking and intense discussion imply separation, read as *exclusion*, an idea that summons up a stratum of infantile anxiety so dense, so exhausting, so self-replicating, that adult reason just gives way to it. How can an artist create new meanings unless there is a milieu of people willing to accept them, play with them, toss them aside or pick them up?

For some geographers, the large space of a region, or even a town, is built up from the many small spaces in which individuals move, perceive and reflect, and it is the large space that is secondary and fictional. The word 'centre', in discourse about poetry, is not a geographical term; it only makes sense in relation to the self, which exists in multiple 'spaces'. Its generator, as a spatial metaphor for a sociological, conceptual, set of relationships, is distance: X is close to something and Y is far from something. Locality makes space unequal: there is a privileged place, most likely of all a concentration of people, and so of human attention.

Perhaps we can derive a major feature of microsocial space, that is factionalism and cliques, from its first generative rules. It emanates from a group, which one is acoustically or psychologically on the edge of or safely within. Listening implies psychological bonding, and this induces partiality; someone outside the bond is an outsider. Whatever channels carry the information must have limits; close attention implies shutting out other stimuli. The word 'clique' contains within it the sentence 'you're not listening to me'. The more intense group loyalty is, the narrower its range.

The centre can derive its attraction, not only from the density of people pressing there, but also from the sparseness of people – and the feeling of being ahead of the fashion. This liminal security of the wilderness where land is not owned or covered with artefacts, however, mingles with the feeling of being excluded, disadvantaged, scorned and undervalued.

The flavours of the discourse around poetry are narcissism and paranoia. If the greatest thing in art is to show conflicts fought out and reconciled, and if what we hope for in poetry is by denying ourselves to become the other, for a brief flare, polarisation prevents the great poem from coming about.

All poets use, up to a certain point, the same information, incorporating endlessly many parts of the outside world; a poet with a weak sense of self will almost certainly fail to persuade us that they are structurally associated within the tense, bounded, frame of the poem, and with the poet. Self-attention starts with narcissism and evolves into artistic awareness. The cohesion of a book of poems is an illusion of reference.

Assets of the Centre: The Courtly Tradition

Literary culture is only a current in an unrecorded river of oral creation, and its minority status makes it reliant on the past, conventionally moving through periods of the sophisticated (Greek-based) Roman literary public roughly from 100 BC to AD 500; the relapse into silence of AD 500–1100, when there was no cultivated literary public; the emergence around AD 1100, in southern France, of sophisticated lyric, closely associated with the courtly milieu, the new vernacular languages, a female-oriented court life, lay literacy, new self-consciousness imported from theology, and hedonism in dance, clothes, and other arts of life; the arrival around 1560 of this style into English poetry, after a false start around 1380, and the substantial continuity after that, with audiences sharing poetic values embodied in sedulously preserved and universally distributed classical texts. The significance of qualitative breaks thereafter, with the Romantics and around 1920 and in the 1960s, is more controversial.

Divisions in the contemporary scene are synchronic representations of diachronic splits; so for example the oral versus written split we have now reflects the terms of the growth of written poetry away from the oral world around the fifteenth and sixteenth centuries. The power of the centre is not in any spatial location, but in its greater command of the resources of print; this is weighted by the general social equation between greater literacy and higher status and income, by the special cognitive equipment of reading (attitudes towards proof and doubt, and ability to resist the short-range field of emotional suggestion), and by the content of what is preserved in print, the historical series of texts that we read and admire. We read them as middle-class people entering a predominantly courtly and aristocratic culture; repeating the historical birth of the professional classes, as a group expert in either reading or reckoning, performing specialised services for the gentry, profoundly affected by their speech norms, and buying their cast-off graces.

The Change of Poetry at the Renaissance

N. F. Blake puts the problem of the Renaissance into a deep perspective in *The English Language in Mediaeval Literature*.[1] He argues that there was a decisive shift of linguistic sophistication from the fifteenth century, and especially in the 1590s, whereby a new sensitivity to the nuances of words, and to the contexts they had previously been used in, allowed a new sense of psychological processes in literature, and of a personal style, which also brought in the personality of the poet as the thing being expressed by the style. Character was newly important in the fictional roles of stage plays, so different from the antecedent Mysteries; outside plays, a new interiority was emerging in sonnet sequences, which are effectively book-length autobiographical poems. In the earlier period, conventional blocks were assembled together according to agreed rules, in a way that we can observe much later on in folk-song, where the old method was never discontinued. Blake argues that

> [a]lthough by the end of the mediaeval period literature had been written in English for hundreds of years, knowledge of the previous literature and language was to all intents and purposes non-existent. English appeared to be a language without a past and with a literature that was always modern. Hence words could not attract to themselves those associations linked with known literary works or linguistic origins. English words were insubstantial things which had to be given meaning by various devices such as repetition.[2]

This implies that awareness of past literary works is what allows words to acquire complex connotations; the breakthrough of English literature in the sixteenth century was an effect of the quantitative accumulation, through print, of knowledge of English itself. Literary self-consciousness is not a phenomenon new in the twentieth century, or the nineteenth; it was a founding act, which allowed poetry to rise from the level of mere songs to the psychological complexity of the great Elizabethan sonnet sequences and plays.

> In comparison with modern English the two important aspects of mediaeval English are a lack of tradition and a lack of precision, both of which were caused by the absence of formal instruction in the language. [...] The lack of tradition meant that words could not acquire the connotative force through literary reference and so they remained as vague stylistic counters instead of carrying localized associations and meaning. [...] The result was that style became more general and decorative than we like and that expression fell into stereotyped patterns.[3]

A greater flexibility produced unique meanings and contexts almost inevitably; this almost compelled the poet to develop an individual psychology, since the old generalised meanings were now obviously stiff and unexciting. A more differentiated semantic grid allowed more differentiated poetry; the grid itself had lost its static quality: the poet was almost forced to become original. Personalisation and introspection were efficient ways of doing this.

This revolution was significantly later in England than in some other European countries, or perhaps France and Italy alone:

> For literary connotation to flourish there must be a closeknit group of writers and audience such as those found in the provincial French courts and such as was to exist in England at the royal court in the late sixteenth century. Although the court of Richard II had the makings of such a tight group, it did not survive long enough to produce any lasting effect in lexical usage.[4]

The intensification of the literary language is a function of the presence of its past, not only through a store of manuscripts, but also through the presence of heightened speech in everyday life, an oral source for what is most purely 'literary'. The habit of attaching the author's name to a manuscript began, for non-Classical writers, at these French courts; this is obviously connected to the new idea of stylistic individuality, and this again is attached to the competition that poets faced at lucrative and sophisticated courts.

'A text was not regarded as an extension of its author's psychology in which his words are sacrosanct because they reveal, if only subconsciously, something of his make-up. Hence the biographical approach to literature is unrewarding.'[5] In medieval literature, a great deal of attention is paid to states of mind – to the progress of the soul, in fact. Entire mystical works were dedicated to psychological discussion. However, these works were normative; they lacked an empirical principle; minds were only interesting in so far as they approximated to the Christian ideal. 'These conditions encouraged work that was general rather than individual, stereotyped rather than individual. [...] The authors used traditional expressions and clothed their thoughts in type characters and allegorical figures with little apparent individuality.'[6] This did not apply to religiosity alone: since chivalrous literature was concerned with ideal behaviour in timeless and tightly repetitive tests of skill, it would not be reasonable to expect it to take an interest in individual character. When literature moved away from the depiction of ideals and topoi, and found the new idea of differentiation and uniqueness, psychology in literature also began taking on nuances, differentiation, serial change, and inner conflict. This took an individual form because the mind is an individual phenomenon; social psychology was much more difficult, and has only recently made inroads on individualistic psychology. Individuals soliloquise, not groups; the sonnet sequences do depict relations between several people, but with an introspective bias.

The literary past was now much more available, following the arrival of print and large-scale literacy, than it had ever been in the Middle Ages. The increase in sophistication followed inevitably from this surplus, and can be compared to the stylistic awareness of rock music in the 1980s when compared to the 1950s; radio and record companies were recycling the past so furiously that the audience couldn't help becoming stylistically self-conscious. Once everyone knew who you were imitating, there was great pressure to develop your personal version of the borrowed style; and also you could deliberately manipulate it as a cultural token.

Russell Hope Robbins remarks, in the preface to his collection of fifteenth-century lyrics, that '[they] lack the storm and stress and psychological conflict which come in later poetic and dramatic art, when the artist becomes a unique person'.[7] Doubt and anxiety came in not with the twentieth but with the sixteenth century; we can even look back at Robbins's fifteenth century and guess that the lack of self-doubt in those charming little pieces was due to poetic conventions of simplicity and directness, rather than to a bluff straightforwardness of human psychology in those days. The song is self-contained but the parts of a book of poetry must be the opposite, to avoid repetition and fading effect.

The difference between self-conscious and unselfconscious in art may be almost entirely subjective even if it is a status boundary. To form a sentence of English already demands many abilities folded over each other and practised simultaneously. The assumption of a zero grade, or of unconscious speech, is part of a social game of competition and rejection. Self-conscious art may demand extra skill, but this can hardly be different in kind from the universal human linguistic power, except to be less simultaneous and less complex. One of the great set-pieces in the history of European poetry is the breakthrough made by the Provençal poets, but their subject matter of love, longing, triumph and so on had much in common with the naive art of love songs; almost certainly, the lack of love poetry from the Middle Ages is due to the prejudice of the clerics, as the only literate group, against recording them; and girls or women were singing such *cantigas de amigo*, *cantilenas* and so on in great profusion, just as pop songs ring out in our towns and cities today. Vernacular texts *of any kind* are scarce before the later twelfth century.

The English poetic tradition (this is somewhat different in Wales, Gaelic Scotland, or the Lowland realm) goes back to the sixteenth century, to anthologies such as *A Mirror for Magistrates* and *England's Helicon*, plays such as Marlowe's, epics such as *Arcadia* and *The Faerie Queene*,

sonnets such as Sidney's. The poet's self-awareness came, at any point
from then until very recent times, from reading in print these works and
their linear successors. Joyce Youings decisively rejects, for the sixteenth
century, the idea of English literary cultures outside London;[8] Phoebe
Sheavyn describes how regional groups, in Ireland (around Spenser),
Cornwall, Devon, Hereford and Cheshire imitated the courtly system by
setting up local groups; these centred on individuals who had spent time
at the London court, and their enthusiasm was for courtly forms.[9] The
creativity of Sir John Davies and Spenser in Ireland, writing poetry in a
language that almost nobody in the country spoke, ironically reflects on
the isolation and self-esteem of these poets in the middle of counties quite
unaffected by them. There was only *one* literary culture in England at the
time, the court system, based on the Italian model, with whatever neo-
Classical, French or Spanish additions. There *were* other traditions in
Ireland, Wales and (in two languages) in Scotland; splendid traditions,
but with a problematic relationship, as it turned out, to the Renaissance,
to print, and to the gentry whose control of rents and feudal dues supplied
the resources to sustain them.

The twelfth-century courtly culture was founded in France and England,
as Bezzola stresses;[10] not in English, however, but in Provençal, French, or
Latin. We know quite a lot about those courts, thanks notably to Latin
prose writers from the circle of Henry II: John of Salisbury, Gervase of
Tilbury, and Walter Map. Walter says,

> I […] can say that I am in the court, and speak of the court, and do not know,
> God knows, what the court is. But I do know that the court is not time: for it
> is time-based, mutable and various, local and erratic, never staying in the same
> state. As I leave I know all about it, on my return I found nothing or little
> which I had left; I see its outside made other. The court is the same, but its
> members have changed.[11]

This is the mutability of human wishes, which also defines us, as humans.
The stereotype of terror that Walter evokes is clearly that being applied,
after almost a thousand years, to intellectual poets: they change all the
time and we can't feel secure with them. John of Salisbury's *Policraticus* is
a guide to the temptations of the court: 'The court loves new friends, is
bored by old ones, it only hears the case of pleasure and profit. […] The
court only loves, hears, honours, trifles.'[12] Both writers dwell on flattery –
a verbal skill that displaces true friends whose compliments are less
adulatory, inflating the currency and making friendship fragile and
conditional. The art of conversation reached a height that can hardly have

been excelled anywhere at any time. The courtier was so close to being an artist, needing to be everywhere the object of pleasure of his or her companions; social success depended on being beautiful, splendidly attired, attractive, amusing. Boredom was the great fear, but the court had the cure for it, as Salisbury's amazing list of court entertainers ('mimi, salii vel saliares, balatrones, emiliani, gladiatores, palestritae, gignadii, praestigia-tores, malefici quoque multi') indicates. The accounts of dress, which we fortunately possess for the twelfth-century courts, including the Provençal *ensenhamens*, strongly suggest that the arts of self-adornment, speech and dance went hand in hand, reaching simultaneous peaks, driven by an outside force that was in fact the court culture itself. Poetry is to speech as the wonderful jewels and robes of the Ricardian court are to plain garb; but the art of courtly conversation is already one elevated far above the speech of peasants. The perceptiveness developed by high-level gossip feeds the sophisticated lyric. The comments made to oneself which permit one to reach the heights in poetry or in dress are precisely the same in matter as those which malicious tattle makes about one's defects in those public fields of contention. Stylisation is the channel of development, and follows the courtly coexistence of multiple selves, the different regimes of social manners, designated by changes of clothes, in force for different social events. Ceremony and frivolity, love songs and bawdy *fabliaux*, succeed each other in an institutional rhythm. This regulation of social manners is self-conscious, although habit made every convention seem natural. The end result of the search for constant amusement is Fashion, so brilliantly evoked by Map, rather than a tempered stability which we could docket and exhaustively describe as Sophistication's Result.

Courtly poetry is the product of a milieu that was stressful and insecure for individuals, where even favour brought psychological insecurity about its loss, and where being closely observed all the time was a source of swollen pride but also of fear of the witticism or malicious envy; where love affairs were abandoned as soon as the other party began to get bored or found alliance with you not to be an asset on the path upwards. If torment brings complexity, sophistication may not be attainable except by going through this mill of impressing people who are spoilt, intelligent and easily bored. This, surely, is why a few thousand people at European courts produced so much in culture as to become our cultural past, whatever our peasant antecedents.

The partisan atmosphere is very like the English poetic scene that I discussed at the beginning of this book, and even suggests that paranoia and narcissism took poetry to new heights in the courtly milieu. Of course this elitism intersects with class, since it was partly wealth and birth that were being displayed. The sense of a split self accompanies narcissism because intense self-examination shows inconsistencies as if under a millionfold magnification. The self splits apart because it is appropriative and because it is so linked to other selves. Where the delights and rules of the court change all the time, we change to catch up with them; and exacting self-knowledge has just this to reveal: a substance so fickle and inconstant as to trickle through our hands, washing knowledge away.

Chaucer is not commonly regarded as a courtly poet, because of the low tone of some of his stories, converted by a sociological error into the notion that this did not appeal to a high-class public. The supposition that the bawdy story, the fabliau, the tales of saucy young wives and cuckolded husbands were not to the courtly taste is refuted by any analysis of the source of the manuscripts, the language they are written in, or even the social origin of the composers. We are missing the real story: the nobles were collectively adept at playing different roles at different times of day, signalled by changing clothes. Liberated by their economic resources and ample free time, they foreshadowed in this the modern culture of leisure, play and hedonism. The command of mutabilities imposes itself also within the psychological design of a single day, as courtiers became attuned to subtle social rules affecting the transitions from one set of behavioural responses to another. The ceremonial regime, although stiff, itself resembled a kind of game, and was only operative within certain behavioural zones, whose edges were signalled by masters of ceremonies. If Chaucer antici-pates the bourgeois taste, this is not because something influenced events before it came into existence, in defiance of the laws of physics, but because the bourgeois imitated aristocratic taste, including poetry, within the limits of their knowledge and economic resources.

If poetry is so subtle in its means of signalling affectively and cognitively important transitions, this is because an internalised grasp of these purely conventional boundaries is an attainment that points to prestigious social experience, of which people are envious and for which they compete. The ability to regard every moment of life as a role, to conform gracefully to arbitrary social rules, and to detach oneself from one's set character, and to do whatever the passing hour commands, is a good index of someone's height in the social hierarchy. This is something that the bourgeoisie had difficulty with, and still today it divides the audience, some of whom are offended by it, perhaps because it reminds them of a regime of manners that makes them feel inferior. Certain antagonisms within the modern literary milieu – loosely, the disagreements between Leavis and everybody else, or the aesthetic wing of poetry – continue this opposition. A symptom of the excessively moral tone of academic opinion has been the visibility of infantilised poetry, withdrawing into immature play because adult play is so frowned upon; the mime of childishness turns away thunders of rage and denunciation. Adult play regularly draws on sexuality, on the command and exercise of fine hierarchical differences. The displayed attainments form series which are extrapolated as individuals compete with previous attainments. This display extrapolation goes on until the behaviour in question becomes, although incidentally, incomprehensible to the inexpert. Rejection of these attainments, and of role-playing, means a dislike of play; a deafness to collusion.

The ability to succeed in different roles, to shine in the seminar and then in the disco, is desired by all, and so supplies a test of competence in life: the more secure someone is, the more diverse their social skills will be. The garbled notion of postmodernism is in part a misunderstanding of this shared game of modern life, where the ability to move between different cognitive modes is what wins points; not only is it this fluency and volatility and absorption in what one is about to toss aside that readers look for in poetry, but there is also a suppressed, resonant sub-awareness that this was what the aristocracy cultivated, enjoying endless leisure in which they sought always to be at ease. The clamour against inconstancy – or, someone's career of writing 600 poems which all say the same things – has a metatext about class affiliation. Role-detachment is not a schizoid weakening of identity, but a practice that gives you social control in varied situations, and dissolves those moments of anxiety or confusion. It is also misrepresented distributionally, as something historically new and danger-ous, when its incidence was vertical, as a skill of the upper classes which has moved partway down the scale.

Ideas about literary taste vary between two poles of the intrinsic and the imitative, the latter holding that what the middle class estimate as desir-able is a memory of the values of the gentry by whom they were formed, and the former holding that what the middle class desires is intrinsically desirable. The process of formation in which a child acquires the values that its parents willingly or unwillingly admire is easy to observe; it arouses thousands of exciting questions which thousands of uncritical poems about family life totally fail to answer or even to raise.

The greater availability of the art of the past, and of different countries, brought about cultural changes in the Renaissance and the Romantic era, which again made art more interesting and brought about internal changes. For analogous reasons, the sixties saw poetry manipulate and vary its own means as never before. It became possible to see the self in the poems as quite different from the self that is *me thinking about my own poems*. The self in the poem could be stretched, simplified and distorted, just as syntax could be once you had discovered what syntax is. This consciousness implies that stylisation, whenever it occurred, was a modern device, a trait of consciousness. If the resulting style was personal, then it is tempting to say that the promotion of personal sensibility to the dominant role in poetry is the main tendency of the modern age in literature, for the past four centuries. This must indicate print as its operative cause.

Gary Waller points out that the arrival of poetic autobiography in the Renaissance coincided with the fierce self-interrogation of Protestantism, most significantly with Philip Sidney and Fulke Greville, and happened inside a court culture which everyone taking part knew involved a theatre of everyday life, a strained, elaborate deception. Feigning and dissembling to deceive others, on a daily basis, went hand in hand with the self-deception, realised as such in sober moments, of the lust for favour, place and wealth.[13] This resembles infatuation, and the being deceived by others, which is what keeps the deceptions of court in place, takes the specific form of duplicitous and vain females, silk-wrapped, glowing with all the refinement of court, and too complex to be faithful. The radical scepticism held by late twentieth-century philosophy about the process of the self is already written in sixteenth-century court poetry, too finished and too ornate for us to read it as realism. The agonised treatment of deception and illusion in Sidney, Greville and Surrey is a critique of subjectivity, unmasking its operations as a prelude to religious contrition and a theologically pessimistic view of the value of individual awareness. As you throw the spotlight on the Self (getting away from action poetry or drinking songs) you find that its substantiality fades, it breaks up and is riddled with discontinuity and self-disbelief. The self disappears when light is shone on it, or the light shines right through it.

The court ceased to be an important factor in English literature in the late seventeenth century, although currents could be received from the French court well after that. While European poetry certainly acquired new techniques and new depth in the seventeenth century, and again in the nineteenth, it is possible to argue that English poetry remained on the same developmental level as the great sixteenth-century writers; and that the attempts to reach a new level, even to keep up with changes in perceptions of the self and of the terms of relationships and cultivated conversation, destroyed the poetic instrument, producing a cultural ideal that could not be attained.

There seems to be a fairly direct link from Surrey and Sidney to sonnet sequences by Meredith, Christina Rossetti and D. G. Rossetti, more than 300 years later. It is curious to mark where this stopped. William Watson and Wilfred Scawen Blunt are late, if unimportant, examples; 1900 seems to be the terminus. The disappearance of this Renaissance genre and poetic self seems to usher in a crisis of the love poem which is also a crisis of fitting self-consciousness into verse. With the Georgians, the course of aggrandisement of self-consciousness goes into reverse. There is an occult link between T.E. Hulme and the Georgians, to which their attitude towards the Renaissance is a clue. If what Blake says is true, then Romanticism merely reinforced tendencies that had been set in motion two centuries earlier; the step from fixed metre to free verse is perhaps a logical consequence of this tendency.

The court, alluring and hard to compete with though it was, was never the only system of values in a society: it always faced an anti-structure, however weak this was and however it was compressed and constrained by its wish not to compromise with the court by adopting any of its virtues. It is time to consider these anti-structures, because they positionally resemble the communitarian poetry we are interested in, and they can perhaps show us the coarse design of the latter, even though all the artistic resources and assets are different.

Anti-Renaissance Campaigns

The Renaissance stands for both the turning towards revived Classical art, away from 'folk culture', and a new ideology of the individual. It is therefore a key moment in the historical theories of anti-individualists and regionalists. By eliding three centuries together, we can say that the era saw, with the arrival of polyphony, rhetoric and the introspective lyric, the separation of a high culture away from what can now be called folk culture; but connecting the unsophisticated or regionalist poetry of today with the untransformed residues of twelfth-century peasant stomps, hollers and catches is so vague as to be absurd. Robbins's suggestion that the fifteenth century did not yet know the individual personality as the burden of poetry resembles a theory of T. E. Hulme's: Hulme defined Romanticism as 'spilt religion', but in fact the kind of art he recommended had ended at the Renaissance; he fluctuated between the two dates. At any rate, he was in favour of medieval art, and against the idea of the personality in art.

I have said that the folk-song continued pre-Renaissance norms; a properly literary culture was unevenly implanted in the country, and a preference for song and recitation over the interiority of reading characterised northern cultural life until the 'new orality' of television and records. Gaelic and Welsh poetry largely missed the Renaissance; MacDiarmid stressed that 'Braid Scots is a great untapped repository of the pre-Renaissance or anti-Renaissance potentialities which English has progressively forgone'.[14] So this opposition, or set of oppositions, is still live today; when we speak of the personality in art, of stylistic self-consciousness, conflict and interiority, we are addressing a single strand of British poetry, and inviting, unwillingly, the hostility of the other strands. The attack on the Renaissance did not start with Hulme, but in fact goes back, as van Tieghem has demonstrated, to Romanticism; the post-Herder Folkists who deify the folk-song also see the Renaissance as a mistake. According to the 1814 introduction by Geijer to a collection of Swedish ballads edited by Geijer and Afzelius: 'it might possibly be shown that everything which in the modern European [poetry] is original and not an imitation is found in nucleus in the romance, or what our folk call the historical and love ballad'.[15] He goes on to suggest that European poetry lost its way with the imitation of classical antiquity, in contrast to which

> the modern [poetry] [...] has up till now seemed little on the path to form itself into a natural whole, but distinguishes itself rather through separation and confusion. It began, yes, with nature or folk-poetry. But it progressed in education only to learn how to despise its source; in return for which it shows at first glance the strange spectacle of an art without nature, or which seeks nature in an uncertain way. If one thinks about the cause of this peculiarity, the closest to hand seems to be imitation of ancient [poetry], through which modern poetry wanted to appropriate to itself in one go all the advantages of an already completed culture and, so as to graft itself on an alien stock, tore itself loose from its natural ground.[16]

These ideas became absorbed into Marxism, and the wholesale rejection of European cultivated poetry since the Renaissance, made notably by George Thomson in *Marxism and Poetry* and Anthony Easthope in *Poetry as Discourse*,[17] went along with a misty-eyed nostalgia about folk artists.

Perhaps the single most important attack on modern poetry is the naive Leftist contention that whatever is folk, traditional and collective is authentic, while whatever is original, personal, introspective, learned and contradictory is inauthentic. The attack on the alienated bourgeois artist took place in two phases, the first being a sophisticated attempt to prove that economic and emotional disaster awaited the non-communist poet, the second being a starry-eyed and affectionate wheeling in of folk artists, complete with concertinas, corduroy trousers and Morris-dancing costumes, to engage the company in dance and singsong pursuing the measures of untouched folk art. Easthope tells us that poetry before the Renaissance is all right because it was collectively composed and unconscious, obeying traditional rules.[18] The programme is very close to those of the Georgians, the Cecil Sharp Society, and the Arts and Crafts Movement, with its venture of a non-alienated workshop in the Cotswolds.

The attack on individualist art has been of some importance in the disastrous relations between Left ideologues and Left poets. The outright dismissal of the authenticity of the conscious artist is in some perverse kinship with the conscious artist's self-doubt; the Marxist says to us both that we must doubt our inner voices and that we are inauthentic because we doubt them. The revolutionary demands unriven marmoreal purity both from his employer and from the poet, and is doomed to be disappointed; the recovery from this disappointment guides the course of his political attachments.

The current of this Romantic attack on the conscious artist in favour of the folk has leaked, over almost 200 years, part of its flow into the regionalist school of thought in Britain. The closeness of the regional poet to 'the people' could not be an advantage unless the people were somehow co-authors of the poems. The ideology of poetry which is concerned with community, family and ancestry, whose gaze is fixed on landscape and religion, which is not interested in theory and technique, is a translation of this folkish ideology, from whose effacing of the individual many consequences flow.

Geijer goes on to say that

[the] principles, which now [from the middle of the seventeenth century] became exclusively valid in literature, namely imitation of antiquity and criticism, were naturally completely alien to the unlearned and set up such a large gap between folk poetry and cultivated that both went their own way without taking the least notice of each other. Thereafter poetry ceased to be an expression of the public and common. It became wholly a learned art, wrought

up with the greatest zeal and an admirable talent; but without root in the great common life it could scarcely get a grip on that with its productions, and it is unbelievable, how little known it was to the folk as a whole, which in the meantime pleased itself with its old poetic lore and its own poetic attempts, however raw and unnoticed these were.[19]

Thomson, representing the Stalinist theory of poetry, says similarly, 'But all poetry is in origin a social act, in which poet and people commune. Our poetry has been individualised to such a degree that it has lost touch with its source of life. It has withered at the root.'[20] Common life? Geijer admits that the Swedish ballads 'almost exclusively busy themselves with high and noble persons; if the talk is not always expressly of kings and knights, so all the same it mentions lords, ladies, ladies-in-waiting (*stolts-jungfrur*)';[21] he explains that the ballads go back to a time when there was no social conflict, and the people liked the nobles, but the evidence admits a different interpretation than the one he gives, namely that the ballads were composed for the nobles by minstrels in their pay, but were sung by everyone who came to learn them. Geijer is clear that most of the corpus of ballads, both stories and tunes, is common to Scandinavia, Scotland, England and Germany; he is confused when he attributes this to a deep past when these peoples had not separated, rather than thinking of people knowing ballads being carried on ships across the North Sea, for example from Bergen to Aberdeen, and teaching them to listeners on the further strand. We can now ask, why is imitating ballads from over the sea such a good thing, when imitating poetry from Greece is such a bad thing? If we look into a Scottish ballad sung by a peasant, using it as a lens through which the 'great common life' is visible, what we see may not be a peasant, but a landowning milieu; and not Scottish, but Swedish.

The splendid court culture of the twelfth century had as anti-structures both the Church and, on the other side, folk culture. It was a regional devolution with respect to Latin literature, which had excluded women, vital to the court. The Renaissance flowering of English poetry faced, still, folk culture, and Puritanism. The Dissenting culture of the seventeenth century was against the universities, because the motive for listening to Dissenting preachers in the first place was that they weren't globally inferior to educated Anglican clerics; against Greek and Latin, for the same reason; against French and Italian culture, as things precious to the upper class, and pagan, because of their neoclassicism and sensuousness. Consider how fragile is this cultural raft: it's vital to read the Bible without commentaries, but reading it in the original languages is unnecessary and damaging; you insist on doubting the powers that be, but rely on solidarity and mere feeling when it comes to your own peers.

So already around 1650 we can find a group of lower-class literati, whose ambitions lead them to reject the most attractive elements of the culture around them; and this situation does remarkably anticipate the polarity in British poetry of the last thirty years. Even then, we can discern literati of humble origins who don't adopt this approach, but who aspire to what is beautiful.

A series of structural oppositions underpins the landscape of contemporary poetry: oral versus literary; academic versus colloquial; religious versus secular; innovative versus 'raising and belonging'; Left versus Right. These mutate or continue previous oppositions, between folk and courtly, native and Italianate, Dissenters versus Anglican and university-trained, bourgeois versus noble, court nobility versus the country party, and 'county' gentry versus 'parish' gentry. Does it not seem as if the regionalist poets had seized on the opposite virtues to the courtly poets? As if their aesthetic armoury were derived from a previous state of poetry which occupied everything that the court rejected? That they are rejecting everything stylised, expressive and original, in an attempt to reverse the differentiation between the individual and the group? This opposition, structural because it affects the design of the text at every level, implies that contemporary artistic poetry is in the structural role of modern courtly poetry, and also equates regionalism with folk poetry, Puritanism and Nonconformism, previous holders of the office of anti-structure to the hegemonic system of the court.

Notes

1 N. F. Blake, *The English Language in Mediaeval Literature* (London: Dent, 1977).
2 Blake, *The English Language*, p. 100.
3 Blake, *The English Language*, p. 168.
4 Blake, *The English Language*, p. 90.
5 Blake, *The English Language*, p. 21.
6 Blake, *The English Language*, p. 21.
7 R. H. Robbins (ed.), *Secular Lyrics of the XIV and XV Centuries* (Oxford: Clarendon Press, 1952), p. lv.
8 See Joyce Youings, *England in the Sixteenth Century* (Harmondsworth: Penguin, 1984).
9 See Phoebe Sheavyn, *The Literary Profession in the Elizabethan Age* (Manchester: Manchester University Press, 1967).

10 See Reto Bezzola, *Les Origines et la formation de la littérature courtoise en occident, 500–1200* (Paris: Bibliothèque de l'Ecole des Hautes Etudes, 1944–63).

11 Walter Map, *De Nugis Curialium* (ed. and trans. M. R. James; Oxford: Clarendon Press, 1983), p. 3.

12 John of Salisbury, *Ioannis Saresberiensis, Policratici Libri VIII*, ed. Clement Webb (Oxford: Clarendon Press, 1909), p. 47.

13 Gary Waller, *English Poetry in the Sixteenth Century* (London: Longmans, 1993), pp. 93–102.

14 Hugh MacDiarmid, *Albyn* (London: Kegan Paul, 1927), p. 25.

15 Erik Gustaf Geijer, introduction to Erik Gustaf Geijer and A. A. Afzelius (eds), *Svenska Folkvisor* (Stockholm: Z. Haeggstroms Förlagsexpedition, 1880), p. x.

16 Geijer, introduction to *Svenska Folkvisor*, p. x.

17 George Thomson, *Marxism and Poetry* (London: Lawrence and Wishart, 1945); Anthony Easthope, *Poetry as Discourse* (London: Methuen, 1983).

18 Easthope, *Poetry as Discourse*.

19 Geijer, introduction to *Svenska Folkvisor*, p. xvi.

20 Thomson, *Marxism and Poetry*, p. 54.

21 Geijer, introduction to *Svenska Folkvisor*, p. xx.

4

Oral versus Literate

Crisis and Expansion of the Middle Class: Georgian Poetry

An important shift in the composition of the middle class occurred after about 1870, with the expansion of the government's paid officials. This new group were serving the lower classes, whereas previously the professionals – teachers, doctors, lawyers, managers and so on – had served almost exclusively the possessor classes. The home civil service grew in parallel to the imperial civil service, numerous in those territories under direct rule. Growing in prosperity and numbers over a long run, civil servants are by now an important complement to the commercial and industrial sectors of the middle class.

Relations between the middle class, including the literati, and the masses seem to have reached a crisis around the 1906 election. Big government seemed to be on its way, and the professional servants of government seemed about to do very well out of this expenditure: their daily work was to be in some sense the servants of the masses, while being better off than them and indeed in many instances telling them what to do. Industrial conflicts reached a peak during the First World War, but had made the centre stage of national politics already in 1910–12, in a dramatic series of strikes; it has been the task of Westminster politicians ever since to be the panic-stricken third vertex of a triangle between workers and employers, always having to face both sides and earn their keep by asking the workers to back down. In an era of enhanced class-consciousness, the politicians' garb and voices clearly signalled a privileged background; what if the workers refused to accept a community of interest with such a government, and simply defied them?

If anyone feels more exposed to public derision, and more dependent on popularity, than politicians, it is poets. The English poet's desperate campaign to be an insider, one of the community, without thoughts of his own, goes back to the Edwardian years, although we know these poets as the Georgians. This cultural insecurity coincides with central instability over Irish nationalism, female suffrage, trade union militancy, and the enfranchisement of the working class.

In the older regime of local government, the poor were helped through charity, distributed partly by individuals and partly by the officials of a parochial organisation, for example vicars and beadles. Money and resources were distributed by the powerful to the powerless in such a way as to reinforce the relations of power. The gentry controlled the organs of local government, and exerted much influence over the parish clergy, frequently appointing their own relatives. The officials of local government were either clergymen or else non-professional and unimpressive. Teachers in parish schools were often discharged soldiers and sailors, thus provided for in their worn-out state. Many people besides the poor were dependent on the gentry for patronage; a young man of talent and slender means was unlikely to receive an education or make a literary career without it. Both gentry and parish officers were insignificant in the new urban aggregations, and nineteenth-century reforms removed education and welfare from the parish. The state grew and grew; its decrees were carried out by a new class of bureaucratic professionals. The duo of squire and parson found their economic and intellectual dominion undermined by new sources of money and a new secular learning, and their political power submerged by new strata of voters. The new professionals could never acquire the same legitimacy as the old masters. What power they did have derived from the centre, passing laws that gave them powers, and raising taxes that paid their wages. Their fitness for their employ was not based on social status but on paper qualifications, acknowledged by their fellow professionals but mysterious to the populace. The rise of the state had a direct effect on poetry, because the readers and writers of poetry were so entwined with the social fractions who staffed local government.

Vers libre came into English poetry through the Georgian predilection for everyday speech, and especially peasant speech, relying on warm imagery of freedom of movement and beautiful health. The whole history of twentieth-century English poetry rests on the Georgians, who seem impossible to think about; but we have to do that in order to assess the potential of regional poetry, why it denies its own history, why what it promises seems to be familiar to everyone and yet unfulfilled. The complex of everyday speech, *vers libre*, populism, regionalism, family conflict, aesthetic freedom, realist subject matter and socialism forms one whole;

and that whole was formulated, stuffed with solutions and with insoluble problems, by the Georgians.

It is in the Georgian period that we find a systematic attempt to escape the rhetorical machine of Victorian verse, which was in important respects continuous with Greco-Latin poetry and the whole Classical tradition. The escape was made simultaneously through use of colloquial speech; through subject matter drawn from the life of the lower classes and the provinces; through the avoidance of the 'sublime'; through free verse; through the return to reading aloud as the central event of poetry; through verse drama; and through dialect. It is this package, more or less, which forms the regionalist ideology. The ready acceptance which the regionalist and anti-literary theory finds today is due to the great age and familiarity of its arguments, even if these are not found in any major theoretical works. Of course, the preconditions for the rapid acceptance of such a programme in 1912 or so were existing values, so that the question of their ultimate origin eludes us; the Georgians found part of their blueprint in the poems of Housman, Hardy and Kipling, who were better poets than they; all were active in the 1890s.

The Georgian poets were revolutionaries; but they were against the process of thought. An attempt to get poetry back to the body led to a preoccupation with dance, and also to the adoption of free verse, seen as a more authentic rendition of speech and other physical rhythms than strict metre. Part of the importance of tragedy is that the choruses are written in a kind of free verse, and in a Greek dialect felt to be primitive; Nietzsche's *Dithyrambs* are in free verse. They are also a kind of dance. Making poetry regionally or dialectally specific brings about the illusion that the poet is in a state of idyllic unity, as if his mind contained only one layer and he never knew doubts or afterthoughts. Phyllis Bentley reassures us that '[d]ialect speech is used by people who are actually in contact with realities; the soil, the animal, the machine-tool are stubborn physical facts, with certain strongly-marked attributes of colour, shape, and smell, and speech which draws on such realities for its images rather than on book-made phrases is colourful and vigorous speech'.[1] A speaker who is involved in some physical activity is also preferred, since it is felt that this shuts out the labyrinths of psychology and hence also the possibility of deception. If you prefer people to be shown at some physical activity, it's because you shun and distrust psychological activity independent of physical tasks: that is, thought and imagination.

The Georgians liked to write about animals, about physical things, and about the lower classes. Is this a coincidence? I would like to think so, but the hypothesis presents itself that they put these things in the same category, and that the appeal of all of them had to do with an inability to think, being physical and therefore straightforward. Given the contemporary ramblings of Dr Freud and the arguments of various cultural critics of the disappeared Victorian Age, one might have expected the 'missing body' to be highly sexual: but there is no trace of this in the poetry concerned, with the exception of Lawrence. The body has become the main signifier, and a renunciation of mediations rich in culture is made up for by a series of scenes of boxing, working sailing ships, working in the fields, or simply walking. A physical act is read as true whereas a symbolic one is felt to be full of tricks.

The Georgian sense of unease was linked to an aesthetic distaste for the physique of the male clerk; the objections to book-learning and a sedentary lifestyle were tied to an image of male pride and sexuality which the City clerk failed to satisfy. The distaste for the writer as literate person, given to reading, came from this identification with the clerk. The liking for poems about animals – in fact strong, masterful, combative and energetic animals – is a projection of this ideal of the male form, and supplies an iconography of it. In visual art, the human subject has been chosen from among atypically good specimens; Georgian poetry was pursuing this deep aesthetic appetite at a moment when advanced painters were getting rid of it, and an insight into physiology led them to prefer anyone whose habitus tended to produce a clear eye, a firm grasp or a sexy walk to an intellectual. This provided an aesthetic basis for a dislike of the middle class. The favouring of a variety of male pin-up scenes (sailors, boxers, poachers, soldiers, etc.) by the Georgians opened up the possibility of another competitive scale of attractiveness within the poetic arena to run side by side with the scale of sophistication. The preoccupation with male grace was ambiguous. The insistence that the way you walk says everything about you might be effective when writing about animals, but involved a fundamental simplification of the nature of humans. This could persuade the poet to enter a game in which poetry was the more desirable the more it excluded ideas, introspection, thought, argument, and the fruits of learning. Georgian poetry has remained popular because it persuades readers to enter that game, and was truly simple and immediate. The politics of those poems about underprivileged people were equally crucial to their popularity, and it has always been obvious to readers in the British cultural sphere what those politics were, i.e. socialism and social welfare. Conversely, communalist poetry by White British groups was imprinted by the Georgian poets, and was following that line up till the 1980s.

The doctrine of simultaneity was felt to be incompatible with reading, where the body is 'switched off' while the brain pursues intangibles. The pursuit of the artist figure who was simultaneously active in mind and body led naturally to the idealisation of the shaman. The appeal of these primitive figures also included the allure of religious power, the culmination of much yearning in the nineteenth century, expressed in the Symbolist movement and the occult revival. The shaman-impersonating poems of the 1960s and 1970s should be set side by side with the Parisian mages of 1880 or so, the Order of the Golden Dawn, and their attempts to call up spirits. The cultic systems of Yeats, Lawrence and Graves are marginal intellectually, even theologically, but central poetically.

Authenticity Visible and Audible

We can apparently gauge authenticity as we read poetry. As we scan we distinguish, fluently and continually, between what is credible and what is not, a high degree of agreement is reached about these judgments, and yet the proofs of veracity must be seen as tenuous and half-unconscious. No, further, there are a great many instances where they cannot possibly be convincing, because what we are seeing is a theatrical performance or a piece of fiction. Language constantly points to an outside that is radically absent and hidden. This area offers detailed resistance to thought, and still we have to invade it in order to assess the idea that one group of writers (regional poets) is more credible than another (poets who have had the misfortune to be educated or to live in London). We can at least draft the history of these prejudices.

Sincerity seems at this point to mean the consonance of what you're saying and what's happening to your body. This throws into question all the mental activity that can't be reduced to physical experience, and indeed the strategy of Georgian poetry seems to be to exclude such mental activity, to thrust it into the negative space where, say, factory workers might have skulked in a Victorian poem of the sublime. The affective body is a manifold of blood flow, muscle tension, sensations in the stomach, on the skin, the work of 300 glands each giving a different 'music' or 'colour'. This definition of the intellect as the source of insincerity is a bizarre contrast to the notion of the body in love as the site of selfish desire and so of insincere words: you're only saying that to get round me. If the Georgians felt guilty about having ideas it's probably because they were idealists.

There is a link between short reaction times and the unconscious. A batsman in cricket, for example, has so little time to think about the delivery he is facing that all the most important calculations of speed, trajectory and so on must be preconscious: they are too complex to be conscious. So it is that the mystery of the unconscious is right there in the performance, in a 30-second segment of time which you can capture on tape. The audience assumes that coordination of voice, hands and facial expression is too difficult to be faked. Deceit is a kind of athleticism.

The issue of synchronisation and side-shift opens up for us a new area of the unspoilt, unbounded and primeval, a virtual particle which only exists for tenths of a second, perhaps less, at a time; and its name is the spontaneous reaction before thought has operated. This one can't quite be labelled a periphery, but it bears resemblances to the other untainted peripheral realms of the regions, the colonies, the lower classes, gypsies, the avant-garde frontier, the experience of women, childhood, etc. The most determined proponent of it was the Georgian poet D. H. Lawrence, whose concern was with

> poetry of the immediate present. This he defined as an attempt to secure permanency in the present's 'wind-like transit', not in the 'finality' of formal perfection produced by the closure of retrospective or prospective experience. [...] His poems cannot therefore begin in generalisation, but in an effort of specific attention to the here and now that destabilises the consolidations of culture.[2]

So the difference between marvel and inauthenticity is one of time: they are the same slice of experience seen at two successive stages of its existence. What interests us chiefly is the fact that Lawrence completely distrusts thought. Thought subtracts value.

The film director Ken Russell recalled in an interview how he had to persuade his actors not to deliver their speeches first and give a facial reaction afterwards, but to produce the facial reaction at the same time as the speeches. It seems possible that the job of the actor is to produce a kind of tautology where the face, the body and the voice say the same thing at the same time. Certainly a temporal side-shift or discrepancy gives the impression of inauthenticity. The good actor wins our consent to what we know, logically, to be untrue. The ordinance of speech would then be based on tubes, linking the several levels of speech behaviour at a moment in time; events at one level would be critically related to events at other levels within the same narrow time-frame, the same tube, rather than to later and earlier events on the same level.

If these three channels of information are so revealing, what is the effect of the print medium, which eliminates two of them and forces the channel of speech into a simplified and stylised form? The first answer would be that print frustrates the onlooker, who has no contextual clues to support or disprove the allegations of the speaker; the issue of sincerity is far less important in print. A second answer might be that the same testing for discrepancy is still going on, but is displaced to other dimensions of the text; both as an inspection by the onlooker, and as a way of encoding conviction and 'simultaneity' for the writer. It may be that the apparatus of regular metre was perceived as a restitution of physical elements to language, so that following the prosodic rules was a kind of test of integrity in the poet.

Once the channels have been coordinated, the reader, whose attention can be described as a set of rhythmic impulses, becomes coordinated too, locking to various time pulses whose predictability (rhythmicity) is what allows sharing: a periodic common space. Attention is not something that the reader can learn, but a quality built into the microstructure of the text, whose ability to bind time in a set of integrating and converging lines is a drama where information is a reward and reinforcement. Rhythm is another kind of tube, stretching horizontally across time with the quality of recurrence, rather than vertically, with the quality of simultaneity. Rhythm echoes itself and realism echoes what is withheld and immovable. The tautology of lips and eyes moving in coordination is effective conceal-ment of the self-referentiality of the unverifiable narrative.

There is an affinity between the discrepancy in poetic delivery and the contradiction in the social order which gives rise to the dialectic. The whole project of radical political criticism is predicated on the visibility of discrepancies where the power order betrays itself: mismatches as chinks through which light bursts from a concealed universe of truth.

Greek philosophy, the art of dialectic, was very closely linked to the art of rhetoric. Cicero wrote instructions to the orator, *De Oratore*, which give great play to gestures, including the technique of bursting into tears; his surviving speeches are incomplete scores, to which the score of mime (memorised before the day of delivery) would have to be added. The authenticity of the emotions being signalled is, of course, incompatible with the fact that the signals themselves are being taught. Rhetoric, so central to Greek and Roman trials and politics, thus has deceit inscribed obviously at its centre; a smoking pistol as embarrassing as, for example, the fact is, for those who believe that Freudian reports come directly from the unconscious, that Freud was an expert hypnotist and was in the habit of hypnotising his patients. Having established that it is coordination and simultaneity in a reciter that carry us away, are we to believe that it is artlessness, awkwardness and the appearance of naive incompetence which are the signs of authenticity – that is, excellence – in a poet? Would such a writer not arouse in us the most intimate indifference, while allaying our suspicions of fraud? Other studies on credibility come from social psychologists; indeed, it seems that there are layers of behaviour signalling intention, of which some are harder to put under conscious control than others. By relying on the involuntary nature of certain facial muscles, tears, perfect coordination, and so on, we lay ourselves open to trained professionals – who in this way become, possibly, the ruling class.

Treatises on the art of the actor differ from treatises on poetics by their practical nature. The most profound of these is Heinrich von Kleist's *Über das Marionettentheater*; it points out the value of the appropriate bearing, gestures and vocal inflections, while pushing the question of inner experience out into the margins to the point where one doubts the necessity of its playing a role in art at all; Kleist raises the question whether the correct physical behaviour does not arouse the emotions concerned, for the actor just as it does for the onlooker. Kleist is perhaps in reality not concerned with the emotions of actors, but with the emotions of poets: is composing a drama, say about Penthesilea, Queen of the Amazons, so different from studying and playing the lead role in the finished drama? So far as I know, no-one has added to Kleist's reflections on this topic.

We cannot separate narcissism, a quality for which actors are noted, from self-awareness, the observation and training that allow one to achieve coordination and visible authenticity. Its absence would mean simply being bad at conveying messages – constant failures of communication. Art is perhaps the opposite of awkwardness.

The *Spectator*, no. 407, from 1712, has a very interesting passage on the reluctance of English orators to move their hands around while making speeches: 'our Orators are observed to make use of less Gesture or Action than those of other Countries'; they speak 'without those Strainings of the Voice, Motions of the Body, and Majesty of the Hand'; this national characteristic has, anecdotally, a distribution over much of northern

Europe, and it is reported that Russians find Estonians cold because the latter make so little use of gesture and facial mime. The same applies to relevant areas of North America. The *Spectator* speaks of problems looking at the extravagant poses of Italian pictures, which seem ridiculous to the English eye. Messages are garbled when two cultural conventions of body language come into contact, and the receiver's code differs from the code by which the message was generated. Eastern European Jews have a notably different gestus and speech melody from the English.

The written standard language is like a big suit inside which the real state of someone's body is disguised. The notation of dialect gives rise to a very specific acoustic image, specific in the way it details the duration and quality of tiny muscular events; the brief durations which are the material difference between Northumbrian sounds and Birmingham sounds obviously resemble the brief durations and specific nature of a performance, where voice, hands and face are coordinated. We can hardly separate this from the current of *vers libre*, which aimed to release the voice by accepting and recording its personal rhythms. Gordon Bottomley moved on from the *Georgian Books* to being as successful as a verse playwright could expect to be: 'Rhythmic speech is best continued and fulfils itself in movement of a similar nature';[3] his plays were choreographed as well as directed, and his last volume was called *Choric Plays*. Behind all this is the sensation of a missing or silenced body, an enervating anxiety that words entrusted to print were becoming ghostly and evacuated.

I noted above that making poetry regionally or dialectally specific brings about the illusion that the poet is a unity. By saying that what is under conscious control is the layer where deception has its say, I imply that consciousness is the source of deception. This indeed seems to sum up the Georgian aesthetic, and perhaps explains why no-one in Britain seems willing to think about poetry. But after all many of the functions of the intelligence have to do with avoiding deception; to switch it out offers a perspective of dull emotional brutality as well as illusions never dispelled.

Dialect Drama and Peasant Realism: *Krindlesyke*, by Wilfrid Gibson

She's a tough customer – she's always been
A banging, bobberous bletherskite, has Bell –
No fushenless, brashy, mim-mouthed mealy-face,

Fratished and perished in the howl-o'-winter.
No wind has ever blown too etherish,
Too snell to fire her blood: she's always relished
A gorly gousty blusterous day that sets
Her wits alow and birselling like a whin-fire.

[...]

Already, dang you, with your hettle tongue:
You've put the notion in my head the curs
Are on my scent; and now I cannot rest.
Happen they're slinking now up Bloodysyke
Like adders through the bent... Nay, they don't yelp,
The hounds that sleuth me: it's only in my head
I hear the yapping: they're too cunning to yelp,
The sleichers slither after me on their bellies
As dumb and slick as adders... But I'm doitered
And doting like a dobby.

                    (from *Krindlesyke*, 1922)

I'm not trying to revive Gibson (1878–1962) as a serious poet; as with so many poets who write about poverty and people oppressed by material compulsion, after time has gone by the emotional compulsion to read his work turns out to be missing. My interest in Gibson is of a sociolinguistic order: he is England's only technically ambitious dialect poet. His self-published trilogy *Fires* of 1912 was one of the foundations of the Georgian style. Three of the founders of this colloquial, realist and peasant revolt were northerners: Abercrombie, Bottomley and Gibson. Note that each of them wrote poetic dramas – poetry as speech, then. As elements that tie them to a specifically northern view of speech and class we can cite stress on the physical; predominance of physical limits, such as poverty and violence; lack of grace; closeness to oral forms, such as dialogue and narrative; fondness for dialect and ordinary speech; indifference to high-flown language and to Continental ideas about literature. A number of reservations have to be made about the selectivity of any thematic approach, the similarity of regional cultures to each other, and the unity of a single chronological horizon. Nonetheless, with these three we may have the start of a conscious treatment of the northern scene in poetry.

Gibson is an exception to most generalisations; in general, it has been impossible to write dialect poetry in England for hundreds of years. *Krindlesyke*, with a few other dramatic poems collected in *Kestrel's Edge and Other Poems*, thus stands out. The regionalist campaign in poetry reached a great volume in the 1940s but really goes back to the Georgians; it was already tangled up with the socialist cause, and with the discovery of a rural poverty undermining all Arcadias. Despite the flare-up of dialect in Masefield (*The Everlasting Mercy*, 1912, and especially *The Tragedy of Nan*, 1908) and Gibson, virtually no English dialect poetry of any value has been written since them. Gibson is exceptional for geolinguistic reasons: deep dialect is preserved in peripheral areas of sparse settlement and poor communications, and the bleak pastoral uplands of Northumberland are just that. Place-names seem to site his dramas in the area to the north of Hadrian's Wall, reaching towards Kielder Forest and the Cheviots: one of the emptiest parts of the whole island. This is a deep dialect area, deeper possibly than the town of Langholm, a short distance to the north-west. But most English people live in the cities – most poets, too.

Krindlesyke, a never-produced drama in blank verse, is set in 'a remote shepherd's cottage on the Northumbrian fells'. It is creaky in its vocabulary of dying speeches, orphans in the storm, long-lost sons returning, and so on, but compels admiration by its grasp of character, narrative and milieu. Its strength lies also in the vigorous tirades in dialect. As the play opens, the youngest son is getting married, while his cast-off mistress and bastard son arrive for a visit; five sons have already run away from home and gone to the bad. It's hard to exaggerate the atmosphere of dislike within this family. Take this exchange, where the mother upbraids the father, after forty years of marriage (*flum*, flattery; *fleech*, flake off):

> *Eliza*. Yes, I was young, and agape
> For your wheedling flum till it fleeched itself from me.
> There's something in a young girl seems to work
> Against her better sense and gives her up
> Almost in spite of her.
> *Ezra*.   It's nature.
> *Eliza*.   Then
> Nature has more than enough to answer for.

The dogma that an injection of colloquial speech makes poetry more lively, rather than less, was worked out by Georgian theorists such as Lascelles Abercrombie, and may simply be untrue; perhaps the examples quoted are brilliant poetic remakes of colloquial material. The idea of a materialist source of poetry could work for Gibson, recording an extraordinarily tart and colourful peasant speech that was unfamiliar to the audience; it has never worked since, and there is now no alternative to making poetry by thinking, by innovation, and by artifice. The project of presenting working-class or unrespectable characters, and situating personal feelings in a realistic social context, was far better carried off by the Georgians, whose socialist orientation guided their style, than by the supposedly Marxist poets of the thirties. Gibson is consistent in his portrayal of material wants and compulsions; the realist approach that this imposed was oppressive and uninteresting. What is the way out of this?

The suspicion is aroused that regional poetry today, along with the whole raft of realist and domestic poetry, cannot succeed because its literary contexts are too informationally simple to evoke social situations, too superficial to evoke conflicts inside them. *Krindlesyke* is 90 pages and perhaps 3600 lines long; Gibson must have had a confidence in the interest of his subject matter which our contemporaries are far from possessing. Perhaps they're aware that no character is interesting without conflict? The lack of beauty in Gibson's poetry is tied up with his characters being too poor, with physical want predominating at every step, and with his avoidance of fantasy. He deserves to be remembered, not just because of his best poetry, but also for failing in this rigorous way. His 'hearthstone' dramas are kitchen sink before kitchen sink, and indeed much tougher, more riven by conflict, more pressed for money, than the characters created by those 1950s dramatists. But forgotten – because realism uses itself up and gets taken out of circulation like old pound notes.

The case against regionalism has, however, to take on the artistic achievements of *The Tragedy of Nan*, *The Everlasting Mercy*, of Edward Thomas, A. E. Housman, and indeed much of Thomas Hardy. Something can be great poetry without being chic.

I have long wondered why the term for thick dialect in Italian is *stretto* (narrow), but in Scots and English 'broad'. 'Broad' in English should probably be opposed to 'refined', as in broad gestures, broad terms, broad humour, broadcloth. It implies that speaking in dialect is an energetic but imprecise activity, like shovelling dirt. It points to a difference of class habitus: if he weren't a peasant, he wouldn't gesticulate so *broadly*. Such haphazard energy also bowls wides; wide of the mark is akin to broad. In the opposite direction, correct speech is akin to writing and thinking, seen as actions involving progressively smaller amounts of energy and narrower tolerances. 'Broad' is, then, in opposition to 'fine'; although, all things considered, we could say that it, and *stretto*, also oppose 'faint'. A Welsh term for English is *yr iaith fain* (or *meiniaith*), 'the slender language', again in opposition to 'broad'. (*Main* also means 'shrill, treble'.)

Assets of the Centre: Doubt and Deceit

Anthony Mellors has proposed that recent decades have seen 'a general and abiding epistemological division between the largely anti-modernist mainstream trend in poetry publication/attention and the continuing tradition of experimental work inspired by modernism and the objectivists in particular'.[4] The difference between the two realms of poetry would be, if *epistemological*, the quality of the poet's testing of primary experiences and impulses, the facing up to or decorative elimination of what resists the unmediated fantasy of the self, the rigour of reflection on experience, careful discussing with other witnesses, the setting aside of theatrical conventions to leave a clear space. This interpretation explains most of the visible differences, while giving a too rapid way of dividing poetry into chic and dowdy; the bulk of the audience can't even follow the explanation of why modern-style poetry is not like the flow of conversations in a restaurant, and wants asserted what this system for making poems doubts. Doubt can become a verbal mannerism and a way of signalling membership of an educational elite: the information in a poem comes from introspection, and while testing can find new patterns in it, it is still the same kind of information after as before. Becoming conscious of what you're doing is no help unless you can find a better way of doing it.

The differences between poetry and pop songs, as they exist today, depend on accumulated, inherited techniques, which we absorb in childhood or adolescence: the history of European poetry and music, made synchronous as divergences in technique. We could ask how far Mellors' distinction between cultivated and naive poetry is already that which separates poetry from popular song. This history is not the past of all classes, all ethnic groups, and all regions. The distinction Mellors suggests corresponds perhaps to the study of philosophy, but certainly to sexual manners and the presentation of the self in a community of literates, where a lack of self-interrogation is seen as crassness which restricts the relationship. The university is the home of a new orality, where the lofty register of poetry is most closely matched to the speech of daily social life. However significant reading is, talking is more so; here poetry can reflect dialogue, not an internal monologue, which is perpetually running down and going into loops. Cultural creativity belongs to groups, rather than to individuals: such poetic associations flare up all too briefly, leaving bright tracks in literary history.

Why is oral different from literary? In a social gathering, there is a nonverbal channel of messages carried by people's whole bearing, their movements, gestures, the tone and volume of their voices, their laughter, and so on. It is from this channel that someone gauges whether the others are glad or not to see him or her; its value depends on presence, so that although it presents a mighty set of imperatives to assimilate, which are very hard not to obey, this information is unimportant the next day. It is not true that this channel carries information inherently different from explicit verbal utterance, or that it is more powerful than the latter: the two channels carry largely the same messages, but the carrying details of speech, qualification and so on are very different. This channel builds up a *context*, so that the value of a statement at any moment depends on the contents of this channel over the previous two hours, or however long the gathering has been there. Simple verbal descriptions of social events are barren, because they fail to evoke this cumulative memory, whose parts are not obscure, but numerous. Reading a book, or listening to a record, are awkward because they are not social; the context around them is silence, the quiet of a bedroom or living-room; any live art has well-known advantages. The advantage of a university, as formerly of a court, is that the page catches this live interaction and dense context, even if this means an excess of information.

The more transient and local information words pick up, the closer they are to live art, and the further away from the defined, permanent meanings. This is the nature of context. Imitation is the chief means by which context enters art: a comedian imitates someone, and it is funny, and social, although someone who was outside the context, and didn't recognise the original, would feel excluded. In poetry, the kind of stylistic awareness which involves parody, allusion, recognition, and sometimes defiance or competitive excelling, is the most knowledge-rich and simul-taneously the most social and closest to live art. We can draw a line of equivalence which says that stylistic awareness is the literary equivalent of social ambience in live performance. We have seen the elements of this in the early development of the literary language as described by N. F. Blake. Literature evolves to bring back what was first lost in the transition from performance to page, and writing that is without personal style, and stiff and repetitive, reflects an undeveloped stage, when the return and translation process has not run its course.

Analysts of these matters say that writing introduces doubt: a story washes over its hearers and they are satisfied inside it, whereas once stories are written down we notice the gaps and inconsistencies in them. The origin of critical history may go back, not quite to the invention of alphabetical writing, but to the arrival of a social order in which there was mass literacy: the breakthrough of the Greek world was due less to 'national spirit' than to a modern writing system and a better technical and social basis for critical thinking. The flourishing of critical history over the past two centuries in the West may not have brought 'the truth', but conclusively shows a superiority of the historian who compares rival versions and studies sources over the previous arrangement of the profession, still attuned to the oral art of rhetoric, and skilled at formal order, panegyric and story-telling. The advance of print affects doubt, identification, solidarity, emotional assimilation, the immersion of the individual in a shared stream of symbolic imperatives; the penetration of print into society is very uneven, and tends to vary with wealth and status. For a fraction of the audience, poetry that is less involving and less emotional is of higher status: eminence varying inversely with gratification. This is the rule forever misinterpreted historically as being 'anti-Romantic'. The split in the poetry audience about doubt is not between those who have read George Oppen and those who haven't, but reflects sociological stratification based on educational level. This strata-split is only realised in poetic terms in this way by those who have acquired the right cultural training, and can in fact realise itself in several other ways, some older and some closer to majority acceptance. Although doubt tends to make the individual autonomous from the currents of assimilatory demands of the others around him, accepting the prestige-value of doubt, and of the experimental style in poetry, is an act of obedience and assimilation to the group; and the poems you subsequently write display badges of recognition, legal tender not only in Britain and the USA. We can ask how much this self-consciousness owes to the behavioural acuity of court culture, how much to the soul-searching of the Church, and how much to scepticism and empiricism connected to the rise of the bourgeoisie and of market capitalism. Emotion in a poem is not-OK because it asks for sympathetic circularity, the attachment that cancels detachment; it corresponds to rhythm at the phonetic level, a convergent imperative that does away with pure autonomy. Suppressing attachment is not primarily an act directed against women, as objects of the affection that is being repressed, but is directed at upward mobility and at assimilation to a desired stratum. A cultural commodity, say an idea or a poetic style, is like a plot of empty ground in which people are allowed to buy stakes. The value of the plot is talked up. It may rise in value relative to thousands of other plots; it may not take off at all. The whole thing is a venture fraught with risk and floating on language. The value of a cultural asset follows the perceptions of the market. The assets of doubt, austerity, resistance to other people's feelings, began to influence the Objectivist share price only thirty or even forty years after the initial flotation: they were not legitimately the poets of the upper middle class while it commercially ignored them. Eventually, they came to stand for exclusivity and long-term growth.

Following writers such as Anton Ehrenzweig and Gustav-René Hocke, we can divide art into an overt and articulate channel, and an implicit, subjective one, which is either not representational, or directly expressive of the artist's physical impulses and states of mind. Because the latter is called style, we can say that it corresponds to the direct exchange of mood-bearing signals forming social ambience; because the engagement of signs within a system of fine discriminations directs the attention and gives them an immeasurably greater impact, the shared ability to relate single poems to a larger poetic context of style, as a literate and cultivated audience possesses it, gives poetry a whole new world of expression.

It is possible to argue that, as the Greeks developed reason, they lost the ability to create myths: all of which are already present at the dawn of the written tradition. Logically, as someone sheds the faculty of doubt, and forfeits the benefits of reason, they should gain in their ability to persuade the reader, and be wholehearted in their emotional projections: this is an assumption which has proved consistently wrong in poetry. I suppose this is due to poets mistaking their medium; instead of clinging to print, which has proved inexorable, they should have moved off to rock music, a world of suggestibility scorning the reality principle.

Cognitive dissonance theory is not really about dissonance, accepted as a universal background, but about the cognitive acts which wipe out dissonance, which are a function of the identity of the group. It would be logical to define 'group belonging' in terms of 'sharing group perceptions', and this would only be interesting at certain points, where perception is ambiguous, and where the group overlay either adds to it or hides part of it. It would be very hard to define *ambience* or *live feeling* without bringing in cognitive dissonance and this force which unwrites it. It also lets us define doubt – as the opposite of suggestibility (and of group belonging), which leaves dissonance alone in the hope of turning it to profit. The extent of ambiguity is indeterminacy, a key political term in recent British poetry.

Someone who sees unmediated reality as bleak and grey and featureless sees community values as an improvement on it, and so perhaps likes communitarian poetry; someone who sees the straightening of dissonance as a loss of information and knowledge may therefore like sceptical and investigative and non-teleological poetry; and this is the ridge dividing the two tastes.

Everything leads us to believe that there is a relationship of mutual exclusion between poetic style and communal solidarity; that stylistic nuance takes the place of sympathetic circularity, as the source of persuasion; that style is the product of a literate social group, preceding print but greatly extended by it; that the doubt violently brought about by reducing the self-assured flow of speech to cold print both makes the old communal poetry ridiculous, and induces stylistic differentiation as a way of restoring conviction; that, because it is superfluous to describe to the people around you their own behaviour and the scene they can see, the writer can only evoke a social milieu by pretending to go outside it, and becoming conscious of its organisation in order to find words for it; that a social group is inherently polyphonic, and that literature tends to recreate this division of meanings.

Deceit

Readers fear emotional betrayal by lyric poets because of the real-life betrayals which have been detailed by virtually every feminist book since 1968, if not before. We need go no further than this picture of purity of intent and accuracy of reporting in sexual relations to see why literary theory constantly produces new reasons for withholding sympathy and disbelieving what the writer says, and never new reasons for believing the writer, identifying, enjoying the experience. Disbelief in male authority figures, and in their symbolic representations of self and others, is also disbelief in their literature. Any survey of modern poetry will find hundreds of poems that complain about being deceived; this is usually within sexual relationships, but also applies to someone's whole understanding of the world. It would be ludicrous to separate the scepticism of modern Parisian philosophers from the practical questions of assessing the offers of lovers and employers. The optimistic tenet of the feminist social revolution is that the sceptical project is a stage B, replacing a stage A of passivity and superstition, and to be followed by a stage C of new emotional integrity, love and trust. However, stage C appears to be a mere textual figure, a castle in the air, and there is no reason to think that stage

B will finish its song and bow off. The positivistic project of building self-confidence, and reverence for female artists and thinkers, goes against every other current of critical thought.

How does one acquire greater acuity? Philosophy is concerned with distinguishing between truth and illusion; the resistance to philosophy may have to do, not with the vacuity and perplexity of the subject, but with fear of its results. It may be that the writings of Derrida, Deleuze or whoever it may be are of little practical use, or it may be that any method that practises acuity and suggests ways in which deceit may be embedded in language makes poets better at their trade.

In the film *Spellbound*, Ingrid Bergman, playing a psychiatrist pondering the causes of her patients' excessive hopes of love and their bitter disappointment, says 'I think it's the poets who are to blame more than anyone else!' If you never trust anyone, you can't be deceived; but you exclude art and, presumably, love and ideals. The philosophical study of deceit must encourage principled behaviour and moral commitment; the pursuit of intellectual consistency must lead to constancy of emotional commitment. The uncovering of deceit also brings about a regret for deceit; if one regards the ability to fall in love as the result of integrity, then studying one's own feelings may be a way of attaining integrity. If your feelings are good, you don't have to deceive other people. Lyric poetry, in the version we have of it, may be simply a by-product, a welling-up of the energies involved in discovering, as an adolescent, what it means to love and to be loved. Close attention to the flaws in one's feelings may be a preparation for love – because inattentiveness may be the result of despair, in someone who is no longer trying to avoid moral depravity. The flaws are spread by time into a domestic scenery.

At a certain moment, reading poetry is like falling in love. One of the central accusations against modernity is the absence of love poetry – a problem that goes back deep into the nineteenth century, and did not suddenly strut on stage with the arrival of structuralism. Love has among its primary requirements passivity, submission, sympathy and loyalty. Love is a means of self-fulfilment, a form of power, but asks self-denial and adaptability as the price. Being in love causes a split in the self, because something essential to it is now outside its control, and capable of complex autonomous action. The end of frustration is only possible through the loss of autonomy. The gaze of the other person is now so perceptive that it can hardly do otherwise than bring intense self-consciousness and doubt. Poetry concludes that one of the greatest obstacles to love, worse than money or other people, is selfishness. The interests of love therefore imply a higher standard than self-interest. The eclipse of love poetry over the past century suggests an inhibition about self-presentation, a withdrawal from articulating the most important feelings, an uncertainty about the duration and constancy of one's feelings, from which intensive attention could offer an exit.

Of course, what the poet says about his or her own feelings, about what happened in his or her relationships with other people, and about other people's feelings, about morality, or about the way to be happy, is questionable. The judge should be a third party. Self-awareness is a representation, it is true or false, and subject to the same critical, truth-finding procedures as government statements, newspaper stories, or manufacturers' claims. The information in a poem does not reach the poet in the claws of a white eagle that has just flown down from the hall of Zeus on Olympus. Isn't the autobiographical, or domestic, project in poetry the relict of a withdrawal from the realms that poetry once governed, a national redoubt like the Kuomintang retreating to Taiwan? The poet is strongly motivated to adorn, conceal and exaggerate in just the scenes where he or she has eye-witness status: the more intimate the involvement, the more it points back at the poet. The proper subject of philosophy is not truth but its forerunner, deceit – which language has evolved in order to carry out, as its proper and central task, under and within the other task of sharing information. The human capacity to deceive must be linked to the imaginative capacity, and this must be linked to the ability to make art. The audience already seeks to assess the value of the information being given it by forming an estimate of the writer's character, and the whole fabric of poetry is already aimed at reassuring the audience on this score. This is the reason for many stylistic choices; the poet is sending the message, *I lack all imagination so I must be telling the truth*; or *I'm writing about my personal experience so I must be telling the truth*; or *I feign all kinds of moral horror at other people so I must be too good to lie.*

The area in which credibility slides is not the validity of ideas, but of the character and credibility of the individuals who carry them and lend them a fickle reality. The dispute is over social structure rather than ascertainable facts. Theories certainly do conflict with the chains of mediation, tradition and association which yield the information recounted by art. In these zones of conflict, theory in a sense has to win, because it offers a judicial method for analysing and discriminating between rival versions, which intuitivism does not. Only a rule that provides for the mortality of theories can offer a way out of plurality and hung councils. On the other hand, theory may have nothing to offer beyond this adjudication.

From Deceit to Epistemology

The self, as the machine that organises and enhances narratives, is a source of ideology. Since ideology is the visitation of self-interest on the realm of ideas, this is tautologous; distortions and the self live in the same place. I suppose there are no lies in an empty room; it takes human beings to lie and also to be deceived. Political ideology is an extension of processes, occurring within the household and within the individual psyche, inherent to natural language. Any analysis of representations is likely to find projective fantasy, and repression or non-reporting; traces of self-interest. However, the personal, or empirical, or individualist, tradition in art also holds that personal experience is the most intense and real, and that reports on the self are more direct and arrive at greater pressure. It is postulated that the self is a source of illusions and that the self is a source of greater truth. For these the poem is a channel.

The gesture of philosophy which claims to examine error and uncover truth is incomplete, because truth is never confirmed, all the tests are negative in their results; the missing source of validation can only be religion. The search for religious truth produced a critique of the mind's capacity for being deceived which anticipates modern philosophy; William Law wrote to John Wesley: 'The head can easily amuse itself with a living and justifying faith in the blood of Jesus, as with any other notion; and the heart, which you suppose to be a place of security, as being the seat of self-love, is more deceitful than the head.'[5] Patrick Walker, one of the most partisan of all historians, says of his own opinions, 'And at the time I think (but I may think otherwise tomorrow, for I have gotten many proofs of my self, and yet my self is a mystery to my self), that if I be not under the power of a strong delusion [...]'.[6] For Protestants, the mind is the source of understanding, of inconstancy and heresy. *My self is a mystery to my self.* The Holy Ghost is invoked to save us from the consequences of our mortality when studying the Bible, yet the existence of heresy demonstrates that the Ghost can neglect us, and Calvin's adducing of demons to explain the inner conviction of men in theological error opens the way to the belief that there is a class of demons, clustering around the act of reading and feeding theological passion, of whom either one or zero may be a Holy Ghost. Walker was looking back on a war of religion; perhaps the Cold War produced an equal amount of rant and partisan feeling, of triumphs of intelligence justifying both sides, and an equal helplessness at the mysteries underlying judgment and identification.

The latent task of the intelligence is to discover the systems underlying the signs of other people. This is as much philosophy as poetry; it is the training for the real tasks of choosing lovers, employers, religious and political leaders. Is to be more sceptical to be more up-to-date? To say that one can perfectly well conduct life, make art, administer a country and so on using fallible sources of data is deceptive only insofar as it creates a verbal ghost of other, *infallible* sources of data. The fear of deceit pours out of the ground at the places where trust is exchanged, where we make bonds and engage in shared projects, and also where language is especially dense and fluent. The incapacity to trust other people means the incapacity to love, or to take part in public life, or in fact to read or compose poetry. To trust no-one, to seize on error and batten on it to the exclusion of all else, is to induce the disaster which distrust panted to avert: a starvation pang of emotional, economic and intellectual distress. Error uncovered yields literary pleasure where it disproves some of your working hypotheses or the flaw in the stable surface opens up a whole new stratum of phenomena. Utter disillusion has to do with a kind of Utopian nostalgia for absolute truth; or it could be a terminal consequence of the evolution of a sophisticated group with too much accumulated knowledge of betrayals, reaching zero velocity in absolute scepticism. Perhaps we accept lower standards of accuracy for accounts of the inner life than for events in the physical world; this may be intelligent pragmatic behaviour given the difficulties of seizing and identifying mental experiences as they go by.

From Gorgons to Girl-Groups: Denise Riley (1948–)

It's possible that new waves of theory have brought nothing to poetry. Perhaps they were bad psychology. Perhaps they were special pleading. Perhaps their integration changed them too much to be recognised. 'Theory' isn't a generator of better artistic practice in the way that systems analysis was a generator of better practice in engineering and management.

A recent poem by Denise Riley is 'Problems of Horror':

Boys play and a horse moves through the woods.
Through perfectly heat-sealed lyric, how to breathe?

He has tailored a calling out of disgust, he spins to see its hang on him;
privately faint at heart he pirouettes [...]
'I've got the measure of this damaged world' – the new barbarian's charmed
sick
with his own sincerity, sluiced in town georgics fluency, solitude skills.
His is the smooth emulsion of a truly-felt revulsion.
He does not mean to be so pure an isolate.

The point of departure is a painting by Claude showing the Gorgon's head: whichever text Claude was following gave the details about Pegasus springing out of the truncated body of Medusa (one of the sister Gorgons), and the origin of coral from seaweed petrified by the Gorgon's blood. (Mythographically, one early image of the Gorgon was a horse with a woman's head, a fantastic anatomy later adapted into an origin myth for Pegasus.) Sight of the Gorgon's head turned men to stone. Perseus fought her by watching her reflection in his highly polished shield – averting his gaze – and the poem is a kind of anatomical drawing of squeamishness, all its organs and nerves drawn in painstaking Dutch style. The attack is on supercilious and contemptuous modernism which names its horror 'political', but denies all interest in the material needs which politics, as the shared code of society, exists to fulfil. Schematised and rigid systems of ideas, such as Marxism or the artistic attitudes of Adorno, can be seen as petrified (turned to stone). This is the origin of one kind of 'theory'. The surface of the shield can be seen as the private domain of reflexivity into which the squeamish withdraw. 'Sealed' may be an echo of 'shield' – 'heat-sealed' from 'light-shield'. The revulsion yields a slick surface, one which allows no grip and yields no textural information. 'The new barbarian' refers to several younger Left-modernist poets, whose names we can safely omit. Their raising of the moral stakes is competitive: the concealed aim is to disqualify a rival for being insufficiently 'moral' and theoretically instructed. They avert their gaze from everyone else in the world of poetry, and of the intellect, so as to attain domination: in his empty, ravaged landscape, the poet with the skills of solitude becomes one of the four most important people left. His claim is still to be selfless.

The winged horse Pegasus has special associations with poetry: the Hippocrene ('horse-fountain') Spring on Mount Helicon is said to have arisen from his hoof-marks (*pege* means 'spring'), and poets are described as being carried off to Helicon, home of the Muses, where they find inspiration. This is, initially, why a poem about lyric poets involves the Medusa. The link is also a riddle – and we may guess that the Medusa appears because lyric poetry involves self-idealisation, and this is akin to the grotesque (since the Medusa is a grotesque projection of the image of a woman), in that idealisation and the creation of monsters are both parasitical on perception. At some level, the myth shows a young man gazing at a woman, being horrified, being unable to gaze at her – and averting his gaze. It would seem that he then *writes a poem* – and that Denise Riley reads the poem. In 'Metallica', a poem included in the volume *Mop Mop Georgette*, the poet says 'I dropped away/veiled in the snakelocks', which apparently has the poet identifying herself with Medusa, the most famous owner of snakes for hair. More probably, 'Problems of Horror' is the poet asking for accurate perceptions rather than wilful projections. The appeal of *the poem* is in its idealism: the poet's moral standards are so high that they invigorate the reader. Only someone who wasn't morally compromised could draw the moral distinctions and expose the self-serving sorrow of these pale prigs. We can become fixated on someone intense and high enough to write such a poem: it is impossible to see someone good without experiencing a profound attraction towards them, which is (already) why so many egoists write pseudo-moral poems.

Dry Air (Virago, 1985) reprises many poems from earlier small press pamphlets along with many new ones. This was Riley's only book of poetry up till *Mop Mop Georgette* (1993). So, two books conveniently collect the bulk of her work, with exceptions worth a fan's energy. In general Riley wrote very few poems between 1985 and 1991. In view of various ill-informed rumours, it is as well to point out that Denise Riley is unrelated to the other two poets called Riley, John and Peter.

A theme running through *Dry Air* is the household, as dreamed of:

> I lived with my children in a warm bright and
> harmonious room which formed the crest of a high
> timber scaffolding – a room on stilts. Outside
> it was a black night, an old railway yard,
> abandoned tracks, a high wind. Our room
> although too small for our needs was glowing and
> secure despite the fact that it had no roof,
> that its walls led straight upwards to the
> black clear sky.
>
> (untitled poem, p. 14)

The book evokes a closed group with its tight bonds, its vulnerability, its dependence on the material world, in the form of housing, its unique atmosphere. But the poems are separate from each other, written over several years, each one pursuing a concrete situation to its last twist. The house is the exact boundary where the natural and affective association of the family comes up against the rational and alienated world of property. Perhaps it's relevant that Riley was studying for a doctorate on housing policy for some of this time.

> the houses are murmuring with many small pockets of emotion
> on which spongy ground adults' lives are being erected & paid for daily
> while their feet and their children's feet are tangled around like those of fen
> larks
> in the fine steely wires which run to & fro between love & economics
> affections must not support the rent
>
> (from 'Affections Must Not', p. 27)

The line about fine steely wires seems like a *prise de position* about the connection between intimate and mediated relationships, unusual for this writer although we can be sure that she was thinking about such links the whole time. It is a pun, referring both to snares, catching birds by the claws, and some kind of transmission, passing energy or control. More typical of the collection is a line from earlier in the same poem, which up till then has been a definition of motherhood:

> inside a designation there are people permanently startled to bear it, the not-
> me against sociology

The designation is probably 'mother', but could also be 'mother of a one-parent family', a category subject to all kinds of opprobrium and abuse from sociologists, politicians and priests. The poet is startled at everything that society and events thrust on her; this attitude of curiosity and detachment may derive from phenomenology, in the shape of Maurice Merleau-Ponty, but certainly it is the tone of the book: one of amazement and curiosity. Conventional emotion would be less ambiguous and full of potential; nonetheless it's a very emotional book. The dry air of scepticism is a flourish of trumpets to open proceedings, but hardly defines the appeal of the work.

Suppose we put the question of feelings into the context of personal relations. Being emotional all the time is not the ideal way to behave towards someone else; far from it. But the absence of feelings does seem to mean the absence of commitment. The surrender of total autonomy is a risk. If you have low affect you adopt a cool attitude towards sexual partners, as though watching something on a screen. This would seem to be, not maturity and balance, but numbness as the result of a paralysing anxiety.

The reduction of risk is eventually a kind of bunker mentality. In the poetic text also, it's depressing if the author has repressed and frozen feelings out of the text, and is offering nothing. Riley's level of emotional commitment to the poem is very high.

Riley was born in Carlisle in 1948 and brought up partly there and partly in Gloucester. There was a cluster of concrete poets in Gloucester-shire in the mid-sixties and she made contact with them, and in fact wrote some concrete poetry, while still at school. A precociously gifted academic prodigy, she was forced to choose between English and natural sciences. This early phase of very close observation of nature (birds and plants) left a mark: she has ever since detested generalisations and confusion and admired precise recording of phenomena. She desperately wanted, at eighteen, to go to art school, but was pressured into taking up a place studying English at Oxford. Dissatisfied, she switched to philosophy at Cambridge, although her eventual first degree was in fine art. Need I point out that she later became a professional historian, known above all for her political activity? A by-product of the switch was quitting the milieu of Oxford poetry, on which she has since passed some rather sharp comments, to arrive in Cambridge in 1968 at the high point of the poetical ferment which later produced so much. People were busy reading the precursors of the nascent Cambridge Leisure Centre,[7] of whom Ashbery and Frank O'Hara stand out. Perhaps more important was the counter-culture that was flourishing at that time in cities and universities. Some distinctions have to be made here. First, we have to distinguish between the merely anti-rational elements, the ones who thought that sex, drugs and rock'n'roll were the revolution; and the New Left, essentially continuing a century of radicalism, who were sober, sceptical, and interested in taking over the apparatus of state and economy. Riley certainly belongs with the rational and intellectual wing, and saw the hippy movement as a vast dip in intelligence and probity. Next, in all the interest in sexuality and social change, a number of people never fell for Marx and Freud, but spotted them on first reading as authoritarians whose paranoid love of system-building had led them away from the sober rules of evidence; Riley was one of these. I don't think she was ever a Marxist, despite her pamphlet *Marxism for Infants* (this was the name of a spoof pamphlet invented by Orwell for one of his essays); she was at the libertarian-anarchist end of things. Within the New Left, one faction was the feminists: Riley was one of these, and that's what she's famous for. Within feminism, you had the people analysing every part of the new philosophy, clause by clause, to see if it was true; and you had the people who paint banners stating 'Our philosophy is the best! yours is poo!' – which corresponds to the difference between engineering and marketing in a manufacturing firm. Someone who thinks critically in the middle of a revolutionary movement is going to be defined either as an enemy or as a leader. In terms of social contacts, however, the counter-culture could not be neatly separated: no doubt they were all in the same rooms, doing more or less the same things, and sharing many of the same ideas. In Cambridge, this movement also included poets; and the poems are about being a counter-culture, because they direct a philosophical intelligence at the structures of leisure and everyday life. Moral science was, indeed, one of the Tripos subjects Riley studied.

Information on Riley's early poetry is scarce. She gives her own account as follows: 'Like several people, I started writing concrete poetry under the knowledge of John Furnival's work, then in the early 1970s wrote and published some "sound poems" and pure cut-ups from, I'm embarrassed to say, textbooks of clinical psychiatry and nineteenth century trials, and thrashed around for a while before deciding that the bourgeois reality of feeling had a lot going for it, too, and so wrote *marxism for infants*'.[8] The phrase 'bourgeois reality of feeling' refers to the proverb, 'When someone says "bourgeois reality" they mean "reality"'. Unfortunately, I haven't seen any of this early work. The association of the words 'subjectivity' and 'bourgeois' was typical of the poetry of the time; Riley, moving against the trend, rejected the dominion of manipulation of found materials and process in favour of interrogating the rich flux of subjectivity. She cut open the orthodox link between subjectivity and deception to pose the *question* whether subjectivity can be telling the truth. The poet she comes closest to, in this project, is Sorley MacLean.

At this point we come to *Mop Mop Georgette* (1993). How is it possible to perceive that a writer possesses great moral integrity, has a beautiful soul, has noble feelings, strives for the good? The verbal account, prepared by the writer, is separated from the reality by a wall, of verbal relations, which can only appear transparent by a scenographic effect. Let me suppose, winding up the tension, that what the reader most longs for in a poet is goodness, the elemental force of attraction, just as, in the visual realm, without beauty you don't get to stand in front of the camera. Such is the force that makes the reader suggestible to every slightest vibration, and makes them relive their own life as the poem rolls by. The ability to love and to be loved is the gift for which any other is merely a propaedeutic. The poem brings the likeness of moral beauty, and we can recognise this, because we apply to it our knowledge of character, the fruit of living in the human milieu all our lives. Recognition does not need proofs. The poet is both hidden behind the wall and standing in front of it, visible, but deprived of the elements of speech; the emergence of the invisible out of the smoke, or the constant yearning and effort which strain towards it, are the sublime.

What is the status of feelings? One approach denounces them, as the uninstructed matter on which philosophy, or politics, effects enlightenment – offering, I suppose, a defence against being swamped by affective states. It would 'defeat' emotion by confronting the reader with the errors it brings about. It would offer sarcasm, and scorn, and, rejecting the identification of the reader with the writer, or with characters, would offer instead the interest of formal relationships; the dry pleasure of spotting a symmetry, or simply of clouds of illusion dispelled. But another approach gives feelings high status. This would be partly epistemological: they are vital sources of knowledge, so that someone who cannot understand his or her own feelings is crippled, and it is worth detailed interrogation to find out what those feelings are. It is partly to do with the pursuit of happiness, since emotions are the most intense kind of experience and nothing can be pleasurable that is wholly unemotional. It is partly aesthetic, since emotions, as moments of uncertainty, of becoming, of crisis, and so on, are fault lines that reveal a situation or a process. It is partly ethical, since one cannot behave ethically without understanding other people's emotions. The resentment against feelings remains, but above all because they let down other feelings: if A is unhappy, it is because B is angry, unfaithful, inconsistent, destroying A's love and trust. The poem does not also deride A's unhappiness. Emotions are dangerous, but a life without emotions is not a good one.

Riley's work is highly emotional *and* dedicated to the search for truth. Her philosophical source is Maurice Merleau-Ponty, upholder of a 'phenomenology' which tried to relate abstract and general ideas to physical sensations, including the emotions; this was a personal and introspective style of philosophy. Merleau-Ponty set out from Edmund Husserl, who used the term 'transcendental subject' to describe the I that interrogates past states of awareness and is set above them; Derrida made fun of this notion, since the fallibility of all past states of the I is present and healthy also in the I of now, or whenever we write philosophy. Subjectivity is bound by truth; if I say 'I love you' it is clearly possible for me to be being truthful. A phenomenologist would ask how to define love, without use of synonyms, and would painstakingly elicit all the sensations, the representations, the thoughts, even the fantasies, which compose the experience of loving. Serious use of language demands this kind of work, which seems very desirable in a poet. Riley is very much in the opposite camp from deconstruction. Recalling the history of sensation is a searching and patient discipline, purifying language.

'Mop mop' is the name of a certain rhythmic pattern introducing a bebop number; the leader shouts out 'Mop mop' and everyone then knows what beat to come in on (possibly, 'Mop Mop' is also a drum instrumental by Sid Catlett?). Georgette is a lightweight material, related to cambric, chiffon, muslin and poplin, used in summer skirts. The only georgette garment which *Angel Exhaust*'s Research Division could come up with belonged to a Barbie doll. Semantic associations for this substance might include *skimpy*, *flirty*, *diaphanous* and *gauzy*.

Merleau-Ponty drew on experimental psychology, borrowing from the Gestalt school the term 'body image' (originally *Körperschema*), which now seems rather well established. Of course, scientific psychology's founding act, in about 1860–75, was to exclude the introspective approach as hopelessly subjective and suggestible. More recent social psychology suggests that

> the contents of the self are so much 'undifferentiated murk'. The self is, in other words, a site for chaos. Its substance lies in a jumble of passing states rather than a coherent flow. The individual who pays close attention to internal experience and who thus penetrates the self will confirm [...] its contradictory and nebulous nature. [...] Inner experience is not sufficiently differentiated or reliable to guide self-analysis.[9]

From close analysis and comparison, Potter, Stringer and Wetherell conclude: 'It is apparent that it is becoming more and more difficult to sustain the "truth and insight" model of literature'.[10] Well, what I'm really interested in are the tonal values. Peter Fuller claims that 'in the ultimate grey monochromes painted just before [Rothko's] suicide he discovered not so much a benign and loving personal God as something like that "blank psychosis" which many psychoanalysts now assume lies at the base of consciousness', referring to the psychoanalyst André Green and his category of 'blankness', to include blank mourning, negative hallucination and blank psychosis, an enveloping grey from which one might come to understand what colour is.[11] Murk, nebula, blank, grey: a consistent décor. Now look at Riley's poem 'LURE 1963':

Navy near-black cut in with lemon, fruity bright lime green.
I roam around around around around acidic yellows, globe
oranges burning, slashed cream, huge scarlet flowing
anemones, barbaric pink singing, radiant weeping When
will I be loved? Flood, drag to papery long brushes
of deep violet, that's where it is, indigo, oh no, it's in
his kiss. Lime brilliance. Obsessive song. Ink tongues.
Black cascades trail and splatter darkly orange pools
toward washed lakes, whose welling rose and milk
beribboned pillars melt and sag, I'm just a crimson
kid that you won't date. Pear glow boys. Clean red.

The bright colours of Gillian Ayres' painting are subjectively mixed with
the colours of make-up and of sixties' glamour clothes, glowing with new
polymer technology. The demon pop world of 1963 echoes the insecurity
of courtly lyric: 'When every look these cheeks might stain, / From deadly
pale to glowing red; / By outward signs appeared plain / The woe where-
with my heart was fed. // But all too late Love learneth me / To paint all
kinds of colours new, / To blind their eyes that else should see / My
sparkled cheeks with Cupid's hue' (Henry Howard). The colours,
representing natural emotion for Howard around 1540, fly in the face of
that nebulous murk of the self we were just gazing into; do they represent
states of mind or are they arbitrarily chosen? And is meaning made by
such bold choices? The word 'lure', actually referring to a device used in
training falcons, reminds me of the mock-ups that Tinbergen used in his
experiments on innate behaviour-releasing mechanisms in gulls. These
artificial but overwhelming stimuli remind me of the psychedelic
sensibility, influenced by Op Art and visual illusions, exploiting anomalies
of the nervous system. Looking at the photographs of Tinbergen's lures is
uncanny, because one realises that this *is* art. Humans seek out
representations of what they know to be unreal because of the autonomous sensations that the images release; the images are organised
around the innate responses rather than something in the world. Possibly,
humans developed the ability to understand the cognitive make-up of
animals so as to deceive them, by lures, decoys, calls and so on, which has
survival value; and art is based on this faculty of deceit. The symbolic
capacity may come out of deceit, which was not originally deceit of other
humans. Is the clarity of Riley due to training in introspection or to an
aesthetic preference? Is the thing which is limpid the soul, or something
else? Are we observing the mind, or training it? Perhaps the poem is an
artificial and designed environment, a lure with a time dimension, where

convincingness is synchronisation and convergence of rhythms.

The use of bright colours in art, clothing and traffic lights or signs may be related to the innate optic responses of humans. The eye likes the colours of fruit, and fruit is coloured to attract the eye, not only of humans. What is this a representation of? Patrick Heron wrote in 1963, 'It is obvious that colour is now the only direction in which painting can travel', as Ayres no doubt agreed. The impact of those big abstracts was a mixture or contest of innate responses (to primary values such as scale and colour) and social suggestion; the heirs of deceased representationalism.

Certain verbal patterns affect us with sensations of elevation, love, aspiration and awe: like neon and other inert gases, the grey fog of being fluoresces with sharply coloured visible light when hit with the right energy. 'It's in his kiss' is a line from a girl-group song of the time about testing a man's sincerity – a practical task for which cynicism alone is not a winning tactic. What looks like someone with a pure soul affects the emotional organs of the reader just as much as if it were a real Pure Soul standing there. Virtual stimuli inspire real emotions.

The frequency with which Riley quotes lines from pop songs points perhaps to the persistence of infantile modes of thought throughout life: strata of the personality rotating at different speeds giving the vortex effect so popular in psychedelic art. Riley's poems are written in clear bold patterns like a Matisse cut-out, which stop immediately before they cease to be vivid. One does inquire, what dusks does this lucidity leave out? The whole of *Mop Mop Georgette* is one sharp beautiful pattern – a sixties Pop ideal remote from the usual concrete-in-the-rain didacticism of the underground. The surface of the poetry is arresting; it never stops moving. This clarity is perhaps not merely the result of editing, but of the attempt to be as true as possible in a relationship by abandoning doubts and ambiguities; the integrity of purpose which makes it possible to love and be loved.

Being emotional all the time isn't the ideal behaviour towards someone else, far from it. But the absence of feelings is also a distortion: the evasion of commitment in order to reduce risk. The dissolution of the whole symbolic realm (into a fog?) produces the illusion of total autonomy, a self transcendent or in a kind of heat death. This self is as if watching something on a screen: a cool attitude towards sexual partners. Precision, indifference... but also numbness, paralysis through anxiety. Poetry, too, becomes interesting if it shows the likeness of faith, wholeheartedness, and love transcending time; Riley's passionate commitment to love and to the poem makes her contemporaries seem grey and tenuous. How to avoid pointing out that the living curve of emotions tends to realise the risk and follow a declining line towards disaster and, at that moment, to austerity and scepticism – the virtues of a banker.

Something Riley has repeatedly protested against is readers being personally attracted to her; responding to the virtual situation with real emotions, in fact. I am reminded of Anita O'Day, according to the sleeve-note of one of her records, refusing to take her raincoat off while singing with a jazz band in Chicago in the late 1930s, because to take it off (and reveal a low-cut dress?) would have distracted the audience from the music. Actually, Michèle Morgan and Lizabeth Scott had turned the raincoat into a glamour object. And the sleeve-notes betray the idea: 'her stance reflected a tough, hip insouciance; she wasn't selling sex. But her singing was another story, showing up the cutesy, kittenish mannerisms of so many of her contemporaries for what they were: pseudo-sex. With Anita, it was the real thing.' Impersonality at the visual level clears the way, it is being claimed, for allure and wiles and appeal at the vocal level. O'Day's vocal ornamentation implies intimacy, and this intimacy encourages men to fall in love. Poetry doesn't take place in a nightclub and doesn't have the same come-hither conventions. However, I doubt how far the poet can vanish behind the poems and prevent an emotional bond developing in the reader. Of course this bond is projective, since the poet is not simultaneously perceiving the reader. The poet's frequent ironic interjections bring us back to these matters. All the same Riley's insistence on truth, as the basis of every poem, does put personal experience at the centre. The insistence produces the effect of intimacy. The act of reading is one of mapping that centre, with its lambent goodness and integrity. In fact, the motivation to pursue the rigours of Riley's fine probing would probably be missing without this biologically important search pattern. The reader also goes through the (possibly quite different) process of *identification*.

'Cut more cut more, mutter my / hearing creatures, snouts / rooting upward for light' is a moment of obvious influence from W. S. Graham, who is perhaps Riley's favourite modern poet: the creatures are the words in poems. Perhaps the problem I have with the reflections is that they seem to come from a position of power, where the hull of illusion is blown off and the difference between reality and error is visible; whereas the poems come from emotional dependency and vulnerability. The precondition under which Riley writes about herself is that events will not be reorganised as self-justification or self-aggrandisement, the evidence will not be carefully rearranged so that every speck of dust points the same way. Instead, we have the conscious part of the mind trapping the narrating, distorting parts of the mind, and measuring their shifts. It is a singular error to mistake this scrupulous fixing for narcissism. The probing is self-consciousness:

> Don't quote the 'we'
> of airs nor worse, of sentient
> humanity, thanks.
> That's attitudinising, in those
> three lines. That's what I do.
> Help me out of it,
> you sentient humanity.
>   (from 'A Shortened Self')

The word 'attitudinising' comes from an era in London theatre of high-cost illusionism, with ponderous super-real sets which took half an hour to strike for scene changes, the time being filled in by processions of thousands of extras in stunning costumes, while the star, possibly Henry Irving, struck super-real poses, attitudinised, wordlessly, above them. Music covered the sound of hammers backstage. The style of the poses may have uncovered a language of posture possibly found also in rock and cinema posters, hyperbolic worldless poses, which must remind us of the lures of Tinbergen.

Perhaps Michael Haslam is a worthwhile comparison, as someone who is trying to write poetry which is full of colour and music, which has *grande ligne*, which has enough elements simultaneously in play to sweep the reader away. The poets formed in the late sixties use either personality or place as the passive capacious site where the natural unpredictability of events can be captured. Haslam was the converse side of '68; a kind of Leveller. Riley and Haslam have both insisted on absolute fidelity to truth as the basis of their poetry. This means searching their own feelings, to which they have first-person access; and perhaps inability to treat the feelings of other people equally involved in the events, because no account of them can be vouchsafed as perfectly true. Is it in his kiss? *Not quite.* Fiction might find it easier to depict the geometry of space between two living surfaces. The lonely speaking voice, locked in love and projection, has somehow to evoke other people as a kind of negative space.

The passive site presents the simultaneity of different channels of social relations, internal experiences, and sensory input. This simultaneity is already there in life: it would be hard to invent an imaginary one of comparable complexity, and anyway the result would have a dead, *in vitro* feel about it, like so many poems. Perhaps the psychological appeal of art based on 'theory' (i.e. based on superior unassailable knowledge) is its sense of certainty, its elimination of ambiguity. A beguiling sixties myth was the idea of the total present, spontaneously and unpredictably happening to all senses at once. It was caught in its lightness and flow by the camera or by improvised music, imitated by other arts. Riley seems to aim for all-over constant variation. For example, the persistent long lines of 'Mop Mop' (which caused the publishers to alter the format of the book) can be seen as an attempt to flood the reader with information, overrunning the pales, line-breaks, with which we normally break up poetic speech with pauses for assimilation and organisation of data. We find metrical run-ons, the sentence overflowing the line-break as if to prevent any pause, and syntactic run-ons, clauses furiously chasing each other without a break for recuperation. This surrounding quality involves information coming in rapid succession from all possible wavelengths, all the senses, powerful abstract ideas, remembered experience, social dynamics, and so on: which is what we actually find in 'Mop Mop', an edgeless rippling plane of constantly shifting forms and rhythms.

The longest poem, 'Stair Spirit', takes this instability as its structural principle, constantly shifting its viewpoint to prevent a dominant pattern from ever emerging. Riley has described the composition of this poem as being like going down a staircase, each line representing a step, with an overall tumbling effect. The displacement of the reader's centre of gravity is like the engulfing, boundless space of a flat abstract painting: 'I want to fall right through / the poem to disappear from view inside it'. If one imagines the staircase as a spiral, by falling we are swirling round and round, converging on a focal point whose angle towards us constantly alters. There is no rational thread holding the poem together; it is held together by its rhythms, if by anything. Surely we have here an echo of certain phases of psychedelic music, for example the Pink Floyd of 1967 taking off into unstructured improvisation. The attractive force of the centre of the spiral is a psychedelic effect. The immersion is a sensurround, like a multi-media experience with music coming from all directions drenched in the other space of light shows and back projections, losing its ground to immerse the audience. Michael Haslam, too, engulfs the reader in shimmering and dazzling effects where reason and realism are being expertly faded out, eluded. The title also refers to *esprit de l'escalier*, the brilliant remarks that one thinks of after leaving the party; but in disconnection from the scene around you:

so strangest disconnections cut between
me, my feet, the stairs, vertiginous, I often
must stop dead in case I'll fold and fall,
I look all down my body to my feet to
check just where they're planted so that
continuity, regained by eye, returns [...]
    I can't
walk down the shortest flight of stairs
without this risk of lost connections.
                    (from 'Stair Spirit')

This introduction explains the poem, since the rest of it is the poet
wandering freely through her imagination: 'so / finger the dado, hand over
mouth, white / dreads speed to white snow streaks on / grey karst rising
behind grey pebbles'. Various of the scenes that drift by are a Greek
landscape seen on holiday; an apparent chant or child's game ('open your
hand the snow walks out'); the experience of insomnia ('drinking unsettled
coffee's / powder that no sleep makes at / the back of the head's scooped- /
out melon'); and evening in a part of Hampstead Heath where homo-
sexuals are stalking each other. The closing lines suggest that the whole
may have been some kind of fugue during a night of insomnia. This
would be a phenomenological curiosity: listening to the mind when bodily
rhythms are still and sensory input is absent would be a way of studying
the triangle made by those three things. In a vast rag-bag of frames and
phrases run together, three songs are quoted, including 'Voodoo Chile'; I
suppose Hendrix's later style, with its improvisation, luxurious drift
through memories and snatches of old tunes, constant self-interruption,
excited reaching-out to bright colours and alluring textures, is a plausible
influence on 'Stair Spirit'.

    Tentatively, we can draw a line linking Riley's distaste for fixed systems
of knowledge, her libertarian politics, and the immersing quality of ideal
sixties events. In each case the excess availability of data floods and effaces
the rigid patterns. A causal factor is the cheapness of information, supplied
by technological breakthroughs. An emerging theme in the sixties was
complexity: a realisation that the rigidity of conceptual models – all of
them up to that time – was conditioned by the limited means of data
storage and data processing. The idea of complexity leads to the unrepeat-
ability of events; this kicks the underpinnings away from authority, trying
to make things regular; and makes real events mysterious and polyvalent
enough to animate poetry.

'Seven Strangely Exciting Lies', in contrast, has a highly rational order-ing principle: each of the seven constituent poems illustrates a kind of deception. The author is asserting that what is being asserted is not true; a shimmer effect exploiting, like Op Art, perceptual ambiguities. The radical scepticism that contemporary philosophy holds about the cinema, the *Vorstellungen*, of the self is already written in sixteenth-century court poetry, an account of the discontinuity and disillusionment when the self ejects the seductive appropriations of over-gay ambitions, infatuations, projects. Where one deceives, one is deceived. The courtly advertisement of the self was too finished and too ornate for us to read it as realism. Emotion is a lure, a pattern which seduces us into ignoring the facts that conflict with it. Despite the ominous naming of mutability, these are some of the most dramatic and passionately moving poems in the book, if not in the whole contemporary poetic scene. In Poem One, the lie appears to be lipstick and hair-dye: the poet, aged about 45 at this time, looks at a covey of ex-lovers and reflects that they 'now sometimes look seedier, more despairing than you, though that's only / because you get to use lipstick and hair-dye whereas they on the whole do not / your vanities, and pleasure in theatrical self-blame, have got you where you are today'. Of course, this is anti-lyrical; it's not a crowd-pleaser to say that the pleasure which keeps you in being is dressing up and bemoaning the disasters of the past. We don't get to hear about the latter: I think because Riley is always writing about immediate concerns, and when the disasters were happening they were too engulfing for her to write anything at all. The praise of make-up is an example of free colour. It's interesting that the theatrical self-blame barely appears in the poems, however much Riley may enjoy it on a private basis: the poems do not simply record dominant affective states. Poem Two, 'Glamour', shows the poet looking through racks of old dresses, from the fifties and sixties, on stalls in Brighton, and wishing to have straight blonde hair. Presumably the lie is her appearance, which is not what 'I truly am'; or else it is her imaginary appearance, which belies her real body. In Poem Three, 'Oleanna' (the title refers to a play by David Mamet), the lie is hard to identify; it could be the belief that 'I thought you'd get through any disagreement just by talking / by persisting quietly. Fool. Steel-rimmed the hole at the centre / through which all hopes of contact plummet down in flames'. The poem refers to a disastrous relationship in which the poet tried to retain moral integrity by discussing everything rationally and refusing to descend to the level of the unconscious and of terrible passions. This theme could reasonably be described as feminist; it's hard for anyone to describe the course of their life without it adding up to an argument for the liberation of women. Evidently the passions played the decisive role, although as part of things going wrong. Riley names this reaction as truthful: 'instead of all that tactile surface junk / there is this sobbing flash, you-die immediacy', but goes on to denounce it as barbaric: 'who longs for decent / and consensual talk, it is that calm and democratic front I'd work to be: / I was not born to that'. So, bizarrely, the *democratic approach* could be the lie in question; one overcomes primitive emotional reactions, which are blind and selfish, so as to converge on the mind of someone else, which, however, turns out to be split, treacherous, squirming. Poem Five is a put-down of various scene poets to go with the many put-downs in the book:

> Not your natural-historical, your exacting tender mushroom-gill accounting
> Others got their Observer books for seven and sixpence too
> Nor your fragile translucent leaf trembling in its behold-me wonder
> Which is a behold-you wonder [...]

The victim here, exhibiting himself as a slender yet strangely sensitive mushroom, evidently belongs to the post-Bunting wing of nature poetry. The poem goes on to more demolition:

> Nor your reassuring conviction that whole governments
> Will pale and stagger under the jawbones of your dismembered syntax [...]

Here Riley ridicules the belief, held by thousands of people who are rarely in the same room as a thought, that 'subverting language subverts the state'. Presumably it is the fifth strangely reassuring lie. Riley is sceptical about other poets. No-one has an admiration and credulity that encompass all poetry: so everyone is part of the sceptical project. Poem Seven, 'Disintegrate Me', is a staggeringly complex series, violent and yet indecisive, of tidal alternations between different versions of agency and the self. The title may come from a poem by W. S. Graham ('Gently disintegrate me / Said nothing at all'). The poem starts with a series of harpy-like voices accusing the poet of being to blame for what happened in her life; she argues that the whole dream of entering the landscape is an attempt to escape guilt, and ends with the even more bitter reflection that there was no guilt because everything is in the hands of chance, where neither wisdom nor intelligence can influence it. The beautiful passage of projection of feelings into Nature is pulled up at the end by the question whether the whole feeling isn't a lie.

In 'When It's Time To Go', a male intellectual presenting himself as an interpreter of politics is peeled by the moral equivalent of a can-opener and dismissed:

> When an aggressively uncontrolled schadenfreude
> reads a personal threat in everywhere
> and so animatedly takes this as 'the political'
> that the very kitchen colander shells out a neat
> wehrmacht helmet of brown rice
> *das schmeckt nach mehr!*

The poem describes someone cruel and self-deceiving. *Das schmeckt nach mehr* (literally, 'that tastes of more') is a German advertising slogan, or part of a simple domestic register. His equation of a heap of rice tipped out of the colander with a German helmet is a parody of the act of finding universal meaning in local objects – the ability to reduce everything to a single phenomenon is literally paranoia, and it's not surprising that the victim also suspects brown rice of hostility. This is not how you find politics in the everyday; you can't sucessfully give objects a symbolic meaning if you also have the problem that you hear objects talking, and believe they harbour malevolent feelings towards you. The poem's linkings are offhand, treating his reading of events as a stage set through which she sticks her hands. The episode takes place in someone's kitchen and so must be domestic: a challenge to those who define domestic realism as the source of all tedium in English poetry. If there is some theory which explains the shape of modern poetry, it is not any of those propounded by our hot-eyed theorists.

To get back to those exciting lies, number four, 'Lucille's Tune', starts with what may be a Shangri-Las-style evocation of falling in love in terms of a traffic accident:

> Riding this gorgeous car I saw in the wing-
> mirror night-black leather coming up blind
> it's the beginning it's the end of the world
> though God knows I've wished it wasn't
>
> an engine of light forgets about everything
> but roaring you into it: blue drenches you […]

Here the immersion in an engine, a desiring machine in Deleuzean terms or Virtual Machine in IBM mainframe terms, is like the vortex-cascade of 'Stair Spirit'. Forgetting opens an edgeless plane of destruction or of the sublime. The engine is rather like the steel-rimmed hole 'full of flames' from the facing page. The lover is called after an old Little Richard

number, 'Lucille [...] there ain't nothing to you but I love you still':
diminished to make the involvement less dangerous. The lie is presumably
in 'first they swear they'll love you to the grave / next they're down to the
woods to dig it for you'. The result is: 'Starry unconscious: sea body: child
maintenance': this striking example of compression evokes the ecstatic
phases of romance before knocking us down with the sequel of pregnancy,
separation and litigation. Just before the end is one of the book's more
overt references to psychoanalysis and feminist theory: 'You can hack off
my breast to write "tits" // but you can't grow them on to your wire chest'.
There has been some kind of conflict with the lover; he is accused of a
callous attitude towards sex, but also of some kind of inexplicit envy of the
female principle, I suppose. Her 'tits', his 'wire chest'. H. F. and M. K.
Harlow carried out a series of experiments resembling Tinbergen's, in
which they reared Rhesus monkeys in isolation from their mothers and
observed them develop attachments to rigged-up pseudo-mothers (lures)
with (precisely) wire chests.[12] These monkeys were unsuccessful in mating
and parenting as adults. Is the implication that the lover's emotional
deprivation, at the moment in the developmental timetable when profound
and authentic patterns of attachment and identification can be formed,
has stunted his ability to love as an adult in a way that is both sexual and
emotional? The couplet is a little too compressed. Is our nature the nature
of newborn Rhesus monkeys? Is love a cognitive skill? Is our human
symbolic activity, its toyshops and *palazzi* full of 'wire chests', a sort of
learning area or a consolation for missing experience?

Having reached the end of the assets of the centre, we can pause and
evaluate their ambiguous nature, and the extent of the opposition to
them. To be sure, the view that the poets listed in my literary map above
as formally radical, and radical or counter-cultural, are the centre of
British poetry is a minority view, if sustained by such anthologies as John
Matthias's *Contemporary British Poetry*, Gillian Allnutt and Fred
D'Aguiar's *The New British Poetry* and Ian Sinclair's *Conductors of Chaos*.
Opposing factions would include the Marxists, who disqualify anything
written in Britain since 1600; the fans of pop poetry, who regard
intelligence as alienation, and extol Tony Harrison or Carol Ann Duffy;
and the poetry of fashion, close to the Sunday newspapers, West End
theatre, and the Oxford English Faculty, which is the visible centre of our
poetry, and can put up James Fenton or Andrew Motion. Poetry that is
complex, paradoxical, self-critical, drawn to crises, unworldly, politicised,
which is not culinary in its handling of experience but regards it as the

product of a continuous act of improvisation, classification and attention, will be regarded by different readers as good or bad for the same reasons. The case against is the case for. The path of invitation is a double one, as the reader toys with the experience described in the poetry and the experience provided by the poetry.

I spoke earlier of paranoia, and the *doubt* of this chapter is the same affection of the mind, but transformed and clarified by thought. Everyone's story is the story of the contest between their views of themselves and others' views of them – an interesting process only if both are being disproved. If one of them is fixed for the course of the poem, or the collected poems, the author's personality becomes solid but is not poetic. If the poet holds that society is always right, and he always wrong, he probably writes no poems. Silence as consent. Speech itself is the product of a divergence of opinion which it aims to close. Speech occurs along the fault-lines of divergence.

Written poetry does not have the sympathetic circularity of art in performance; it cannot draw on the myth of denying the differences between people, which Georgian and communitarian poetry dress themselves in; it rises to its highest peak by admitting the movement of anxiety, about the esteem of the group and the value of the self, into the fabric of the poem, moving through rage and dread into self-knowledge and authentic utterance.

Notes

1 Phyllis Bentley, *The English Regional Novel* (London: Allen & Unwin, 1941).
2 From Boris Ford (ed.), *The Cambridge Guide to the Arts in Britain* (Cambridge: Cambridge University Press, 1984), VIII, p. 84.
3 Gordon Bottomley, *Lyric Plays* (London: Constable and Co., 1932), p. viii.
4 Personal communication.
5 J. Brazier Green, *John Wesley and William Law* (London: Epworth Press, 1945), p. 68
6 Patrick Walker, *Biographia Presbyteriana*, I (Edinburgh: D. Speare, 1827), p. xii.
7 This is an alternative to the phrase 'Cambridge School', which refers to dozens of disparate groups. The word 'school' derives from the Greek *skholē*, meaning (among other things) 'leisure'. For a definition of what this centre meant, see Andrew Duncan, *Secrets of Nature: Origins of the Underground* (Cambridge: Salt Publishing, 2004).
8 Personal communication to the author.
9 Jonathan Potter, Peter Stringer and Margaret Wetherell, *Social Texts and Context: Social Psychology and Literature* (London: Routledge and Kegan Paul, 1974), p. 157.
10 Potter, Stringer and Wetherell, *Social Texts and Context*, p. 22.
11 Peter Fuller, *Beyond the Crisis in Art* (London: Writers and Readers, 1980), p. 47.
12 See *Scientific American*, no. 207 (1962).

Part II
Poetry of the North-Western Periphery

5

'A Native Ardour of their Minds which Brooked No Master': Poetry in the North of England

The North is classically Cheshire, Lancashire, Yorkshire, Northumberland and Durham, Cumberland and Westmorland. These boundaries and names were changed in the 1975 reform of local government areas, and again in 1996. The 1992 census showed 14,500,800 people in an area which includes all of these plus parts of North Lincolnshire culturally taken as being northern. This is about 30 per cent of the population of England and Wales, impressive since the region's share of the medieval population was only 15 per cent: the North is a recently underdeveloped region. This state was dissolved primarily by better communications; the end of local autarky left a lingering resentment of outside forces, and the decline of regional dialect, brought about by an infrastructure of roads, railways, ports and canals, is the material substrate of recorded speech, that is, literature.

Poets from the North (listed by date of emergence) would include:

- Around 1905: Wilfrid Gibson; Gordon Bottomley
- 1910s: Lascelles Abercrombie
- 1920s: Herbert Read
- 1930s: Basil Bunting; Kathleen Raine
- 1940s: Os Marron; Norman Nicholson; Roy Fuller; Hubert Nicholson; Francis Scarfe
- 1950s: James Kirkup; Ted Hughes; John Arden
- 1960s: Tom Pickard; Barry MacSweeney; Ken Smith; John Riley; Peter Riley; Spike Hawkins
- 1970s: John Seed; Colin Simms; Michael Haslam; Denise Riley; John Ash; Geraldine Monk; Tony Harrison; David Chaloner; Grace Lake; Brian Marley; Tony Jackson
- 1980s: William Martin; Peter Didsbury
- 1990s: Ian Duhig; Michael Ayres; Chris Bendon.

Note that I don't think all of these are good poets; they are just there as straws in the wind. The list shows the artistic results of new literary centres forming after 1960. The centres are self-sustaining now the fire has been lit; the social milieu of intelligent poets is available also in northern cities. A glance at the names mentioned will show the plurality of possible responses to northern economy and society, the importance of ideas and of *time*, the ambience of ideas hot when the poet was learning how to write. Many of the best ideas came from America.

The following study is not one of relations between texts; that would assume that the poets had lived in linguistic environments composed purely of texts, and that we could ignore the tiresomely complex land-scape of conversations and interactions in which the poets led their lives, absorbing language at every step. Resemblance between two texts may perfectly well be due to a shared cultural structure, carried in conversa-tion, shaping literature but not transmitted by it. The relation of any northern writer to the cultural past of the North is tenuous and difficult; it has not been a cumulative and self-referential culture, as the South's possibly has been. This is why poetry tells us something about the ideo-logy of the region; it enacts certain structures which exist both before and after the recitation. They are intermediate between formal ideology and concrete objects, and affect ways of ruling how individuals in a group ought to behave, what the niches available in social space are, allocating social rank, and the boundary between the self and other people. The sheer quantity of available language might face us with too much diversity for thought to be possible, but the wish to reach a wide audience has persuaded writers to use their liberty to act just like everyone else; either imagining a collective narrative fund in order to dramatise it, or really finding it.

Wilfrid Gibson's life is negative evidence for the prehistory of northern poetry. There doesn't seem to have been any poetic community in Newcastle that he could hang out with; the poets he recalls as his friends, in some rather touching poems, are those such as Edward Thomas, who hung out at the Old Nail-Shop in a certain Gloucestershire village before 1914, and the usual London Georgian literary figures such as Sturge Moore. Abercrombie also lived in Gloucestershire at this time. However, by the time we get to the 1940s, poems of farewell to Abercrombie by Bottomley and J. Redwood Anderson suggest a northern pool of poetic ideas. Ander-son also dedicated a volume to Gibson. In the *Anthology of Contemporary Northern Poetry*, edited by Howard Sergeant in 1947 (a singular aesthetic nadir, I'm afraid) we find several poems featuring magical moments, where the supernatural steps in both as the personification of the landscape and as the frisson of the Poetic. This was perhaps the first book of its kind, presenting 52 poets with next to no poetic flair. We can suggest that northern poetry was virtually starting from scratch in the 1950s, as James Kirkup and Ted Hughes got going, while a local infrastructure of publishers and magazines dates from around 1960. There is a startling take-off around 1959, when Ted Hughes and John Arden must have been two of the most technically advanced writers in the world. But there wasn't a *thematic* start from zero; there was a ghostly ambient idea of what a northern poet should be like, and what northern poems should evoke: these themes (the supernatural, the Dark Ages, nature, bleakness, ruggedness, struggle) are present in the 1947 anthology.

The following account is, necessarily, scant and simple compared to the complexities of the past of northern society and culture. There is as yet no book on culture in the North; a full account would cover historical sociology (family structures etc.), literary institutions, the lives and ideas of numerous individual poets, and the history of regional ideologies – for example Liberalism, Methodism, Anglicanism, Positivism, Chartism, the Labour movement, and feminism.

Underdevelopment: Assets of the Exterior

The North is a region rather than a nation, because its thinkers have, since at least the seventeenth century, seen themselves in relation to the South, and hence as having quick access to one pole of a spectrum of qualities, and obstructed access to the other pole, where southerners could compete too effectively. Paranoia about the South – a view, essentially correct, that history written from Westminster, Oxford, Whitehall and so on distorts life as lived in the North – went along with lack of self esteem; anything from the North is simultaneously despised and sentimentalised.

Underdevelopment is visible in the forms of self-consciousness that give rise to historiography; this record has been largely written by south-erners little interested by our region, and decisive advances, away from a mixture of marginalisation, befuddled municipal pride, and legends, have been made even in the past ten years.

Let's quote three topic poems about the North.

Envy, the founding parent,
Odalisque along the lines of conversation.
The whine, sardonic vowel-smears,
Hope & Anchor flounce,
Possibility dismissed immediately in sneers.
[...]
From Hunslett clear to Chapel Allerton,
Tony Earnshaw's balding pate to Norman Hunter's kneecaps,
Bones of back-to-back punishment,
Time-clock severity, Armley gallows (drop on the last chime).
Workhouse spell spun on the skeletal loom around a bronchial breast –
Third pew back – secret reprisal for Wesley's lidless glare.
             (Jeff Nuttall, from 'Goodbye to Leeds (Hate)', published 1987)

I love the archaic North,
The gothic loneliness,
The bare cathedral of the cold
Where, in the stunned ice,
The winter woods display
A stripped elegance, and frame the rare
Rose-window of the midnight sun.
             (James Kirkup, from 'To the Ancestral North', published in
                             The Descent into the Cave, 1957)

I have seen the names of Vikings
Scattered through the firmament like dross
The starry dirt that drifts without a compass
In the locked out vacancies beyond the night
Viking names clocked on the woolman's card
And the fierce tribes sounding small down Batley's alley
And the vague clash of old conflicts hollow in the dawn
Where sombre clogs move to the turning day.
[...]
The blue March wind blows on the Humber
The great rectangular warehouses don beauty
For I know that I will never have to work in them again.
             (Brian Higgins, from 'The North', published in *The Only Need*, 1960)

What we see at first is a kind of auto-exoticism: northerners look at their
own home through southern eyes, and see it (and themselves) as exotic
and strange. The rise of a provincial literary culture in the 1960s must have
made this problem obsolete. However, the presence of unprocessed (and

therefore non-literary) landscapes must strike anyone who studies northern poetry; Victorian England responded to the rise of a new world of objects and activities by re-creating the Middle Ages in art. The problems of dealing with subject material for which no conventions exist, and of attractive false optics, have been most significantly theorised by Roy Fisher (from Birmingham).

Two glimpses, almost missing, almost unreadable, from the 'deep' history of the North. We can suppose that the Celtic church brought to Northumbria Irish literary habits, along with other practices. If we had a Northumbrian literature from that time, which despite misleading and nebulous statements we certainly don't, it might follow the Irish pattern. Frank Musgrove points to the east–west axis of cultural connections, for those centuries, as an alternative to the south–north axis (so infrequently the other way round!), more mediately Italy–France–south–north.[1] So Christianity and its cultural complex came east from Ireland, overlords and settlers came west from Denmark. There is, so far as I know, no trace of the lexical and rhetorical exuberance of Irish Latin, or of an equivalent to Irish vernacular prose, in Northumbria. If this tradition existed, it did not leave traces to influence later centuries: the kind of cultural memory made possible by literacy and urban centres was simply not there. It seems likely that Anthony Harvey was right to claim that the 'diacritic h' of modern English spelling was a feature borrowed from Irish, and therefore a reflex of the period when culture in Northern England and most of Scotland was carried by, or influenced by, Irish monastic culture.[2] The original Anglo-Saxon spelling system had two special letters for the sounds we represent with -th- (the ones in *fourth* and *that*); the first appearances of the digraph using h are in the North. This is perhaps the only relic of a period of the North which is likely, in what has not come down to us, to have included local versions of the favoured Irish genres, such as nature poetry and hero-tales interspersed with poetry. The diacritic h, much later generalised to form special digraphies -sh-, -gh-, -wh- and -ch- for the English sounds not depicted by the Latin alphabet (and intermittently for the alien Welsh -ll- sound, as in the eighteenth-century spelling Lhuyd for Lloyd), was well known in Irish spelling, unknown in the standard Anglo-Saxon script, and quite irrational for a language, such as English, in which the -h- sound is a phoneme (as it is not in Irish). (It is used twice in modern Welsh spelling, for the sounds appearing in *wyth* and *coch*, respectively.) The generalisation still stands that culturally legitimate currents come from the south-east, and currents from either west (Ireland) or east (Scandinavia, Flanders, Hamburg) remain at 'folk' level and are not elevated to the school syllabus. The other glimpse is an illuminating comment by Dick Leith (in *A Social History of English*) that the distribution of Scandinavian settlement meant that for three centuries the English of the North was cut off by another language from contact with the English of the South, and so inclined to evolve away from it.[3] The exact conditions under which areas such as Yorkshire came to speak English, and how English dialectal influence flowing in from the North met and mixed with influence from the South, are mysterious. The region was penalised, not only by lack of urban centres, but also by having a non-standard, low-prestige language, without a literary tradition, and excluded from the written record because the literate wrote in authorised languages. Any works that were created were lost when the language itself was forgotten. The North has lost its literary past, and people who cared for reading have read southern books.

The North was closer to a subsistence economy, not producing enough surplus to permit the existence of a rich aristocracy; it was less able to sustain that other feudal institution, rich monasteries which produced manuscripts, and less likely to afford either patronage to poets, or well-appointed libraries preserving and recopying the past of regional culture. The principle of storage relates both to money and to manuscripts.

Jewell's article on the origin of the North–South divide identifies the early twelfth century as a moment when written sources start to recognise the North and northern characteristics.[4] This coincides with a new settlement in the deep North, based on a breed of Norman landowners hardy enough to like a land of oats and beasts, and willing to supply permanent armed readiness in return for the land grants. We can take this as the political and linguistic foundation of our North. Jewell cites descriptions given by southern writers, which dwell on pride, violence, refusal to be governed, lawlessness, vengefulness, inconstancy. William of Malmesbury refers to 'a native ardour of their minds which brooked no master'; 'men of the north be more unstable, more cruel, and more unesy', says Higden.[5] Even the slightest interest in reducing the judger to a subjective agent will throw up the notions that (a) if the people of the South were more deferential than the northerners, this doesn't represent progress but a feudal oligarchy; and (b) the writer has a set of rules for when submissiveness is required and 'pride' is a vice only in terms of these rules. The inclination of commoners to change sides suggests that their loyalty to the gentry was not unconditional, but allowed them to bargain and improve their position.

The monarchy was a southern institution. The monarch of England rarely visited the North, Edward I's personal campaigns against the Scots being a rare exception; royal estates and palaces were to an amazing extent concentrated in the South. Defence against the Scots was organised by regional magnates without assistance from the Crown, which more or less relinquished any tax revenue from the North. People who wrote histories, from the *Anglo-Saxon Chronicle* (biased towards Wessex and its royal house) onwards, concentrated on the monarch and acts of the royal household, its successor the government, and Parliament; a bias excluding the North, and one that academic historians have only recently tried to counter-balance. There is a historiographical deficit, a missing set of characters, narratives and literary formulations, poorly compensated for by fierce legends and resentments. Almost everyone in the North has noticed, therefore, that high English culture comes from the South and is not about them.

Keen says of medieval Northumbria that '[the] gentry families [...] lived in fortified tower houses, half as squires, half as cattle thieves'.[6] Such ferocious characters might inspire great ballads, but regions such as these were bound to be tardy in urbanisation, the growth of retail trade, education, and in producing publishers and local authors; their destiny was to read books from outside, but whether these would come from Manchester, Edinburgh, New York, London, or some other affluent urban region, was yet to be fought out. It's hard to see the lack of literary figures from the Borders, or from the English North-East, as due to southern hostility, as Colin Simms has claimed.

There are two versions of the pre-modern history of poetry in the North. The first is dynamic and tragic, and refers to the dying out of indigenous technical knowledge in the region since the triumph of Standard English in the fifteenth century. It assumes that there was a flourishing literary culture before the dialect's loss of prestige, although its great productions are never cited; it is paranoid, asserting that southerners came to the North, found where its prestige was hidden, and took it away. It ignores all conscious agency (e.g. the tastes of the northern gentry as patrons) or geographical make-up (sparse population, low urbanisation) of the North: history is made in the South. The North itself is virginal, pristine, helpless, unconscious. The second version is plainer; it points out that the alliterative revival was not northern but West Midlands in locale, finds a lack of significant northern compositions at every stage of literary history, and posits a much more even development up until the arrival of the reading habit, and of local publishers, in the later eighteenth century.

Both accounts have to deal with the problem of the ballads, so excellent and so isolated; neither can offer us much significant poetry outside the ballads. The ideological match between northern literature of the fifteenth century (the alliterative *Morte Arthure*, Malory, the ballads) and northern society, with its free farmer-warriors, is close, which suggests that any other kind of writing would have lacked a market. How can you have courtly literature without a court, or bourgeois literature without a bourgeoisie?

Gregory Bateson has defined the process of schismogenesis in the formation of social roles. He describes it as follows: 'If [...] one of the patterns of cultural behaviour, considered appropriate in individual A, is culturally labelled as an assertive pattern, while B is expected to reply to this with what is culturally regarded as submission, it is likely that this submission will encourage a further assertion, and that this assertion will demand still further submission. We have thus a potentially progressive state of affairs [...] Progressive changes of this sort we may describe as complementary schismogenesis.'[7] He goes on to describe a symmetrical schismogenesis, as when two rival groups both engage in boasting, and flat statement becomes less likely from either one the more boasting has occurred. This withdrawal into complementarity may illuminate the case where the poets of a region feel themselves, as poets or as people, to be not complete and unimpaired, but partial, because a more privileged region within their world-horizon excels and excludes them. Poets in this case might seize on virtues culturally 'available' to them with a despairing greed, acquiring a fierce regionality by dint of insecurity and perceived inferiority, which they will lose as soon as they relax. The first undiscernible moment of dissimilation, which paranoia confidently ascribes to the conscious acts of individuals, would be interesting to see. Clearly, anyone starting up to speak is conscious of a certain protocol about occupying social-acoustic time, about using honorifics towards the listeners, about what they are allowed to say, about what the listeners will accept from them; this kind of rule applies even more strongly to literature. Its operation may have shaped the text, but it is not legibly inscribed within the text. Some of the roles or flavours adopted by Northern writers may have been comic, egalitarian, rough and strong, simple-minded, but honest and authentic. A reviewer for *Angel Exhaust* wrote of the 'virile Northern verse' of *Sir Gawaine*; tetchily, I wrote back that the poem was written in Staffordshire dialect. The revised article deleted the adjective 'virile': the alliterative diction could no longer have the manly quality if it came from Staffordshire. Northern poets might, in this perspective, have ceased to be virulently northern in the 1960s, when they acquired self-confidence and became natural and diverse, expressing their personalities rather than a stiff, theatrical role.

Fine Discriminations

Just as the speech of the most high-status groups in the North comes from the South, so also do many of the fashions and status objects. Any northern patriot must develop, then, *resistance to prestige forms of speech*, with various corollaries: inhibitions about poetic language; tendency to lapse into pre-modern forms when emotionally moved; *Sprachkrise*; anxiety about dialect and discomfort with the standard (i.e. South-East Midland) language; distrust of abstract ideas and tendency to break poems down into sequences of physical events; excessive belief in the self-evidence of interpretations of life; impoverishment of the verbal realm.

I failed, for years after I came to London, to locate the rubbish dump: the sign by the entrance road referred to a 'civic amenity', which I naively thought referred to some beauty spot maintained by the council. Where I come from, a rubbish dump is called a rubbish dump. Southern English is mimsy-mouthed. I associate this with the habit of the London Left of wanting to change representations rather than changing the power structure and the distribution of income, and in fact altering reality. Northern socialism is much more about giving poor people enough to eat. A lot of people in London work in decorative occupations, such as advertising, where reality is merely something waiting to have value added to it. But shifting representations about is the art of deceit. A lot of writers in the North think that refinement is inauthenticity; and I attribute to the use of terms such as 'rubbish dump' qualities such as *virtue* and *integrity*. The term 'civic amenity' is called more 'poetic': but it's orotund, squeamish, anxious, turgid, incomprehensible and false, so what *kind* of poetry are you going to write, like that?

English literature grew up, until the late seventeenth century, around the court, after which it was concentrated in London anyway; the North was short, not just of people speaking with southern accents, but also of elaborate social ritual, of theatres, and of writers. There is a link between the fuss and frills of polite society and fine writing; the plain language of the North goes along with a lack of political and social articulation, of mediations to fit daily events into larger patterns. The writing of poems about private life is damaged by the underdevelopment of a historical framework to put them in. Intelligent political poetry could only follow serious historical thinking and collection of data.

The cultivation of fine writing in the South owed something, not only to the foliation of language in a social structure with more layers, and where more shades of flattery and status discrimination were necessary, but also to the development of the skills of literacy, concentration, quiet assiduity and so on for business purposes, in a region where the family fortunes didn't depend primarily on a strong arm and a large retinue. The North retained a strong oral culture much later than the South. Sir John Forster, in about 1580, claimed that 'we that inhabite Northumberland are not acquaynted with any learned and rare frazes',[8] the difference being not merely phonetic but in the use of new layers of vocabulary, mainly French and Latin in origin. There is a division in poetic taste between those who think that a rich lexicon expressing a finely divided grid of discriminations, besides using techniques such as paradox and irony to suggest even more discriminations, is good; and those who find this annoying, narcissistic and evasive.

One of the Georgian preoccupations was to get away from the symbolic and back towards significant actions – the more physical, the better. This could be a political attack on the way mediations are currently coined, and so an anticipation of the politics of representation which became big in the 1970s. But, in psychological theory, being unable to deal with emotional material symbolically is a symptom of psychosis, and emotions that the subject can't work out by thought and analogy can express themselves directly, as violence or rape. Such a disorder could even be re-described as the absence of mediations, which are typically brought about by the descriptions of oneself by others forming the elements of self-consciousness and of a firm sense of the self. I admit that this abstract awareness brings about a crude loss of energy; not everything is acted out. What we find in these poets is a torrent of cruelty and violence. This is what critics objected to back in 1912, and it's also what critics objected to in Ted Hughes in the 1960s and subsequently. If you open Bottomley's play *Britain's Daughter* (1921), you find in the opening stage directions a young woman, hanging up, stripped, having been whipped; 'In the right foreground rises a weed-hung, salt-encrusted mooring-post. A young woman, NEST, is tied by the wrists to a ring in the post higher than her head.' This is pretty 'primary', I suppose, but one can prefer the equanimity and decorum of Victorian times. Interfering with other people's bodies is less human than interfering, or interacting, with their minds by means of language and a shared symbolic system. The first lines of the play are sung by a soldier: 'The rat is a sociable fellow, / But I cannot abide his tail; / I like to hear the long bone crack / When my little dog's teeth get into his back'; he then says, to an old woman, 'Fat hen with no rump feathers, / When will you weary of squatting in your dust-hole?'[9] This theatrical ruffian is reminiscent of so much *voulu* bravado of the 1960s, extras in Westerns trying to look as hard and surly as possible. In the sixties, no doubt the whipping would have taken place on stage. There is a certain kitsch given out by poets trying not to be refined and delicate. Why couldn't it be a nice *clean* mooring-post? Who ever heard of a mooring-post that was covered at high tide?

Hughes-like cruelty is a tone in some Georgian poets, but Abercrombie only dwelt on cruelty in his first play, *The Sale of St. Thomas*; Gibson throughout views suffering with compassion, and as the result of a social system. Later in the century, the theme of Vikings was popular with northern poets. In fact, the heaviest settlement of Danes was in Lincolnshire and East Anglia, which became the richest and among the least warlike of medieval counties; the northern fixation on the Vikings, and the Dark Ages in general, is part of a recent wish to be primitive and bloody and heroic. So the Georgians react against Hellenistic ideals and plump for the Dark Ages; Hughes extends the reaction even further and goes for even mistier and wilder 'savages'. What Vikings represent is a fantasy of exaggerated masculinity; naturally, this can acquire a homoerotic tinge, as when James Kirkup writes 'From that elemental land / Of iron whitenesses and long auroras / My Viking fathers sprang / In armoured nakedness' ('To the Ancestral North', in *The Descent into the Cove*, p. 20), where the last phrase is distinctly fetishistic.

Manchester, Capital of the Nineteenth Century

An interesting list of the largest towns in England, descending as far as 2000 inhabitants, in 1377 and the 1520s, shows only five northern towns out of 42 in 1377 and still only five out of 42 (although a very different 42) in the 1520s. The generalisation about sparse settlement in the pastoral North, which goes back deep into prehistory, thus still holds good in the early sixteenth century, when East Anglia was the richest region. We are surely justified in associating less urbanisation with fewer specialist or skilled workers and a less monetised economy. We are not, then, expecting the miracle of English history, which is the industrialisation of the North and the conversion of high wastes to the most advanced region of the world, with an export economy and skilled to a degree barely conceivable a century earlier.

The rise of the North in the late eighteenth and nineteenth centuries was so startling that it altered the configuration of British politics. We must see the industrial regions of the nineteenth-century North as a new country, one comparable to Prussia, Japan, Pittsburgh, Chicago: intoxicated by expansion; furiously insecure about seizing enough markets to pay off the money borrowed to buy the new machinery; seeing commerce as almost a passage of arms where only the strong thrive; envious of older cultures; opposed to the past and to poetry. The Victorian North saw the expansionist progress ideology of three types: the working-class movement expecting to take over the wealth of industrial civilisation from its non-productive owners, the free traders expecting to satisfy the whole of the industrial needs of the Empire or the world on an unlimited growth curve, and the supporters of industry expecting to displace the South, the political power of the landowners, and all the non-industrial sectors of the country. What we probably miss today is the expectation of the time that the North would follow the path of its differential and faster growth rate, would completely eclipse the South, buy it out, and reduce it to a kind of holiday resort, a quaint old-world place like the American view of England. It is the stumbling of this expectation that shapes twentieth-century northern history and political reflection. Details on the phase of the growth curve changing shape are supplied in Musgrove's *The North of England*; around 1900, modernity flitted away from the North. Northern suspicion of the traditional and continuing English culture was a resentful reaction to its image of the northern world, and to the fear of becoming psychologically enthralled to political enemies. There is a whole contamination theory which led to the attribution of guilt (for the aristocratic principle, for example) to specific works of culture, so that abstention from them kept you ritually pure; this is not so dissimilar from an old-fashioned American distrust, as displayed by Caspar Goodwood in *The Portrait of a Lady*, of the Old World and its ideas as corrupting yet seductive. The internal process of the new industrial civilisation was one of merciless competition over prices, expressed as ruthless depression of wages and squeezing of conditions; the new society was led by men who had triumphed by force of character, avoiding bankruptcy and keeping their equally stalwart men on the leash. It must have been frightening to lie awake thinking that such men were competing with you and would close your business down unless you got the better of them. Such struggles were like wars, absorbing the consciousness of those involved to the exclusion of all else. Weakness and sensitivity were mythologised as the mothers of all defeat and poverty.

British industry matured in the later nineteenth century. The arrival of share-owned companies, with limited liabilities and employed managers, replaced the boss and the drama of the self-made man, and was unacceptable to public perception of the business process for a long time. Inheritance of wealth by heirs unwilling to enter the business themselves, the Corporation Act and other changes in business law, the rise of investments in the Empire, brought a new model of wealth without daily combat, and of the idle rich, spending all their time amusing themselves. This implied a physical move to fairer and more fashionable places, from Manchester to Cheshire, Surrey, or the Riviera. A new profession of financial servants arose to look after this money. Inherited wealth became more typical; the type of the self-made man waned at the top, and the goal of social ascent was increasingly a salaried position, working for someone else. Over a century from about the 1870s, and at an uneven rate, control of manufacturing industry moved from owner-managers to boards representing shareholders; capital could be supplied either by bank loans or in exchange for equity. These changes in the pattern of ownership, together with the geographical concentration of corporate headquarters in the South-East, close to the financial markets, meant that the most important men in industries sited in the North lived in or near London – a management hierarchy expressed in spatial terms. External financing meant that even local factory owners had to relate, almost primarily, to stockbrokers and bankers in the City of London. Trading problems made the controllers of debts the effective bosses. This made it emotionally possible to assign all trading problems to malevolent human agency, and to locate this in the South, where the North was being done down. Accepted ethical standards are missing by which we could confirm or refute this; any concern that needed to obtain a capital injection to survive may have been resentful at how much of the equity and the control it had to concede, and how high the service charges were. All the same, it's inconsistent to demand control of a firm that you are running at a loss, and the value of equity in such a business is rather chancy. Subsequently, the manufacturing firms, and regions, could argue that their bad trading figures were due to the exorbitant cost of debt servicing. By the 1960s, the belief that British industry was in crisis was almost consensual; and the stabilised triangle of state–employers–unions was being circumvented, in the direction of the national fortunes, by the triangle of factories, finance and commerce. There was a latent dispute over sharing the proceeds of making commodities, and it seems that the manufacturer came off with the smallest share; supply-side unions were fighting over leftovers rather than the original cake. The apparent success of a prices and incomes policy during the Keynesian era of state management concealed worsening figures for profit and investment; the running down of the manufacturing base was effectively volatilising the precious jewels over which all the noisy fighting took place. The ratio between investment in plant and research and profits distributed as dividends or debt servicing was out of control, and was reliably generating future crises. Policy was visibly being made in the South, and the North was visibly sliding towards disaster. When the crow came home to roost, in the form of mass unemployment, in 1981, the response of rage was directed not only against capitalism but also against southerners. A key term is 'power of speech': because control over northern businesses was effectively vested in various offices in London, the relationship between northern workers and southern bosses was one of utter dependence, intimacy, and yet remoteness. What someone in a meeting in London EC1 said was binding for people working for a factory, about to be shut down, in Salford: what *he* said went, *their* part was to listen. This made listening to a poet from the South or South-East problematic. The disintegration of an industrial order has brought a crisis of mediations. The conditional failure of the two agencies of modernisation, the London government and the London financial quarter, discredited the modernisation process in poetry also.

The twentieth century saw an industrial revolution in the South-East and Midlands, a new and undefined industrial civilisation outstripping the North in growth rates and profits, and soon in overall output. We no longer have to oppose Manchester and Bradford to Canterbury and Westminster, but to Swindon, Birmingham and Harlow. In culture, there is a vertical succession of self-misunderstandings: each successive generation in the North has been more prosperous, more cultured, and less religious and less radical than its predecessor. English culture has been poured full of elements derived from the new industrial-nonconformist world, but that world has itself become more middle-class, less aggressive and radical, and in effect more southern.

The political neglect of industry has also been cultural: poetry has a skeleton in the closet here, because of historical attitudes that rejected industry as a subject for poetry. This is especially true of successful industry: who today thinks of writing poetry about the growing industry of the Midlands and South-East? Decay is so picturesque; working people are so much more acceptable when in misery than when prosperous, loud and proud. The converse of this was the rejection by the new industrial towns of *belles-lettres* and poetic culture, which remained concentrated in the South. The sequel was a deficit of technique: poets today want to write about de-industrialisation in the North (and South Wales, Cornwall, Strathclyde and so on), but the technical problems of writing about subjects such as trade, manufacturing, the firm and the city are an accumulated debt, problems that make them flounder or turn to teeth-grating simplification. The verbal realm is much smaller than the realm of practical thought and behaviour, offering the poet the task of verbalising what has up till now been unconscious and pragmatic; this project is called modernism. Our use of the word 'poeticism' proves that poetry is narrower than the reach of experience and intelligence. Non-traditionalist poets go to the borders of this poetic domain and struggle with the unknown. Their reward is to make something original.

The world of nineteenth-century northern industry now appears as a vanished civilisation whose Cyclopean red, black and purple buildings dominate the urban landscape, where a new population lives by an exotic, hedonistic code.

Songs and Recitals

The emergence of a significant retail market for books, and of printers, in the North took place after 1780, with the development of better roads and a mail-coach system. These new industries started with the reproduction of the past, for example Bishop Percy's *Reliques* (1760), a collection of old ballads (part of the repertoire of the minstrels, we may suppose), and Joseph Ritson's *Northern Garlands* (1784–93), printing songs from a communal tradition, and concentrated on songs during the nineteenth century – continued in modern times by folk singers, inspirations or rivals to poets of today. The structural oppositions of oral to written; dialect to Standard; sung to printed; working class to educated; communal and social to personal; jolly, boozy and flattened to introspective and sublime are fraught and were still of deep, even devastating, importance in the 1960s.

The books of songs weren't necessarily used for reading, instead of singing aloud. It is hard to exaggerate the popularity of singing before the invention of the gramophone. The rise of reading – even of the housing conditions that would permit it – was hindered, if never arrested. The separation of the lyric poem from the song, something vexed for so much of the history of Western Europe, was taking place painfully and rather unsuccessfully in the nineteenth-century North. It seems that the growth of something more ambitious and introspective did not take place in an empty, open space but was attracted to the already existing poetry culture of the South; northern poetry either picked up 500 years of development for free, or else failed to realise its own destiny, depending on your point of view. The undoubted national greatness of Wordsworth and Swinburne *may* not be wholly unconnected to their ferocious radical politics, fascination with narratives and ballads, distrust of southern literary and moral conventions, and interest in common speech.

We do see, from about 1840, a sub-literary genre of dialect poetry, in regional newspapers, which continued until after the Second World War. As A. S. Umpleby points out in the preface to the Yorkshire poetry anthology *A White Rose Garland*, the nineteenth-century weaver poets were keenly aware of social and political issues, thus becoming the grandparents of British socialist poetry. Umpleby dates the rise of interest in politics to the middle of the century, i.e. presumably as part of the Chartist wave of the 1840s.[10] Dialect poetry of this sort seems to have been largely confined to Yorkshire and Lancashire. A. L. Lloyd, writing about industrial folk-song, also points to the weavers and the miners as the sources of most of it.[11] A later generation of dialect poets in the West Riding was often linked to the Independent Labour Party. The latest book in this line that I have been able to trace came out in 1972: *The Muse Went Weaving*, by Fred Brown (1893–1980), who went into the mill in Huddersfield at thirteen and 'tewed', as he put it, all his life.[12]

Poetry in nineteenth-century Manchester is discussed in an important article, 'Class and Cultural Production in the Industrial City', by Brian Maidment, and illustrated in *The Poorhouse Fugitives*, his anthology and study of poetry by self-educated nineteenth-century poets, chiefly those from Lancashire.[13] Maidment divides the poetry of self-educated men in the nineteenth century into three types: Chartist and radical writing; Parnassian poetry, often using 'the most complex and elaborate traditional forms within the British literary tradition', with 'the ambition to rival the educated classes in poetry'; and 'deliberately homely rhyming', often using dialect. In the light of the tentative remarks made above about a more hierarchical society using more complex language, we can see that the problem facing the self-educated poets was that of either writing a poetry close to the spoken language of their own class, which would impress nobody, or writing in a language which, because of its resemblances to the ornate language of the upper classes, would arouse the audience to question the relevance of the style to the poet's real daily life. The theme of solitude in northern poetry was probably revived by the extreme problems of being a poet in a society that only wanted songwriters; a few groups of people following radical lifestyles provided the air that a modern poetry could breathe, instead of dying or leading an artificial, monologic life in the brain of a solitary poet. Such nineteenth-century groups are the ancestors of all literate groups of today who do not follow a traditional middle-class lifestyle. The logic of the audience taking such a class-based view of poetry, rejecting it where it did not faithfully portray the lifestyle of their income bracket, was bound to abolish the reading of poetry in favour of literary biography, which guarantees the accuracy of its data. So we end up with a public that would rather read interviews with a poet than read his or her poetry. The shadow of social reality is that someone unimportant is therefore uninteresting and should not devote attention to themselves beyond a certain measure. Extended, this principle would imply that rich people are interesting without striving for artistic form and that poor people cannot develop complexity of language as a way of creating personal value *ex nihilo*. The engine-driver Alexander Anderson wrote the following in about 1881:

> Dare I fix my vision further, deeming that we mould this mind,
> But to look in steady splendour on the toiling of our kind?[14]
> Heart! but this were something nobler than the poet ever felt
> When the fought-for happy laurel clasp'd his forehead like a belt;
> When the liquid fire of genius, rainbow colour'd, flash'd and glow'd
> All its mighty beams above him with the splendour of a god,
> Wider in its stretch and grandeur than the brain could ever dream
> To look down on our fellows from some planet's blinding gleam,
> Watching with seraphic vision, grasping with delighted soul,
> All the goals to which they hurry as the moments shake and roll,
> Linking with an unseen quickness vigour to the tasks they do,
> Touching each with fresher impulse as a nobler comes in view.
> Then when triumph crowns their striving, start to hear the heaven sublime
> Fill its azure arch with plaudits echoing from the throat of time
> (from 'A Song of Labour', in Maidment, *The Poorhouse Fugitives*)

This is very well written. One can see that the sublimity might call forth accusations of pretentiousness from his social superiors, and possibly even his social equals; he would have been less vulnerable, although not necessarily more poetic, if he'd written unambitious pious and realistic verse. The social fabric has massive conservative energies driving people back into the boundaries set around their movements. The elements of pretension are many, but include the claim to autonomy: by philosophising, Anderson is claiming to be in control of his life; and the claim to knowledge, implicit in the scope of the poem and conjured up in the delirious perspective of watching the Earth from a different planet, implies that he is as good as his rulers. Using a Greek word (epithalamium) might be ambitious in itself, when a classical education was the property of the moneyed few. We can see that a viscount who advanced these claims might encounter less resistance, even if he were less gifted. The use of 'splendour', then 'splendour' again, then 'blinding gleam' might be called hitting the same button three times, and the 'liquid fire' that 'flash'd and glow'd' might be a fourth instance. But I admire the fabric, and there is a real movement of argument in the verse. Intellectually ambitious verse is just as much part of working-class culture as stubbornly narrow and unthinking realism. The theme of the poem is the superior interest, as subjects, of industry and technology to visions; Anderson remarks that 'this knowledge is a master whose first aim is to unteach', a Hegelian notion that anticipates the critical attitude to knowledge of many poets since 1960. I believe that the view that upper-class speech resembles the gorgeous discourse of poems and plays is wrong in poetic terms. Certainly, we have today a breed of poets of working-class origins who are completely insensitive to style, and regard their biography as the source of the flawless value of their work. Modern poetry is the province of the Left, and divisions within it are divisions within the Left, surviving because of a dislike for internal debate. If linguistic research is a free source of personal value, then poetry subverts the social order – which is the premise that induced me among others to get involved in poetry as a teenager. This value is not merely self-referential, because its gold standard is the attention of other people, readers. But poetry that is without readers cannot be subverting the social order, as contained in the minds of individuals who are not, certainly, being altered by what they do not read. Hence the innovative poetry written by socialist poets is written off by most of the Left because it is not going to be a best-seller. Apparently poetry can only be socially subversive by being formally conservative; one can only change assumptions by taking everything for granted. This is the situation we live in, and seems to be imprinted by what took place in the nineteenth century.

The culture of the northern working class also includes religious writing, drawing on a stylised and elevated literary tradition traceable back to the first century AD, if not, truly, to Israelite literature and the depths of the first millennium BC, and offering an elevated diction to the humblest Christian. The problem of relating individual experience to biblical types, biblical speech to personal poetry, remained acute. The temper of intro-spection was changing in the nineteenth century. What we seem to be seeing is the replacement of the religious vocabulary of self-examination with a scientific, psychological one, a revolution of modern times. The new society of the industrial zones expressed itself through religion and, increasingly, through working-class politics; a tradition of public litera-ture poured out through hymns and oratory. However, nobody wrote hymns in dialect, which thus led a niche existence in a cultural periphery. It seems that the preachers of all Nonconformist sects strove to master Standard English and the oratory of educated men; their superiority to the Anglican Church was based on feeling, not on form. Their picture of the Established Church as a ruling-class conspiracy, based on hierarchy and family connections, organised and given a deceptive elegance through the sinister institutions of Oxford and Cambridge, is recognisable in the propaganda of the 1990s. The Anglican Church's piety and belief in social justice have been consistently under-rated, but in any case the Christian Socialist movement was from the 1840s an attempt to face the new society – and is recognisably the ancestor of middle-class guilt and of some of the chief strains in modern English poetry. Radical verse often took an eschatological form.

Literature is as restricted by technical development as any other activity; the reader may care to test this by experiment, but anyway let me assert that there is far more going on around us than can be easily turned into words, and that describing, say, a party, or a week of your life, so that nothing was left out, would be extraordinarily difficult. If one examines what is easy to record, it turns out that it is what has already been written about. What is omitted is a trickster world, producing results you didn't wish for or don't understand. Primary processing is difficult and exhaus-ting. In 1800, the life of industrial urban cities was outside the scope of literature; this has only very gradually, and partially, been changed. It is unreasonable to blame southern writers for this, since it was the responsibility of northern writers; if very few of these feature in our nineteenth-century history (Wordsworth, the Brontës, Mrs Gaskell, Surtees, marginally Harrison Ainsworth) it is partly because the subject matter proved intractable. The tolerance for industrial themes which arose around 1960 has since been reversed; the Thatcherite attack on industry, as a dead horse needing to be replaced by service industries, was a new form of this intolerance. However, the New Left's attack on the Old Left can be seen partly as an attack on the politics, cultural institutions, and most of the people, of the North.

Increasingly skilled industrial activity demanded increasing amounts of study, reflection and serious thought; Musgrove quotes an account from 1849: 'The cotton mills of Manchester abound with hard-headed, studious, thoughtful men, who pass brooding, meditating lives';[15] if it hadn't been for these studious people, there would be no left-wing movement as we know it today. Such people wanted freedom to read; and still do. Their work demanded thought; experience of the vagaries of the market, and of the changes visibly being wrought by technology, made them familiar with a world of economic relations; consequently, they wanted literature to give an account of social life which was not abusively simple, and which captured a sense of progress, speculation and optimism. Beside the sentimental recitals and pub songs we have the heady soarings of the Manchester politician Ernest Jones (1819–69), which, like the poems of his fellow-Chartist Ebenezer Jones, float in some misty Hegelian or Swedenborgian realm of the sublime. This working-class literature is confused because it is mixing the most supernatural elements of religion with the quantitative world of science and sociology:

> But science gathers, with gigantic arms,
> In one embrace, the South's diffusive charms;
> Nor these alone, she rears the bright domain,
> Throughout the world expands her hallowing reign –
> Then bold aspiring as immortal thought
> Launched in the boundless, mounts the aeronaut;
> While o'er the earth they drive the cloudy team,
> Electric messenger, and car of steam;
> And guide and govern on innocuous course,
> The explosive mineral's propulsive force […]
> (from *The Revolt of Hindostan* [1849])[16]

A car of steam might easily be propelled by Jones's poetry, I should think. 'From Freedom born to Time, transcendent birth!' Finding the middle ground between the excessively banal and the excessively uplifted and phantomatic was to puzzle socialist poets for more than a century.

I don't find anything urgently worth reviving in the poetry of nineteenth-century Manchester; nor, tacitly, does the expert, Brian Maidment. But I don't think this failure was inevitable: there could have been a great poet within the parameters accepted by the audience (and, probably, challenging them). The record shows both work for public performance that sticks tightly to collective rules, and work that is heady, speculative, excessive, sublime and chaotic. Between the two, there were ample possibilities. The Left poetry of the present century inherited these, tightly intricated with problems. The homely poetry of the time can repine at its lack of an audience today; I find it tedious, but I am not the target audience. A new mass reading public might have taken over the popular literature of the preceding era, but did not.

The verse of Lancashire and Yorkshire weavers, printed in local newspapers, especially in Manchester, did not perhaps die out without progeny as working-class radicals acquired an education and a new, classless culture. It had an oral and collective (and flattening) bias; and these features reappear in the 1960s in the upsurge of poetry readings. The new poetry of the sixties did have origins partly in Liverpool and adjacent regions, and in Newcastle; although this localisation has probably been exaggerated, and it would be wiser to suggest the USA as the place where the mutation originated. Early phases of the new, direct address, 'anti-literary' poetry of the sixties may point us accurately at the heritage of 'Ab O'th'Yate' or Edwin Waugh; names such as Jim Burns or Brian Patten don't seem too far away from that linguistic world. Reading is a middle-class activity, and most books are by middle-class people. By no means everybody on the Left accepts that reading a book is a valid way of behaving: many see it as selfish, individualistic and non-solidary. It was possible in the sixties to define the preference for the printed word as middle-class and obsolete; the superior vitality and morality of 'the Reading' is in fact advanced as the thesis of *British Poetry 1964–84* by Martin Booth, a critic known more for his left-wing integrity and enthusiasm than for his poetic sensibility.[17] Significantly, Booth also favours the poetry workshop, and was formed by his participation in one organised by Philip Hobsbaum called The Group; this kind of warm face-to-face contact suggests the university as the home of poetry, as indeed the readings had largely student audiences. The classroom is modern orality, if not exactly a minstrels' gallery; if estranged from rhetoric, it teaches the arts of dialectic. This live poetic society solves the problems of isolation, self-absorption, crankiness and despair which have afflicted so many provincial artists struggling on their own.

The model of *communal and oral culture* prevalent in the North had strong traits of its own: sentimentality as opposed to self-consciousness; communitarianism; fear of originality; liking for commonsense empiricism and for shooting dreams down (as anti-social?); fear of the imagination; belief in the importance of being 'rooted' in a community, as a source of authentic knowledge that poems can record, and a consequent inability to think about social relations or explain why they are that way; beer, beer, beer; fetishistic belief in the spontaneity and authenticity of linguistically undernourished and retarded forms, especially if they are old and to do with song; automatic leftism and class consciousness; Tourist Board view of the past, unsolved problems in dealing with anything except the immediate present. Unfortunately, the aesthetic limits of flattened, joky, beer-and-sawdust 'social' poetry seem to be clearly inscribed in the weavers' dialect poetry of the last century.

The opposition between oral and written is global, as codified most impressively by the Canadian scholar Walter J. Ong in *Orality and Literacy*;[18] if oral culture includes Homer, the orations of Demosthenes, Chinese opera and the sermons of Donne, it is not in itself limiting or flattening. Audience expectations can be high or low. The conflict between *flattened* (unpretentious, collective, easy) and *heightened* (intellectual, innovatory, strange) poetry was decisive in the formation of the new literary order, as repressive traditionalism collapsed in the 1960s; education, simultaneously the main benefit of the collective purse to the lower orders, the main way of segregating and recognising the lower orders, a solvent of traditional values, and a rift between the new poets and their perceived community, was too fraught for poetry to expand its information base without arousing social tensions which ruined the cosy collectivism of the reading. The revolution of the sixties caused a scattering of artistic tastes over a wide area; the poets who did not repress and deny this sailed out of the popular taste of readings, but wrote something that looks good in print. The poets who imposed on themselves the dogma that *anything more intense than speech is elitist and false and selfish* committed artistic suicide.

Ruggedness and Isolation: Northern Mythology

The shared mythology of the North includes a theme of *pride and individualism* involving domineering and blustering; a belief that the strong have the right to decide everything; interest in conflict and tests of strength; touchiness, preferring to sacrifice politeness for the sake of defending symbolic status; fixed clusters of associations between grimness, bleakness, ruggedness, sullenness, Viking ancestors and so on; admiration for a sharp tongue, nimble in insults, carried out in a pithy, half proverbial language, whose self-assurance excludes doubt; hardheadedness, especially in resisting ideas of any kind; resentment of authority figures; privileging of inarticulacy; and problems expressing emotion.

Ong has claimed that a stress on conflicts, in which larger-than-life heroes noisily triumph, is characteristic of oral literature.[19] The emphasis on size and dominance in northern poetry may, then, be inherent in the weak development of the literary mode. Since we do not find it in southern poetry, we can speculate that a physical norm of dominance, demonstrated by combat, is replaced by dominance expressed by social prestige, where culture is part of the legitimation process and conflict is simply marginalised. Cultured poetry is intensely competitive: the competitive urge may shift from a desire to have the largest and most dangerous hero figure into a desire for stylistic supremacy. This relationship of mutual replacement may also explain why poetry about heroes ignores stylistic development.

In the medieval North, farmers held their land by 'tenant right', which meant that they could not be evicted at will; paying only minimal rents and Crown taxes, they were obliged to provide military service against the Scots, and to find horses, weapons and harness to that end. It was a military society; R. L. Storey speaks of the 'northern military complex'.[20] We can even claim that the boundary of this militarism was also the boundary of northernness. This military basis for landholding applied supremely to the counties of Cumberland, Westmorland, Durham and Northumberland, but also to the whole of the country as far south as the Trent. (It also applied, within slightly different dates, to the counties of the Welsh marches, and to Wales as an unruly dominion of the English Crown.) The light horse of the northern hills were led into battle by magnates, *les seignurs marchers del north*, whose power depended essentially on their ability to inspire their followers and to win, not on owning the land and ordering their tenants about. While non-military tenants lost their land, which meant for example that women were unimportant in the transmission of social power, it was unfeasible to exploit the arms-bearing tenants, so that the percentage of gentry and nobles in northern parts was much lower than in the South. This meant that high medieval civilisation was a scarce thing in the region. The ordinary yeomen were far better off than southern serfs, but the economy was far less monetised and opened to trade; war, indeed, was the business of the North, more so than farming. Storey's article on the North of England in the fifteenth century cites the poll tax records of 1377, giving the North 15 per cent of the total population, but only 5 per cent if we exclude Yorkshire, which had a commercial and international wool economy and was a different kind of society. A century of Anglo-Scots wars from 1296 onwards wiped out much of the accumulated rural capital of the Borders, inducing a move backwards into pastoralism and military virtues, reducing commerce and town living. This scorched zone resulted in, among other things, a gap between the dialects of Northumbria and Scotland. The monarchs wanted the inhabitants of their own border regions to be as warlike as possible, to slow down enemy raids, foragers or invasions; this made them unwilling (at times, unable) to subject such men to the process of law, and so the Borderers became hardy and outside the law; their reiving made ordinary farming unprosperous in those parts, which also slowed down alien armies, among other arrivals. Nicholas Udall, visiting the Borders in 1598, said that he found the people 'strangely compounded, barbarous more of will than of manners, active of person and speech, stout and subtle, inclined to theft and strife, factious and seditious, full of malice and revenge, being nursed up in these vices from their ancestors, apt to quarrel rather with blood than speech, though scant of neither'.[21]

Dating the ballads is difficult, but any Middle English ballads that survived in oral recitation (as they did not in manuscript) must have been modernised and refashioned along with the language, while there are reasons for thinking that the ballad tradition was conservative, and declining, in the seventeenth century; so the fifteenth and sixteenth centuries are the candidates for the composition, or finishing, of the ballads as we know them from written and oral recollection.

While identifying that the values stylised and ennobled in these fifteenth-century texts (Malory, alliterative *Morte d'Arthur*, the ballads), so similar to each other, correspond on another plane to the real-life values of the warrior-farmers and warrior-landowners of the North, we also recognise that they are exemplars of an international style which had a long history behind it. The mythical Arthur was thought to have lived in the fifth century, while the texts of Taliesin and the *Gododdin*, from around AD 600, depict a social order in northern England or the Scottish Borders which bears striking resemblances to that of the fifteenth century. Stress is laid on warrior feats, on metal, and on horses. The task of delivering energy at an area no larger than a lance's point, within restrictive limits of timing, was precise and delicate; Lynn White has pointed out how the pennant on the knight's lance was a cross-bar, so that when the tip of the lance had entered the adversary's body, it could be retracted without going so far in as to unbalance and unhorse the lancer.[22] The delicacy of these high-speed interactions, the focusing of thrust on small areas, the need for high-class metallurgy, make them psychologically akin to working with machines. The harness of the horse is the predecessor of driving-belts: from horse to horsepower. In the charge, the horse is part of the delivery system of the lance, supplying the impetus which, concentrated on a tiny surface area, gives the lance's tip its penetrative power. The bow is an early form of stored kinetic energy. Both represent the extension of the body by mechanical means, and we need to imagine the limits of the naked body to understand their appeal.

Stover and Kraig describe the Beaker People, of 3000 to 2500 BC, as the first heroic-metallurgical culture to arrive in the British Isles;[23] the spread of chariot warfare, from about 1400 BC, has been conjecturally described as the forerunner of the knight as heavy cavalry, using armour, the stirrup, the lance and the horseshoe in one technical complex of revolutionary impact. Because precious objects and military skills are the sources of social power and success, eulogistic poetry celebrates them, and heroic narrative recounts the use of the skills. The state can be founded on the hard edge of the sword because of the latter's functional relationship to the soft parts of the human body. The equations governing the design of swords include the consistency and resistance of human flesh. The stability of physiology, and of the dynamics governing rigid blades moving to shear or pierce the integument holding the human body together, means that the chivalric complex is a 'cultural recollection' of aristocratic cavalry corps going back to the Bronze Age. The high speed of the interactions makes observing a large number of them peculiarly necessary to understanding them, which would be conducive to accumulating narratives of past encounters; the need to excel, the penalties of weakness, made comparison vitally interesting.

If Malory was a Yorkshireman (which is controversial, although the surviving manuscript of his work is written in a northern dialect), the untiring stress on heroism and violence and feats of arms in his epic may have been realistic rather than drawn from some misty world of romance. Storey stresses the importance of retinue violence between magnates of a county: failure at passages of arms led not only to loss of life but also to loss of land.[24] The Crown tolerated this in order to have warriors ready for service at short notice. Property replaced armed retinues as the basis of social power and prestige. Family warfare within counties became obsolete in the fifteenth century; defence against Scots became archaic in the sixteenth century. The minstrels, still a feature of northern gentry life in the sixteenth century, declined as lavish hospitality ceased to be politically useful, and the gentry retired into a new private or family-based existence in smaller rooms, ancestral to modern middle-class life, and even engaging in the new individualist practice of reading. Their books came from the South, or from the general European culture. The rise of lay literacy occurred in the fifteenth century. The minstrels merged with the peasantry, who preserved their basically aristocratic art until the collectors arrived, but did not add a new repertoire. Scott places his 'last minstrel' (in *The Lay of the Last Minstrel*) in the 1620s, and was probably not far wrong. Ballad composition continued later in the North. There is a ballad on Lord Derwentwater, a Jacobite with estates in the archaic region of upland Northumberland, who was executed in 1716; this (brilliantly recorded by the singer Shirley Collins in the 1970s) is unforgettable (the executioner holds up the severed head, says 'Behold the head of a traitor', 'and the head it spoke, and said, "You lie"'), but is surely a throwback.

The conditions described would have produced an alarming set of values: marginalising women and culture, preoccupied with tests of physical strength and willpower, hierarchical and despising the weak, inclined to boasting above all other qualities of speech, stubborn and proud. The problem of writing a northern cultural history is proving that these characteristics, so outflanked by new conditions, hung around as values into the revolutionary nineteenth century and emerged as myths in poetry in the twentieth. I am unwilling to believe that a value system is so slow to adapt; nonetheless these descriptions seem very helpful in understanding twentieth-century northern poetry. Fantasy is a (real) structure with the value of time relaxed; myth represents a social structure, but can outlive it.

'She seemed to have the fondy flummoxed, till his wits / Were fozy as a frosted swede.' The understanding of deceit as a test of strength, common in Wilfrid Gibson's poetry, strains the relationship between poet and reader, suggesting that the latter is weak-headed if he swallows what the poet is putting over. A patriarchal reading of all relationships as unequal produces such a politics of language. The relation between North and South tends to be pressed into this pattern, with the South producing high-flown poetic beauties, religious and philosophical theories, and the North hard-headedly breaking them up into pieces and hanging onto its indifference. A northern patriotic version of history has never been worked out except by fragments, but ghost doubles do struggle against the accepted, southern, version of historical narratives in a kind of giganto-machia. Some of the popular psychic assets of the North are beautiful hills, hard rocks, difficult heavy industries, strong men, beautiful women, sharp tongues, hard heads and dark beer, and anyone who impugns either the ultimate value of these things, or the North's title to pre-eminence in them, might be advised to go and take their thesis somewhere else.

What is striking about *Nan*, and Gibson's verse dramas, and Gordon Bottomley's *King Lear's Wife* (in the first *Georgian Book*), is the promin-ence of family conflict at their centre. The conflicts in Gibson's plays seem to come from the fathers' savage wish to dominate, which produces an imitation, expressed in faithlessness, theft and flight, in the sons. The pattern is reminiscent of two nearly contemporary Scottish novels, *Gillespie* (by John MacDougall Hay) and *The House with Green Shutters* (by George Brown). This father–son conflict is also fundamental in German Expressionism, a contemporary style. The arrogance, blustering and intransigence of both sons and fathers supplies the action as well as the most vivid passages of poetry in Gibson's dramas. What distinguished John Arden from other political playwrights of the time, and made him a great playwright, was the reflection in his heroes of an older northern ideal of ambition and self-aggrandisement, bursting out in language of great richness. His Brechtian withdrawal of identification does not diminish the protagonists, as so often with other writers, but draws them into a deeper literary space in which their alarming energies are shown off to greater effect before being exposed by the perspective of history. The protagonists of plays such as *The Workhouse Donkey*, *Serjeant Musgrave's Dance* and *Live Like Pigs* are coarse, domineering, but larger than life. I believe all these plays should be acted in broad northern accents. Arden's work resembles that of the other West Riding poet, his exact contemporary, Ted Hughes; and the potent, unreasonable animals of Hughes's poems could be projections of these potent, unreasonable heads of family. It is this theme of pride and competition that I am going to discuss for the rest of the chapter. The word 'rugged' means 'wrinkled', became attached to anfractuous scenery, and then to people, first of all meaning 'surly, rough, inconsiderate'. I speculate that this last shift refers to this potent-unreasonable personality type, with the mountain representing power, danger, refusal of emotional links, glowering silence. A repellent quality became an admired one.

It is time to see through the alleged bleakness of northern poetry. It is implausible that this stems from the weather, which is after all only a couple of degrees colder than the South. It isn't the landscape, since most people don't live in the craggy and mountainous parts. It is more reasonable to look for the bleakness, isolation, aggression and so on in particular family structures, which immediately become limited in history and subject to change. The self-made man is a less common, less intoler-ant phenomenon, today. These formations aren't specific to the North. They are also subject to alteration by conscious political action, so that it now seems possible to argue about the behaviour of the characters in the plays. Indeed, the thought arises that Gibson's way of presenting behaviour, in a dense social and familial context, is ideally suited to such discussion, that it resembles the poetry written by feminists in the past thirty years, and that poetry which is less realistic and more individualistic evades and frustrates such discussion (unless perhaps it presents its results as *faits accomplis*, finished and untouchable ideas). The values that Gibson shows in his characters are the work ethic; Puritanism; materialism; stress on hard work as the only test of character; contempt for anyone soft-headed or easily got the better of; worship of physical strength; admiration for hard-headedness and for dominating someone else. This system is inimical to poetry, or to any fine language. The history of northern poetry may be missing for internal reasons, not because of control rays being transmitted from Influencing Machines in the South.

The familial revolt of characters within the Victorian realist matrix of Masefield and Gibson's works both resembles and contrasts with the revolt against the parental generation of modernists of the same period. This question of revolt or conformism hangs over the subsequent eighty years of English poetry. The hypothesis is that individual self-determination, implying both vanity and aesthetic choice, is so controversial and fought over in an authoritarian family that a poetry which immerses itself in such subject matter is unable to contemplate subjective linguistic freedom. This may be a complete chimera. Still, a poem can be beautiful as well as virtuous.

Perhaps modernism was only possible because the existing authorities were so positivistic, capitalistic, colonialistic, and swollen with a belief in progress that the rebellion was a furious outburst, which at the same time *imitated* the bad fathers, seizing their authority in various secret, disguised, and fantastically mutated forms. Our concept of artistic revolt is much less exciting and more reasonable. Children are no longer – except in extreme and illegal circumstances – subject to violence from parents, teachers and employers. Social control has changed its methods; and presumably the notion of what is curbed and repressed by society, the self and its unmodified impulses, has changed as well.

In Sergeant's anthology is the poem 'Mountain-Love', by J. Redwood Anderson. Anderson was one of the lesser (in fact totally ignored) *vers libre* poets of the First World War era (his first book came out in 1913). He published a book called *The Vortex* which had nothing to do with Vorticism, was a teacher at a public school, lived in Hull, and later went to live in Wales in order to sit at the feet of John Cowper Powys. In the 1940s, he published a mystico-Buddhist idealist cosmic epic in three volumes. What his poem shows is the psychic identification of man and mountain: 'By closest sympathies / Lovers exchange their qualities', the two lovers being man and mountain. This is a gloss on the adjective 'rugged'. But what are the qualities that he finds so attractive in the mountain?

> it stood as in a cold black fit
> of anger and of hate
> [...]
> cried
> aloud in baffled and bewildered pride
> And all men feared it (not the abyss,
> but the black lake and precipice
> [...]
> something as strange as human love,
> something as cunning and as kind,
> as sweet, and pitiless, and blind
> and grey in cruelty.

I confess I am at a loss to see how love is 'grey in cruelty', although I do not find it absolutely impossible; Anderson's proverbial manner assumes knowledge that it does not lay out. All the same, we can observe that (a) this is a pretty poor look-out for marriage, (b) it echoes the relationships in Gibson's plays (although these are not in fact based on love but on self-assertion and habit), and (c) the link of love and cruelty suggests a sexual interpretation of the whipping scene in *Britain's Daughter*, which after all is one implication of a beautiful, semi-naked young woman on stage. Perhaps solitude and cruelty are due to a failure of mediations. Further on in the poem, we find these lines:

> there were moments [...]
> that his face seemed
> no face: but one of the blind crags that move,
> huge and forlorn, behind the mist.

We are seeing in live action the transformation of the man into the mountain.

> His brow was like a hard
> boulder of stone [...]
> and the proud
> head, where the long white hair
> drifted, was like some solitary, bare
> high summit with its mane of cloud.

Only the word *patriarch* is appropriate here. Almost we seem to see R. S. Thomas or Ted Hughes rearing into these clouds, grimacing and declaiming. 'Mountain-Love' was collected in the volume *Pillars to Remembrance* (1948), where we also find 'The Old Gods', describing the pagan gods as withdrawing to the mountains in rage and hate; they are equated with the powers of the human soul 'which he must obey'. So mountains here stand for what a Freudian would call the id; intemperate passions are not small, within a human heart, but expanded to vast proportions, towering over the town and enveloping it; nature is defined as the realm of infantile emotion. In 'Lake and Crag' we find more imagery of solitude and grimness: a lake seeks out solitude, its last passion when others are burnt out; the crag is 'proud, solitary, mighty, and aloof' – like Gibson's arrogant bad husbands, perhaps? 'Lynceus' is a Morrisian medieval legend about a castle (of mountainous size) full of haggard, enchanted revellers waiting through centuries for the prince to arrive; the watchman, Lynceus, on the pinnacle, scans the horizon. Here the position of dominance and authority is defined but remains vacant; the suzerain never quite comes to take up his place among humankind. In 'The Cliff –

> The cliff?
> Rather the depth of strata'd stone,
> flesh of earth's flesh, bone of earth's bone:
> the hidden belt of rock that came

– serried layer and contorted fold –
up from what old
rage of forgotten passions? what unguessed
desire? what storm of subterranean flame?

– the anthropomorphised hero-scarp, having heaved itself up apparently in a bout of psychotic rage, remains quiet for millions of years, 'triumphant in the solitary consciousness / of great deeds done', and finally falls into the sea – an act of self-oblivion seen in oddly sexual terms ('exultant, naked, free') as the cliff dissolves in its union. Again, this can hardly be seen as praise of marriage.

The solitude of these Cyclopean emotional objects is the result of violence; Anderson seems to be designing a landscape dehumanised in an almost eugenicist way. Other voices have fallen silent. Yet the emotions, which are in his phantasy the causes of these geological shapes, are social in origin: the sense of rejection, resentment, the urge to excel. Even the absence of human emotions is a form of revenge, a move in a cruel social game: if you don't feel for me, why, I won't feel for you. The apocalyptic *mise en scène* of the Incorrupt Man in the wilds is akin to many scenes in Welsh poetry (starting with the exile-hermit schema of Gildas's *De excidio Britanniae* in the sixth century). Symbols are ambiguous, and the heroic solitude can point, not only to bad quarrelsome sulking rage, but also to the tradition of political resistance and protest in Britain, which goes back, equally mythically, to Gildas, his contemporary Arthur, and the failed resistance to the Anglo-Saxon invasions. At any rate it points to a bulging pride, and this is what I find thickly spread in Northern poetry.

Snowdon was the fastness to which Welsh guerrillas withdrew, time and time again, to evade ponderous English field armies. Mountains can, then, be the realm of isolation and freedom. (Apart, of course, from disqualifying the South-East and East, partly alluvial and wholly free of mountains.) We can look in Anderson for the struggles of marginalised legitimacy; his cliffs and mountains strive for size in order to compete with something else, the rejecting master which we can hesitatingly identify with invested authority (given Anderson's obscurity, this would include poetic authority and accepted taste). The description of 'the solitary consciousness / of great deeds done' can refer to someone who is not conventionally successful and has progressed through shame and humiliation to serious endeavour and to defiant self-respect; a single parent, I conjecture, an impoverished radical, an underground poet, or one of the long-term unemployed. This stubborn independence is able to be either bullying in marriage *or* political virtue. Anyone who is trying to become socially radical has to go through the stages of withdrawal, of intellectual isolation, and of official disapproval.

Lexical oppositions are only useful if we grasp the behaviour complexes that generate them. Anderson's size complex draws us into the structure of competition and compensation; the refusal to be second. The mountains are only there in the poem to be bigger than someone else's hills; some men are bigger than others, my feelings are bigger than yours. The suggestion that there is a metropolitan middle-class taste which belittles provincial (or working-class? or female?) poets fits very well into this landscape. The game is one of acquiring and displaying psychic assets almost like consumerist families in the furniture shop. Least welcome of all would be a critic who sneaks in and says 'these aren't your mountains at all, they are just figures in some infantile scenario of introjection and appropriation'. Anderson was distracted by manipulating millions of tons of living rock from realising that his poetry is qualitatively under-developed. The struggle for size (typically expressed and advertised by the trilogy: Anderson indeed wrote a poem in three volumes) is egoistic in a quite arrested way: it would be so much more interesting if the camera pulled back to show two figures competing rather than just one, glowering, alone, and armoured against change. Anderson's dramas seem only to have one character; surely an adolescent problem. Maybe if the mountain was happier it would only be a little bump in the grass.

Someone purely alone is a *monachos*, a monk. The hermit custom of the Celtic church goes back to Saint Anthony, in the second century AD, withdrawing into the Thebaid – an act of protest against the (anti-Christian) Roman Empire of the time which can anticipate any cultural revolt in Western history since then; our official culture includes models of withdrawal and protest. Quite a few of our saints' lives draw on this hermit tradition, including that of Guthlac of Croyland, but especially, because Northumbria was converted by missionaries from Ireland, those of the northern saints of the Celtic church. So quite a proportion of the few northern texts we do have from the Middle Ages use this knot of images: solitude, holiness, desert places of the earth, physical ordeals, spiritual struggle, triumph. Anthony had to struggle with demons dwelling in his desert, a theme that found its way into British saints' lives and so points forward to Hughes's conjuring with evil spirits. Severance from the evil influence of women was rather too prominent in the system of the Egyptian ascetics; notions of sexual and poetic purity have shifted a bit over the last century. R. S. Thomas oscillates in the semantic space between *monachos* and monarch; self-control is a substitute for, possibly preparation for, controlling other people. The cultural preference for virginity points to a vision of the personality as a fragile pattern, sealing its sense of authenticity into elements which are too fine and fleeting to be touched; elevating constancy to the point where change (and dialogue) are seen as corruption. How far is this from stating that poetry that changes is corrupt, that thinking about poetry corrupts it, and that writing poetry different from that of the nineteenth century is merely fashionable and weak-headed? Not *all* northern poetry is based on these principles.

In *The Cry of the Curlew* (1940) we find complementary examples of Anderson's themes. In 'The Farm-House', there is a 'never-ceasing war' between the farm and the moor; the latter is seen as a principle of sterility, locked in a test of strength with human effort. 'The Moors', in the poem of that name, 'live in cloistral brotherhood. / They have renounced desire, made faith's last sacrifice': sexual sterility is seen, once again, as a form of authenticity, isolation permits one (one's ego?) to grow to giant size, but is ultimately ruinous. If I become attached to someone else, my feelings will become much smaller; if I don't become attached to anyone else, they will go away altogether.

James Kirkup (1923–), in his 17-page poem *The Last Man*, included in *The Submerged Village* (1951), wrote the definitive version of the solitude theme, going deeper and reaching greater heights than others. His hero is alone because of pride ('Love of my own image was the crime'); the Anderson-like ruinous orgasm is suicide by jumping:

> Like thin paper placed upon a tongue
> of flaming fire, all my body now is accurately seized
> with twisting heats, more absolute, at last,
> than love's wild easy passion.
> Now! swift epileptic agonies of searing lust
> wither the soul's evaporations into freezing dust!…
>
> falling from hell to falling hell, and falling,
> falling in doom's interminable well

Perhaps we can see the poem 'The Submerged Village' as being about a landscape of happiness, unobtainable because it is homosexual and forbidden; an account of sexual alienation, then, as 'What were the feelings of the wild springs, the sweet / wells that without warning began to feel themselves / rising, filled with an overwhelming dread?' is a moving account of spring's awakening in a society where such acts were still punishable by prison sentences. Kirkup creates striking pictures of landscapes bound by ice, rather than water. The crime of 'loving my own image' is, ambiguously, loving one's own kind, i.e. other men, expressed through the poetic image of a mirror down the middle of the bed. But everyone who writes either about Vikings or about isolation is writing about men without women.

Another mountaineer poet is David Craig (1931–), author of a whole book about mountains; he is in fact Scottish, but has lived in Lancashire for many years and appears in the anthology *Northern Poets One*. He is a Marxist, and presents a left-wing view of mountains: they aren't property, aren't converted into use, and are egalitarian because climbing them demands only physical strength, stripping away status and possessions. His vision of geology as a deterministic, inflexible, inhumanly long-term process based on law is, however, an occult version of patriarchy: the eagerness to set aside human wishes is part of a Marxist abolition of political rights in the name of a deterministic law-based historical process manifesting itself as knowledge in the hands of the pure authoritarian few. One constitutes a solitude in order to have monarchical power there.

Such overbearing male behaviour was bound to call forth a vigorous reaction from women, and indeed we find a hard-talking streak of feminist poetry from the North, most memorably recorded in the anthology *Purple and Green* (the suffragette colours) from Rivelin Grapheme Press. Already in *Krindlesyke* we find the amazingly sharp-tongued Bell Haggard, who claims as her ambition to be a 'tinker's baggage', delivering some of the most tart and withering tongue-lashings in the language. Take for example this tirade against her son and common-law husband:

> Ewe's milk you'd bleed
> If your nose were tapped. Who'd ever guess my dugs
> Had suckled you? Even your dad's no more
> Than three parts mutton with a strain of reynard –
> A fox's heart, for all his weak sheep's head.

Cutting down three generations in one generous sweep, she goes on to invite her father-in-law's participation (*deafy*, gone bad; *kittle*, tickle):

> You deafy nut, you gibbet, you rusty corncrake!
> Tell me what's kittling you, old skeleton,
> Or I'll joggle your bones till they rattle like castanets.

Salty as the Yorkshire feminists of *Purple and Green* might be in full flight, one doubts that they are quite as scalding as Bell Haggard. Someone who says 'Where I am mistress, there can be no master' doesn't need to read *Spare Rib*. After putting paid to every male around in this blood-curdling style, she settles down to keep house for them all; Bell's way of speaking ('I / Who've always done the choosing, and never yet / Tripped to the beck of any man or bobbed / To any living woman') resembles that of the men she reviles, and she admires what they admire. History doesn't attribute such diction to the Georgians; history is wrong.

It is arguable that art is mainly a symbolic way of dealing with contests, which primate society ceaselessly calms and assuages and yet ceaselessly generates. But it is also the case that the energy of art comes from various forms of argument and competition, the rich technical vocabulary of rhetoric coming from formalised dispute, where contradiction is the challenge that presses the mind into invention and precise formulation. It is possible for writers to quell impulses to conflict and self-aggrandisement so much, reaching such equanimity, that their books are boring. This book I am writing offers (apparently) a balancing after conflicts have burnt themselves out; it doesn't offer a dramatic exhibition and pitched struggle between opposing forces, as Hughes or Arden do. Literary pleasure may need displays of primitive vigour, the Bussy D'Ambois and Tamburlane characters stalking around stage delivering tirades. However, the corollary of aggrandising your own assets is disparaging other people's; provincial resistance to the centre can have all sorts of positive results, but we cannot list among these a furious hostility to artistic innovation because it happens first in some metropolis and wasn't invented here. Page rage isn't an artistic response.

This hypothesis of a regional thematic has to be tempered by other data; the hermit-apocalypse theme is important in the poems of Peter Abbs (from Norfolk) and Emyr Humphreys (from Wales), and the psychic identification with mountains is common in Scottish and Welsh poetry. One could write a whole thesis on the poetic use of stones and geology by writers from all over the country, although the meaning 'I am obstinate', 'I am going to refuse dialogue', 'I am going to say the same thing over and over again' seems amazingly constant. *Briggflatts* starts with an instruction to carve something in stone. This asset is marked as regional because there are no mountains in South-East England; the antithesis of soft and hard, so often applied to oppose South and North, was bound to overflow and occupy clay versus rock.

Ted Hughes has carried these themes of strength and conflict to a higher level, yet it seems that they were already present in the air of the North, that they were recognisable as non-southern, and that this was part of their attraction for him.

Beneath the Surface of a Great Nerve: *Goshawk Lives*, by Colin Simms

This remarkable collection by the Northumbrian naturalist, poet, and sometime Objectivist is the latest in a bibliography of some 40 items. The amiable and far-sighted Mr Gilonis has drawn my attention to the connection of six of these works (*Parflèche, Celebration of the Stones in a Water-Course, No North-Western Passage, Rushmore Inhabitation,* 'The Compression of the Bones of Crazy Horse' in *Poetry Review* 67.1, and 'Carcajou' in *Eyes Own Ideas*) in a large-scale unified work on the Indians of the north-west states of the USA. Some of the earlier poems are in dialect: separately, North Yorkshire, Northumbrian, and Cumbrian. Simms is a northern nationalist (and sometime activist for northern autonomy); the crisis of mediations animates all his work.

Goshawk Lives (verb or noun) is a collection of poems written over about fifteen years, linked by the species of their subject matter. Some of the pieces are rather slight prose moments; possibly a relief, as 31 pages of Simms is rather a lot. But there is a big swatch of the all-sails-spread edgeless onrush, too:

> glacial-melt-water valley little into fieldland so that it was forgotten by the farmer
> a sinuous scar healed over by the machines except its corn grew darker in the shallow
> it brought them up from the south, hirundines black arrows skimming the little clouds of midge
> even if they were going east to west, here they turned north and the birds of prey already knew it
> where it grades to the river there the spread of the bright green was, and the marsh-marigold yellow
> in the willowgarth's annual growth so fresh green it bewildered like its birdsong the willow-warblers
> leading up to something on the water cyclical yeasty bubbles showed the first sulphur-yellow wagtails
> and up to something the draw led, under the skylarks, sparrowhawks had always been, in this

like so many birds of prey in two sizes.

before they had left the land egg-collecting boys knew that, but their
continuity was broken

so that when the sparrowhawks came back after insecticide and persecution
they were in three sizes

or even four if you looked closely enough and they didn't allow you to do that

so it was not so bad nor so impossible

the males of the new hawks were near the females of the old hawks in size and
looks anyway

near enough for the confusion to be allowed in a country that had eight names
for Cow Parsley

they were not long enough about the entry of the warblers and the martins,
the sparrowhawks

the bottom end of the dry hollow a natural funnel for the insects finding shelter

in an unpoisoned place, the top end a shallow space where the wind waited

to take their songs away the new farmers who had taken down hedges, trees,
fences to enlarge

make every inch pay as if space could be stretched the wind behaved again as
in the days of loess

(from 'Spring')

Again:

On the dead air it was effort to rise on slow wings what the herons must feel
fatiguing

longer and longer flights between fewer pools and more regulated waterways
as laid barracks.

Gos had played with one in the air on their way from the railway to the old
grainland at height

the massed starlings of winter further north didn't aspire to mob at, and the
heron had played back.

Pigeons' conspicuous convergence flung together over the grey-plover stand
until they rose and fell

quiet as a shadow across the retina. We are secret people, huddle, come and go
as the place does know.

turning to use the sun to pick out the groundbirds by their shadows the gos
levelled to fly alongside one

back-marker, twisting with it and gaining then slowing to stalling speed with
the plover alone now

and taken with one foot at the edge of reach like off a low ledge, a flurry of
wings to the ground

and one wing shaken out over the corpse like a shield from the carpal joint
fanwise forward.

bringing to mind how the bird had judged to the point in the stroke of the
     wingbeat a calm dense foggy
morning air precisely where the reach of the mailed foot would be at that tree's
     protuberant raised-root knarls
were scored by the squirrel scrabbling its indecision the roughbark tiles so
     often traversed there they
carried hair of squirrel, fox scent, a tarry of dead leaves the brush of the gos'
     wing scraping just once.

(from 'Winter')

And a shorter untitled poem, complete:

ghost moths go feeling-out the outfield holding
both us lost fielders before we go, grey ashflakes in this light
uncertain censering against cicely and hawthorn moulding bright
from nowhere out of the earth the hawk unfolding
furrow from a soft ploughing grassheads spread from his mowing
manœuvring talon to maw, stalling-speed chopped at the blockhole
resuming rowing the heavier for the early vole

Let's pause to notice that this incredibly broad narrative tone, with its
exhaustingly long lines, its relaxation, lack of tropes, capacity to notice
everything in its slow sweep, effortless rising to flash-moments of spurt,
death and transformation, its tranquillity, geniality, alertness, odd didacticism, furious concentration which is never sensory deprivation, unruffled
registration of tiny details in a superordinate frame of extraordinary
complexity, clarity and resistance to upset, is great poetry. I could quibble
with the metrics of these super-long lines, often well over 20 syllables,
clearly derived from field notebook entries, but they fairly do sweep me
away; so let's cite the hexameter of mediaeval didactic poems – hooching
with information, capacious, calm, sweeping – and leave it at that.

The uplands of Britain are full of sheep, and most of the people out on
them are shepherds; Simms isn't interested in sheep, but mainly in raptors.
At this point we can note the transition from cold observation to
identification, and the kind of emotional choice that occupies parts of the
outside world; we cross over from the search for absolute truth to the
world of Nietzsche. Sheep have a biology too. The dialect project, of
course, isn't so far from the pastoral of Theocritus, written in fourth-
century BC Alexandria in a pseudo-rustic Doric dialect. But Simms stands
out among writers on nature for his rejection of moral allegories or
religious instructions to urban Man; among writers on raptors, for his lack
of preoccupation with the kinetic, bloody, stirring, air-ace moment of

snatching the prey; he is unusually interested in many other moments of a goshawk's routine, and is free of cruelty. This chastity is no doubt why he hasn't become a media and TV star, but it also means that his work doesn't lose any of its effectiveness with long familiarity. The hawk's eating for him isn't wildly different from other forms of energy exchange; no projections or hang-ups.

Simms reminds me of Alan Ross, because they have both written effective poems about cricket. Ross's comment about Wally Hammond's batting action being impossible to catch on film even with an exposure time of only 1/500 of a second ('Like some prototype birdman / Straining at silk moorings, he conveys / Ambiguity, both imprisonment and release') strikes me as a good example of someone trying to identify reality – physical behaviour and the operation of the brain and nervous system – at the subliminal level, to slow down time and to focus conscious attention steadily on what is characterised by being *without* conscious control. The batsman isn't consciously controlling his stroke: the time-lapse between the ball giving away where it's going to pitch and the stroke being largely shaped is far too short. So the unconscious is capable of far greater precision than the conscious: it's a battery of control systems which are more reliable the older they are. Breathing is obviously more error-proof than thinking about philosophy. Freud goes right out of the window here; the old systems, the mathematics of hawks stooping, are more complicated than the conscious mind. Simms's cricket poem takes up much of *Eyes Own Ideas*. It's a natural subject for him: the actions of split-seconds – the ball launched from the bowler's hand, the batsman's stroke – exploded and as it were exegesised by the vast white and green space of the pitch, a dozen taut alert brains rather than the two of naturalist and goshawk. The ball is a recording instrument; trajectory slows down the ultra-short interval and delivers it to understanding.

What competition lays bare is subtle differences of action and coordination, as characterisation, a central Simms theme, has to do; a realm of differences between values even smaller than the original values themselves.

Modern poets have sometimes been able to make out the Before as a new site of the sublime, meaning the state of perception before language, of awareness before deceit, of social groups before the arrival of hierarchy, property and social roles, even of poetry before stylistic polarisation. It is traditional for the sublime to be cruel and intractable. The physiologist Libet is cited by *New Scientist* for his experiments proving that behavioural reactions preceded conscious awareness, that conscious reception of events was half a second after perception and unconscious brain functions had already calculated the response long before that.[25] So consciousness appears as something external to the mind, registering results that have already happened; responsible, too, for the verbal record and for deceit. Simms is preoccupied by this first half-second during and after sense perception, he is interested in splitting it and getting back to the first fractions of a second, rather than expanding it to include all the sequela of articulation and rationalisation. (Of course, I simplify the detectible operations of consciousness, which has important roles to play in learning and in ambiguous situations.) The data of the senses – the ports of entry from the outside world to the internal environment – cannot be the same as what surrounds our skins, and the translation is repeated as it enters a verbal, or literary, form. The mediations are socially enhanced or controlled. Perhaps there is a primary flow of awareness, a kind of polymorphous, depolarised flux of moments without proper names. Moments of perplexity reveal the unnaturalness of any linguistic self-description: the real me is represented as if on stubborn stone, missing detail. Disrupting the verbal code reveals a plurality of superstructures, underdetermined by the flow, which is more complex than they are by at least one dimension. Embedded in this network of suspicions and hopes are three intuitions – of alienation in economics, of the prevalence of deceit in public, corporate and official discourse, of the complexity and artificiality or autonomy of the long process between primary experience and verbal consciousness – which I take to be constituent of the modern Left, basic to modern poetry, and the source of our melancholia. The mediating literary codes from the Civil Triangle (London–Oxford–Cambridge) may be irrelevant to poets from Wales or the Borders. Language tries to capture *Geist* and releases phantoms. Somehow, occultly, this is linked to distrust of the city, of the South, of people who derive profit from ownership and secondary business activities, of accumulated culture, of poets who aren't writing about animals, and even of French and Latin words. This distrust conjures up a Nietzschean view of the world as infinite surface, where what appears to be a depth beneath the visible is some teleology of social control and enticement. Simms is operating in this area but avoids overall statements or promised ways out. I would say that he is animated by a constant fear of deceit, and of deceiving.

There are a number of variants on this attempt to get back before verbalisation. The attempt in the sixties to get behind two thousand years of literary habits and attain immediacy is one. W. S. Graham's attempt to

switch off and make conscious the rules of language reveals a belief that
there is something before language. Simple disruption of the linguistic
machine, as in Tom Raworth, has gone *pari passu* with a project of interrogating awareness during its suspension, to find out what its real nature
is, even if this can only emerge as an energy profile cracked out from
hundreds of different *linguistic* emissions. Raworth, by abolishing the
representational function of language, reducing the world-surface to a
stage set, hopes to make visible the manipulations of language, glimpsing
the Pristine Unmanipulated the instant after it has disappeared. David
Chaloner is fascinated by the way perception can be exploited by false
signs. But the work of art perhaps *is* a landscape of false signs, a self-
adornment; acquisition is symmetrical to demolition. Adrian Clarke and
John Wilkinson are, in different ways, stripping out metalanguage from
the verbal flow in the hope that an account without interpretation is more
truthful. Denise Riley's poetry is usually searching the self-account for
truth, on the assumption that the immediate data of consciousness are
often wrong and self-deceiving. The pristine of our spontaneous wishes
and of a released socialist society is the missing which in their poems
corresponds to the flights of birds, verbally detained, in Simms's poems.

> Looking at it, it has to be the individual character
> of a bird that confers nobility; a captive bird, its world released from reason,
>   reflex, and reaction,
> behaves complicatedly towards what it could be, towards one of the changing
>   personalities it could have struck.
> True feeling in a world removed from sentiment.
>
> (from 'Winter')

Simms refers to a hawk reasoning. He isn't a Behaviourist; I suppose the
surviving Behaviourists are protected in some reserve somewhere, safe
except for the odd weekend's recreational shoot by real scientists. The
world seen by a hawk's eye is sufficiently complex and ambiguous for a
reasoning process to be necessary; the senses yield no meaning. The
human world also does not deliver itself to the senses without mediation:
conscious thought uncovers the truth. We are only *assured of certain
certainties* because our cognitive channels don't have the capacity to
handle the full ambiguity, the multiple part-patterns.

Simms's meditation on the jizz (the preconscious impression of a glimpse
that already tells you what species an animal is) is also a meditation on
writing – on the deep underlying rule which tells you what to cut out of a
poem and what to leave in. The word 'essential' or 'necessary' is self-

referential; any pragmatic definition has to grope with characterisation, jizz and differentiae. I can't write down the rule that tells me what has to go in a book review and what doesn't, but I spend my life applying it. Could you recognise Colin Simms's poems from my description alone? This would be a good test. Poems aim to utter what it is about a situation that makes it different from all other situations. Words are distributed at points within the originally unbounded realm of perception where they locate characteristic and behavioural differences. But language is carrying other well-formed patterns of discriminations than only lexical ones. If we, as well as high-performance raptors, can reason, we can recognise situations from many different clues, so the essential could be an overall aggregate, or plural. Editing and selection of detail are completely subjective.

It takes me longer to get a poem's meaning than to recognise the poet's identity, which happens within the half-second, by unconscious but highly reliable scanning. So the poem is reduced to a behavioural surface like walking, a display of the personality, almost bodily adornment. We are good at using physiological differentiae to recognise individual humans, recalling alliances and allegiances like a mouse identifying individual mice by their scents. What do we signify with poems? What is the act of meaning?

Competitive games benefit the spectators more than the players, by making visible tiny differences in performance; the act of playing is, like poetic style, a self-characterisation. This playing with time-values almost too short to perceive must remind us of dialect: the differences between two dialects draw us into a world whose timescales are much finer than discrimination between two phonemes within a single voice's phonology. A world too fine to codify – but saying that humans are good at discriminating between voices is like saying that goshawks are good at flying. So written English, especially Standard English, is simpler than what we perceive, a kind of bureaucratic levelling. The urge to get back to the body-voice agitated the Georgians – the finest hour, it may be, of English dialect poetry. The group, as for example Lawrence, Gibson, Masefield and Hodgson, were also preoccupied with animal poems. Ted Hughes picked up this theme from Lawrence and Edwin Muir. Lawrence, like Simms, is interested in immediate responses, and in the unreasoning but highly tuned actions of animals. Their advance into *vers libre* came from the same interest in the body and in fine time-discriminations – authenticity located in the shortest time interval. Inauthenticity is perhaps a matter of timing – the opposite of coordination. I suppose one of the allures of jazz is that, by confronting rhythms of different periodicity, it conjures up speed differences in a scale of time so small we can't hear it, confronting us with the sublime and the hallucinatory. I suppose the concept of the individual is bound up with this ability to discriminate between voices, which again is bound up with the importance of alliances in anthropoid politics: you form alliances with specific individuals and so have to recognise them; an individual you have known all your life may be either your ally or your enemy.

Note that I am adumbrating a position here without nailing either Simms or myself to it. He says:

> season accessions reason below barrens earth opens hard
> access of gos and secession from reasonableness human hesitation on land
> excess is aggression any essence is all-in-eye yet the bird watches
> not either of us, but movement, as if the rattlesnake's vertical pupil makes no
>   sense of us, and we do not even know what he sees
> or what we see or name as seen. Beneath the surface of a great nerve
> only partially warms, like permafrost, even in sight we don't understand
> manned in each other's space none of us in the gos's course.
>
> (from 'Gos')

This is not an easy passage, but it is about cognition, not about a specific moment. Simms seems to be comparing the incommensurability of the mind and the world that it perceives or otherwise builds a model of with the incommensurability of the snake's world-view and that of the human it observes. I think 'access' refers to a physiological event, like 'an access of rage', seasonally governed and possibly to do with having unfledged young, eyasses, in the nest. Awareness is a physiological state dependent on the physiology it resides in; the realisation that a perception is affected by the species that is experiencing it ('manned in each other's space') leads to the phenomenological investigation of the observer as a factor of the observation, associated especially with J. H. Prynne, Andrew Crozier and Denise Riley. The previous passage ('Fellow, the eyes stream on recognition [...] eyass-excited') possibly describes the hostility of the range-'owning' goshawk to one of its own kind, recognised similarity the trigger to manning the palisade – in contrast and symmetry to the moment of disrecognition and dissimilarity we have just seen. (There is another version of the same passage on about p. 14.)

We can identify two impulses and high achievements of poetry, towards *drunkenness* and *attentiveness*. Alertness is a tuned state of brain and body, almost melodic. Reading is not about information transfer, it is an autotelic vibratory state of the reader's cognitive apparatus. We can look backwards, away from the paths of air where birds may be seen, and towards the human observer. The merit of the poems is, I take it, their depiction of a perfectly calm and alert Watcher (with several notebooks stuffed in easily available pockets), in the likeness of a huge recoilless mirror plane to within a few micrometres, with optically perfect characteristics; and it is this calmness which by mimesis affects our mood – inducing attentiveness directly, unconsciously, by exhibiting it. The alertness does not need the birds.

Let me quote another passage, from an untitled poem:

'Bitter let all sweetness be, let all these apples be crab!'
Rhubarb-and-ginger jam well-left on cold stone slab
straight from the pot to get its smell, whitewashed larder
harder than when it set, wonder the warmth of its ferment
ice under bog, frogs' courting stun-warms some tundra
the goshawk picks them off in amplexus, leaves skins to mildew
skin off the jam, same maimed dark stain of the discarded.

This is a charming domestic sketch, whose first line is an acoustic hallu-cination suggested to Simms by the goshawk's mating-calls. The braided theme of exchanging slight amounts of energy also brings us to compare human softness in wanting the lovely smell of the jam with accipitrine squeamishness in spitting out frogskins (even ones with a residual sexual charge). The tundra was in Alaska, the jam in Washburndale.

Recently, I spent some time with my brother in eastern Scotland travelling around looking at Pictish stones. What had at first appealed to me, their bizarreness, disappeared after I had seen enough of them to have clicked with their visual language: disguised by the primitive technique was a wealth of animal themes, something simple, present in all cultures, appealing to two-year-old children around the world. Simms got as far as the Pentland Hills (originally *Pict*-land, or *Peht*); their sixth-century missionary, Columba, also brought the Animal Style manuscript illumin-ation, which after the conversion of Northumbria (from the North) in the seventh century became possibly the greatest cultural achievement of the region; its pages an example of semiotic surplus. Ian Finlay's book on Columba stresses the zoomorphic ornament, which he relates to cultic practice and to the East: 'borrowed by the Celts from their eastern neighbours', Scythian in fact.[26] Possibly the apparently abstract whorls and swirls that grow out of the animals' bodies are really attempts to reintroduce the fourth dimension into the picture surface, taking the image back to the memory-image of the animal, and to depict movement, by which we *recognise* it. Finlay talks about Columba's cultic relationship with cranes; for Simms, it's hawks. The aesthetics of animal poetry are too primordial to be simple. To get behind Simms's animal poems we would already have to have explained the animals of Dark Age manuscripts (and stones, metalwork, and so on). The animals go right through from La Tène to Romanesque. Perhaps the difference between Pictish and Romanesque is largely one of better-quality metal edges for working the stone. I don't think this is an influence within history, but two examples of a biologically rooted fascination. What, you will rightly ask, *is* our biology? The clever neurological box which converts from observation through the eyes to imitation, the government of coordinated behaviour patterns, is present in many species who imitate their own kind: humans imitate other species as well. This box governs imitation, the realist impulse in art.

If attribution of motive to birds and sheep is a problem, attribution of motive to humans is a greater one, and there is a maze of rationalisation which acts to conceal motives. We don't know why we watch animals. If you say 'children watch rabbits following an instinctive information-gathering programme so that when they are older they can catch and eat them', that's cute, but you're only a split-second away from saying 'verbal behaviour during sexual relations is inauthentic, a lure, a dazzle pattern', because you have said, not only that instincts for pre-human things, such as breeding, are hard-wired teleologies, but also that introspection is inaccurate and even locked out of the engine room. Critique of language is a euphemism for critique of speech. The consequences of this proposition for poetry are possibly fatal. If people told the truth all the time, there would be no philosophy; and no Stock Exchange Rules or auditors, either. There are excessively patterned behaviours in language and other forms of culture; the excess suggests that there is not a one-to-one relationship between utterance and the world to be described; the surplus then carries out functions quite other than description, or indeed introspection.

Perhaps introspection and self-accounts are always right. We never get to see biology; it's a depth, it doesn't come to the surface. Maybe it isn't there. Where's the test? How can we ask introspection whether introspection is right? How could we grade the answer?

Froth and Delphs of the Atlantic Fringe: Michael Haslam

Michael Haslam (1947–), the son of a Protestant solicitor in Bolton, Lancashire, was at Cambridge in the late sixties, at the same time as Denise Riley, Martin Thom, Nick Totton and other poets, when the so-called 'counter-culture' was happening. He acquired from reading David Jones an abiding interest in pre-modern forms of writing and in the Welsh mythology recorded in the *Mabinogion*. In the terms of Cyril Fox, he belongs to the western current of British culture, with a continuity of sensibility with the regional past, and a sheltering scepticism about influences from the metropolis and across the Channel. After Cambridge, Haslam returned to the Pennines (more precisely, to a commune in Hebden Bridge, in Calderdale in Yorkshire), from where he doesn't seem to have stirred much since. Hebden Bridge is, or was, a kind of counter-cultural village; Ulli Freer lived in a nearby clough in the seventies, and Asa Benveniste also lived there. Martin Thom lived nearby. Anecdote shows Haslam and Maggie O'Sullivan passing each other, during the 1990s, in the Job Centre, but not exchanging a word. Haslam has worked as a manual labourer, carrying out various building tasks, as he has described in his poems, using the skills acquired in fixing up the derelict building that the commune adopted. He has also taught poetry to extension classes, been an editor (of the magazine *Folded Sheets*) and a publisher (of Open Township). But mainly, it would appear, he has dedicated himself to perfecting his poetry. It was not until 1986 that a decisive proof of his gifts was published: this was *Continual Song*, the composition of which may have occupied him for many years. Earlier pamphlets, such as *The Fair Set on the Green* (1975), *Various Ragged Fringes* (1975) and the Arthurian poem *Son Son of Mother* (1978), identify his themes without bringing them to a head. A note at the back of *Continual Song* states that it has its origin in 'my actual practice of rewriting and by some instinctive principles transforming everything I've written, with some sacred exceptions, over twenty years'. This, a masterpiece, was followed by another pause, broken by *Aleethia* (1990, billed as 'a kind of epitaph to *Continual Song*'), and *Four Poems* (1994), which, along with Haslam's poems published in periodicals, makes it clear that a new phase of creativity is now under way. *A Whole Bauble*, which came out in 1995, collected a great deal of his earlier work along with large amounts of new poetry from 1994–95.

The English poet Haslam reminds me of most is Traherne: they share the same mystic bliss induced by everyday phenomena of birds, rain, clouds, plants. But he is also portraying himself: working, in moments of idleness or clumsiness, in love, in distress. He is driven to write by moments of beauty, but he is also blunt and down to earth. He belongs to a generation for whom pop music was one of the most important parts of culture; it would be naive to look for points of direct contact, but those who remember 1967 may recognise something of the feel of 'Strawberry Fields Forever' and 'Itchycoo Park' and 'Dear Mr Fantasy' in Haslam's idea of what constitutes magic and spontaneity. His belief in the trans-formation of the everyday supplies him with some very ordinary props – an ordinariness that pop music never got away from.

One of Haslam's virtues is his sweet nature. I don't mean that he eliminates struggle and damage from his world-view; rather that many of the urban poets are locked in a struggle for strips of territory which makes them obsessed by perceived rivals and authority figures, and also by the vision of being excluded by these rivals. In the upshot, they are unable to write about their own everyday, because they are too preoccupied with status; and too busy scoring points to make beautiful things. Is there any point winning a fight to compose a chosen kind of poetry if it is not beautiful? A too strong sense of party makes it hard to describe any social intercourse, or in fact any passage of life. This contentiousness, formerly part of theological quarrels, today attaches as much to academic life as to politics. Haslam, leading an unconventional and unprosperous life in a remote hill region, following an unfashionable philosophy, is certainly justifying his life by his work: it is at stake in every poem he writes. But he does this justifying simply by describing it, not by introducing his enemies, those who would deride him, into his poem, or by contracting it to a ritual of satire in which their speech is altered to disprove itself, and he vanishes behind the camera, invisible and in control. The period is one in which British society has been rent by powerful conflicts of opinion: few books of poetry give a portrait of the social ideals dividing people as impressively as *Continual Song*.

I suppose I have to use the word 'hippy' at some point. I think Haslam was one, but only for the brief period – of late adolescence, of collective enthusiasm – when that was possible:

I met the emanation of a school of thought myself
one time, when I was clothed in purple and scarlet and
gold, with all my edges frayed or flared and flapping,
hitch-hiking one April way back on the old Colchester
Road, in 1969, when I was burning in the sense of being

on my own. I took myself to be a devotee of light,
attempting to escape the Empire, when I came before
The Living Phoenix, face to being in the world itself
A mirror, stepped out of my crystal stupor, and I swear
I sang out what had all the makings of just one pure
tone. And soon I'm shaking in the afterdazes of the star
of Venus, rare green light in rare green weather, fits
of rainbows, colour, cloud and hailstones.

(Continual Song, 77/08[27])

The lineation of this poem is totally different in the book from the version published in *Grosseteste Review*; guessing it was prose, I wrote to the poet inquiring, only to learn that he completely rewrote the poem to match the width of the page format of each printed version. This sheds light back on his broad narrative style, with its striding long lines and multiple enjambements. The only real controversy about Haslam is whether his work is too compromised by crank cosmologies to be convincing; as he has remarked,

> Archaic images attract because of a felt lack of stick, of presence, in the grounds and premises of modern academic discourse. The archaic package comes complete with its own solid-seeming spiritual vocabulary. In recent years it has been sold as the 'alternative': whole sets of crankish and incredible beliefs. And yet, I'm attracted, in poetic practice. The terms seem to fit, together, and to accurately match experience.[28]

This question will be addressed at length. Anyone who describes in poetry their ideals in life will be furiously attacked by those who own other ideals; the subject is quite rare in poetry, perhaps for this reason, and beliefs slip out as telltale symptoms.

The failings of Haslam's early works give us some hints about his poetic success in maturity. We find that they lack the articulation of verse into lines and sentences, which enables a poem to move from one end of the page to the other, the relation of the parts to each other being expressed by syntactic structure. Awkwardly placed single lines are unable to establish contact with each other:

THE WHISKY
is aqua vitae
an elixir aphrodisiac
a music
raising sight beyond crest

of wave blown back to spray
streaks in spindrift
   (from *Various Ragged Fringes*)

Without a more continuous compositional line, the acoustic effects which
are the special excellence of Haslam's mature work could not have come
about. Adapting to forms of past poetry, and of discourse outside poetry,
was therefore the step towards his most daring and original moves. But
already in the early work, he was using run-on far more than other poets
of the underground, where it was common, in Raworth or MacSweeney
for example, for every line-break to end the current syntactic unit, so that
the reader had to carry out the composition. Discontinuity was being seen
as virtue, meaning the liberation of the poet from the social system, or the
past, or something.

The prominence of metrical and syntactic run-on, the composition in
verse paragraphs, the stress on the immediate moment, the stress on
personal experience, the building up of different sorts of information to
make the immediate moment vivid and complex – these elements link
Haslam to Denise Riley, however different they are in their ideas. *Various
Ragged Fringes* includes odd snatches of Prynne: 'Phoenicians were the
most promontory of semicolonists [...] The archaeology of trade is dis-
count, bound in books & sheafed'; 'The goods go out to remote fringes,
from / centres, changing hands are charges for / higher prices yet; the
mark-up is a function / of an endless set of lochs'. The structure of this
poem on the fringes of the Atlantic littoral, with its visits to Cornwall,
Wales, Ireland and the West of Scotland, implies a kind of comparative
geography, as well as an account of Celticity – didactic aims that point
away from the poet himself. The answers to these questions do not tell us
how to lead our lives; whereas tracing the poet's own course between
happiness and sadness is close to the core of our own existence.

Continual Song starts with three quotations, one of which is in Welsh; it
comes from the Triads, and runs: 'Three unceasing songs were of the
British in former times; Bangor, and Caer Gariadawg, and Ynys Widrin,
in English Continuale Songe'. One thinks of various Celtic legends of an
island where singing never ceases; a reflection of the aim of monasteries to
sing God's praise in perpetuity? Bangor was a monastery. The English
equivalent of the last name is Glastonbury: Widrin comes from Latin
vitrina, and means glass. A glass object of sub-Roman times will have been
a goblet; and we can equate this with the Grail, kept at Glastonbury, at
least in mythic terms. In Poem 25/60, we read:

I broke my breath on baffled vast
expanses of Atlantic Vitrine
Aquamarine Serpentine
Sea-green and azure silver

Vitrine is the same as Widrin. It means a glass-like rock. Later in the same
poem we find:

The brittle rash of arms
The laughter of the earth
I broke my breath
it smashed to bits
a globe of glass on granite

The globe of glass could refer to the goblet. The poem refers also to the
Romans ('Purple Imperial the past') and to Christian myth ('A Christian
his last / coastal romance death and rebirth'). It refers too to the idyll of
Bran and his companions on Gwales, recounted in *Branwen Daughter of
Llyr* ('The sound of people singing on promontories / the birds').
    Another passage might refer to a Grail:

ecstasy
of No Extinction, beckoning or beaconing
on deep green glass
close to the source.
Just one Green Spring is all it takes
to fill the bowl
of a becoming whole.
                        (*Continual Song* 32/53)

Haslam is obviously familiar with what we call New Age beliefs. His
writing would be greatly weakened if it were underpinned by some occult
system. There is certain evidence against him:

1. the presence of apparent tutelary spirits, Aquila and Alaunna;
2. a reference to a book, *The Hidden Church of the Holy Grail*, in
   passing; clearly the poet was reading this highly suspect publication;
3. a reference to transmigration:

the brief life which the Druid thought just flitted
through the hall, fleshed out with feathers. She is
emblematic mistress of the lucid transmigrations,
dumb speech to the wise, Hello! to my
life's brief bedfellow. She's

the blindfold soul pursued by dogs
of the inhuman world –
an object of remote control, who touches home
The Sanctuary Rock, with fingers crossed
Over the water,
as the options close.

(*Continual Song* 18/67)

4. various other fragments of occult systems.

However, these do not deaden the poetry and subdue it to the arid proof
of some demented dogma: they are always motivated by the poet's
immediate life experiences. Haslam's elevation of daily circumstance to
the centre of poetry follows the Protestant shifting of the focus of spiritual
attention away from popes, saints and monks to secular daily life, the
turning of the nobility during the sixteenth century away from great state
and towards domesticity and private pleasure, and the revolution of everyday life as preached by Lefebvre and the Situationists and mediated to
Haslam by J. H. Prynne. The poet aims for complete simultaneity and
whole transience, in a realm surpassing, sometimes, Hebden Bridge for a
walk on the moors or an excursion to Southport. Tracing a few repeating
themes persuades me (to my relief) that there is no overall symbolic structure, occult or otherwise, to *Continual Song*. The book is not withholding
itself from the reader: everything is plain as daylight, and everything is
transient: if you don't glimpse the bird flying by, it is gone, but it had no
lesson to teach. Glass is a metaphor for this vanishing quality: immersed
in the immediate situation, we are neither anxiously foreseeing the future
nor chewing over the past. The technical difficulty was no doubt to
generate situations which are sufficiently complex to absorb our attention
and make us forget the outside world, but simple enough to disentangle
and resolve themselves and make way for the next. I have mentioned
'mystic' writers who exclude the everyday in order to write about the
eternal, with themselves either monumentalised as fragments of these set-
in-stone Eternal Dramas, or excluded, rolled back and drowned out by
the majesty of utterance of whatever Invisible Monsters they are the
secretaries of. The test to apply is that of coherence: if we find Haslam's
poems clinging simply to an idea that they illustrate, he is being run by the
idea. We can consider Poem 30/55, for example. Stanza one concerns the
poet cutting himself when his hammer misses the chisel, and six doves fly
off to 'seal the suffering'. In stanza two, a series of statements: the voices of
the dead are distorted; the sun is turning blue; the message was a dreamer

going into code; the shape of things is a set of echoes. In stanza three, we come back to the pain, and to the emotional pain of a separation, leaving the poet dressed in tatters; he takes a break and looks for a protective glove.

I can see no coherence for this poem as an illustration of an idea. It contains ideas, but the poem does not stop for them. I am left with the possibility that the coherence is the poet as actor; this is aesthetically credible, and confirmed by looking at pop songs, which are held together by the singer as actor; or by poems (which I posit as stylistically related) by John James and Denise Riley, which rush from one topic to another but suggest that life is like that, and that our living experience is happening on disturbingly many layers at once. This could be antinomian if it implies that government and church are imagining people in crudely simplified terms. Some of the poems are more unified, but they are never lessons. Haslam's technique is overwhelmingly empirical, in the sense that it is both concrete at every step, as if it were a series of photographs, and inconsistent, composed of different streams of information or awareness, which are themselves in motion, so that many geometrical relationships are possible, and no pattern can become fixed and dominant. No doubt it follows from this multiplicity that each pattern is trivial: this is the humility of the poet. He is not wise enough to present a truth which is constant from minute to minute. He is not a sage, an instructor. He lives in the world of phenomena; thus he has avoided the depressing deadness of an Edwin Muir or a Kathleen Raine. Nonetheless it is with this strain of English poetry that he belongs; he is not a wholly new thing, nor one that offers the reader perplexities and obscurities.

His use of phonetic echoes is striking:

a ragged carreg
skerry sticking out
a cragged blackness
points from blue to blue
(from *Various Ragged Fringes*)

Kiddies playing in the classic sandpit
of a seaport city park kick sand
up in the air –
it swirls and anticlimacteric falls
in crystal trails.
(from *Continual Song*, 76/09)

I caught her eye once when the lid was closing
and it sounded like a doom.
I blanch and flinch
and earth and all her train whirr through
to drink at the flash brink
                    (from *Continual Song*, 72/13)

Hello, you failure
falling hollow
lapwing squealing squeaking whatsoever
You who sever
on the gale
You waste your breath
on sins and springs and windows
wishing, willing, a Remission from the moor.
                    (from *Continual Song*, 53/32)

This is ornament, even though ornament may be the most important part of the poem. Resemblances to the verbal ornament used by the Russian (Cubo-)Futurists don't have any metaphysical implications; the most positive results of the method were achieved by Boris Pasternak in poems that were otherwise rather traditional. The feel bears other strong resemblances to *cynghanedd*, the Welsh system of obligatory harmonies of sounds, which Haslam, who cites phrases in Welsh, must have come across. The relation between wISHing and remISSion is an ambiguity, because the phonetic link is not also a semantic one. This relation competes with the explicit and rational sense of the line; there are apparently multiple patterns competing for the same site. They shimmer. Phonetic relations are important to the memory process: superfluous relations, such as RAGged–carREG–cRAG, conjure up memories that aren't there, and make different words bear illusory resemblances to each other. 'Crag' resembles itself, but also other words, which we easily remember, but cannot piece together into a statement. This phonetic linking is like rhyme, so it is not bizarre or wild; like rhyme, it emphasises links between the words so related, and so gives them an ominous or resonant quality. The play of anticipations and repetitions teases our sense of temporal location and yet deceives it; time seems to stand still. On a record, the use of echo or reverberation literally alters the timing of the music, creating secondary acoustic images which confuse the primary sound, yet make it more suggestive. Stylistically, the poem's impact is psychedelic: the phrases shimmer and resonate in a way that dislocates our sense of time, and this shifting effect makes us hypersuggestible; images refuse to depart because they cannot be rationally assimilated.

Making a dull poem suggestive has no effect. Using these secondary patterns of phonetic association multiplies the effects of synaesthesia, dazzle, wonder and rapture, where these are already going on. These means make us dream, but I would argue that they are not irrational in nature, any more than vibrato is an irrational musical ornament. The irrational would be the assertion of the false and the denial of the true; which is not happening in Haslam's poetry.

Distortions or ornaments only work within a pattern that is already definite and ordered. I feel that Haslam's precision in placing words derives partly from working as a builder:

> labouring with scutch and wire-brush, at Little Manor, Heptonstall. A
> crash of plaster-dust reveals a date over the door: 1681 –
> that rings a bell with a Miscellany of marvellous *things* – all London
> bells ring in the delph, the den, the concave quarry of the ear, and in
> it echoing I heard:
> *The Lord, the Lord is my – Waterfall*
>
> Re-hammering time after time along a line, I reckoned with the issuing of
> Reason from the Nation, taking care not to and yet, damn it, my hand slipped
> and I chipped a little sliver off the date. The thing's defaced.
>   (from *Continual Song*, 41/44. Lineation varies as described above)

'Delph' is a local word, more expectable as 'delf', from 'delve'; it means a quarry. Such hollows or pits usually appear for their resonance in Haslam, as here, as dips that hold and delay sound, like globes that hold water. Froth is another favourite thing of the poet, and both resemble the principle of echoing in phonetics. There is also a possible subliminal resemblance to Delphi, the site of an oracle, another special kind of sound. He says:

> I need my small recuperations filled
> with providential chances brought to hand
> by drift as secret news of one
> subjective rosicrucian sort of
> world of truth. The living forms
> I live my life in rainbow light
> and dwell in illustration.
>   (*Continual Song* 12/73)

The Rosicrucians were an initiatory occult society, but Haslam is simply looking for a life that has patterns he can intuitively believe in; and we can connect to this, because life is not dominated by reason. He knows that each poem is a gamble, guided by the certainties of intuition: the alternative is poetry written to a predictable pattern. The course, frequently miraculous, of each poem justifies his belief in destiny – which goes no further than that. The patterns of phonetic echoes set up anticipation, of which the recurrences are of course fulfilments: through anticipation and fulfilment a rhythm unfolds which is completely within the grasp of our senses. Haslam's notion of destiny is fulfilled by the richness of the linguistic web he involves us in. The sense of assurance, of a higher order of events, is strictly evidenced by the metrical and syntactic run-ons. He seizes symbols because they are needed as straws to make the swirling of his poetic winds visible. I daresay his beliefs about cosmology are very different from mine, but his artistic cogency is indifferent to religious divergences. The passage about the bird flying into the room is beautiful, and it makes the idea of transmigration beautiful, whatever we may think of its credibility.

> Wind encompasses its self-consumption
> in vacuity and leaves all else
> in sway rotating.
> Water on the wind. All Else
> is Ellen. As Continual
> as Weather Wind and Wells.
> (Call it 'Brigantia' or else 'Tall Tales'.)
>   (from *Continual Song*, 27/58)

I presume that this is an image of the poet, because the passage uses the key phrase which is the title of the book. Rather than achieving some power over and outside Nature, he sees himself as a natural energy, which simply uses itself up and disappears. Haslam seems singularly free of illusions, except for the temporary ones arising from excitement, paradoxes such as the wind seeming to produce a voice. I believe Ellen May is a folklore figure involved in well-worship, rightly or wrongly associated with Helena, mother of Constantine, who lived in the Roman province of Britain; Brigantia was the very large tribal territory which covered most of the North, presumably including Hebden Bridge.

The traditional opposition was between the multiform and ever-shifting world of the senses, and the stable world of eternal verities vouchsafed by ideas, or the world of the spirit. Haslam's world belongs to the former domain, because it is ever-shifting. If a poet subscribes to some belief system, that must make the course of the poem predictable, since it exemplifies the knowledge already existing. Moreover, if the system gives its servant power and control, that power must act to restrict the number of possible outcomes still more. The movement of Haslam's verse, carefully based on *The White Stones*, makes each moment unique, and so perilous, giving way and never relapsing into control. Someone who writes in this way cannot also have a spiritual system which fore-ordains things.

Notes

1   Frank Musgrove, *The North of England* (Oxford: Basil Blackwell, 1990).
2   Anthony Harvey, 'Some Significant Points of Early Insular Celtic Orthography', in Donnchadh O Croinin (ed.), *Sages, Saints, and Scholars* (Maynooth: An Sagart/St Patrick's College, 1989).
3   Dick Leith, *A Social History of English* (London: Routledge, 1997).
4   H. M. Jewell, 'North and South: The Antiquity of the Great Divide', *Northern History* (Leeds), 27 (1991).
5   Quoted in Jewell, 'North and South', pp. 19 and 20.
6   Maurice Keen, *English Society in the Later Middle Ages* (London: Penguin, 1990), p. 133.
7   Gregory Bateson, *The Naven* (Cambridge: Cambridge University Press, 1936), p. 176.
8   Sir John Forster, in D. L. W. Tough, *The Last Years of a Frontier: A History of the Borders during the Reign of Elizabeth I* (Alnwick: Sandhill, 1987), p. 31.
9   Gordon Bottomley, *Gruach and Britain's Daughter* (London: Constable & Co., 1921).
10 See W. J. Halliday and A. S. Umpleby (eds), *A White Rose Garland* (London: J. M. Dent and Sons, 1949), p. x.
11 A. L. Lloyd, *Folk-Song in England* (St Albans: Paladin, 1975).
12 Fred Brown, *The Muse Went Weaving* (Youlgreave, Derbyshire: Hub Publications, 1972).
13 Brian Maidment, 'Class and Cultural Production in the Industrial City', in Alan J. Kidd and K. W. Roberts (eds), *City, Class, and Culture* (Manchester: Manchester University Press, 1985); *The Poorhouse Fugitives* (Manchester: Carcanet, 1992).
14 He is referring to the task of recording the details of working lives.
15 Musgrove, *The North of England*, p. 271.
16 In Mary Ashraf (ed.), *Political Verse and Song from Great Britain and Ireland* (London: Lawrence and Wishart, 1975), pp. 197–98
17 Martin Booth, *Driving through the Barricades: British Poetry 1964–84* (London: Routledge and Kegan Paul, 1985).
18 Walter J. Ong, *Orality and Literacy* (London: Methuen, 1982).
19 See Ong, *Orality and Literacy*.
20 R. L. Storey, in S. B. Chrimes, C. D. Ross and R. A. Griffiths (eds), *England in the Fifteenth Century, 1399–1509* (Manchester: Manchester University Press, 1972), p. 130.
21 Nicholas Udall, in Tough, *Last Years of a Frontier*, p. 32.
22 Lynn White, *Mediaeval Technology and Social Change* (Oxford: Clarendon Press, 1962).

23 Leon Stover and B. Kraig, *Stonehenge: The Indo-European Heritage* (Chicago: Nelson-Hall, 1978).
24 Storey, in Chrimes et al. (eds), *England in the Fifteenth Century*.
25 John McCrone, *Going Inside* (London: Faber & Faber, 1999), pp. 120–39.
26 Ian Finlay, *Columba* (London: Victor Gollancz, 1979), p. 18.
27 The 84 poems of *Continual Song* are numbered both from the front and from the back.
28 Michael Haslam in Denise Riley (ed.), *Poets on Writing: Britain 1970–1991* (Basingstoke: Macmillan, 1992), p. 27.

6

Celticity Cumulative and in Decline:
Poetry in the West of Scotland

The main feature of the modern history of Celtic languages has been their shrinking geographical and cultural hold: 'declining Celticity'. The successor, in every case, has been English or a related dialect, identifying the Celtic cultures with the past in a double sense. There is as I write no possibility of any author making a living by writing in Welsh or Gaelic. Gaelic is at the present time spoken by about 2 per cent of the population of Scotland, Welsh by about 25 per cent of the population of Wales, Cornish by no-one except in evening classes, Cumbric and Manx by no-one, Irish as an everyday language by about 1 per cent of the population of Ireland.

The psychological trauma of the Gaels is partly a regret that modernisation was not more effective and partly a lament for lost autarky.

> The life of the glen people was a living whole, for it revolved about its own axis and its centre was within itself; the mind could consider it in isolation from adjacent regions and see it satisfyingly, as unity. But given over to sheep and shepherding the district would be meaningless by itself, its centre would lie outside it far away in the woolmarkets and factories of the south; it would decline at once from an intelligible whole and become no more than an insignificant and not even necessary point on the circumference of a life centred elsewhere. (Fionn Mac Colla, *And the Cock Crew*) [1]

This passage from the Highland novelist Fionn Mac Colla, overblown and nationalistic though it is, reveals the sense of loss of the modern Celt, and also the state of autarky which obtained, in pre-modern times, in the remote mountain areas where Welsh and Scottish Gaelic survived. This autarky also, paradoxically, puts an author in a commanding position: society is visible, comprehensible, and all its members are intensely conscious of a belonging together which a skilled author, by mastery of language and shared memory, can exploit. The individual is explicable because you can *see* what he is thinking about and encompassing. None of this applies to a society where trade, increased population and the division of labour make work and exchange more opaque. The besetting temptation of writers from the mountain areas is to write about this solidarity – in which objects speak for themselves because everyone who sees them shares the same classifications and symbolic structures – where it no longer exists.

These close communities, confined by mountains, were much smaller than the borders of the language; unity at that level has been conjured up by external pressure. However, regional unity was promised, as it were, by the residues of past cultural systems. When scholars speak of Highland society in the eighteenth century and Gaulish society of the third century AD as if they shared the same cultural horizon, we should not dismiss this but should look, for example, at continuity of agricultural techniques, and at how far European society reached a technical peak in the Bronze Age which it hardly excelled until the end of the Middle Ages and the advent of new material equipment. The Christian world of forms was, so far as we can see, younger than the classical Celtic one; both have exerted a powerful influence on twentieth-century artists struck by the fact of being outside them. The most sensitive question that can be asked of a modern Welshman or Highlander is 'How Celtic are you?' Part of this is bad faith in failing to assimilate, psychologically and artistically, the real Celtic (or north-west European) society of the twentieth century. But part of it is a legitimate greed in wishing to appropriate the past, even when this can only occur through fantasy and antiquarian curiosity. Because our life is a long run, it is reasonable to listen to the old, and to retrieve the long runs of the past.

Poetry does not need to be read by foreigners; but my account of these matters is not written in Gaelic or Welsh. The commodification of poets and thinkers as goods laid out for English visitors to pick over, disparage and graciously purchase may be shocking for Celts. Faced with the long-term decline of the languages of the North-West, the poverty which has marked Scottish and Welsh societies so deeply, and the long-term material problems of poets writing in minority languages, or away from the cities, I would be unable to bear the knowledge that I had criticised this poetry unfairly. What is sold to tourists must tend to become kitsch. It is the depth of my incomprehension that makes it kitsch; the intelligentsia of nationalities in long-term decline and subject to domination become angry and sensitive to slights.

Classical Celtic poetry was brought to an abrupt end by the Anglicisation of the local noble families who provided its financial support. (In

Ireland, the families had their lands confiscated or simply perished.) The local classical forms of culture were ended in Wales and Ireland in the seventeenth century, and in Gaelic Scotland in the later eighteenth century. Which elements passed, through an adaptation, into folk culture, and passed on some of their cultural genes into twentieth-century poetry, is a hotly disputed question. The 'remote and rich antients' to which modern Scottish and Welsh poets have looked, through the written tradition or the spoken, may be Duncan Ban or Dafydd ap Gwilym. The relation to this classicity of anyone in Wales or Northern Scotland who writes poetry is a good way of approaching their political biography. There are difficulties in sketching in prose a set of elements that would represent the overall feel of these ornate and highly integrated aristocratic styles of verse (how would you describe a sonnet of Shakespeare to someone who had never read a sonnet?), but the following description will suggest what to look for when we are wondering about 'survivals'.

J. F. Campbell attests the structural principle of traditional Scottish Gaelic poetry: 'It will be seen that each of these lines is complete in sense. The passage might be finished at the end of each line, without making the rest nonsense, which is a peculiarity of Gaelic poetry.'[2] Eoin MacNeill remarks that '[the] Irish metres required each line to give nearly complete sense. In the couplet, the approach to completion of self had to be nearer still. In the quatrain it had to be perfect.'[3] The rule is related to oral delivery, where there is a need to be continuously interesting, and to minimise carry-over of sense; print's sense of time and short-term memory is different.

Here are some passages from the earliest manuscript of Scottish Gaelic poetry, *The Book of the Dean of Lismore*, written down AD 1512–26. I have lineated the English (which was printed as prose) to emphasise the structural divisions.

It is no joy without Clan Donald;
it is no strength to be without them;
the best race[4] in the round world;
to them belongs every goodly man.

The noblest race of all created,
in whom dwelt prowess and terribleness;
a race to whom tyrants bowed,
in whom dwelt wisdom and piety.

A race kindly, mighty, valorous;
a race the hottest in time of battle;

a race the gentlest among ladies,
and mightiest in warfare.

[...]

A race whose assembly was most numerous,
the best in honour and esteem;
a race that made no war on church,
a race whose fear it was to be dispraised.

Brilliant pillars of green Alba,
a race the hardiest that received baptism;
a race who won fight in every land,
hawks of Islay for valour.

A race the greatest and most active;
a race the comeliest and calmest of temper;
a race the widest of heart,
the best in patience and in liberality.

Sons of kings, who deserved not satire,
in whom were manliness and dignity;
men untamed, noble, hearty,
who were open-handed and generous.

A race the best for service and for shelter;
a race the best for valour of hand;
ill I deem the shortness of her skein,
by whom their thread was spun.[5]

And so on. This eulogy of static ornamental repetition, with the quatrains internally balanced but so free of run-on that it doesn't matter which order they are recited in, was written by Gille Coluim and mourns the train of events which led to the abolition of the independent MacDonald Lordship of the Isles in 1493. Another poem, written in the early sixteenth century in praise of James Campbell by Giolla Padraig, and translated by Watson, runs as follows:

A hand whereby a slender blue blade is reddened,
(but) without violence to the schools;
cattle-flocks they carry home with them as a golden reward;
it serves his praise well.
[...]
heavy is his pursuit at the coming of each time of straits;
his foray is not like to be turned back;

above his warriors is a satin banner red like brown gore;
wrath and rage are around the fierce warrior.

[...]
James, who is the protection of men,
has won wealth of love from every train of poets;
for dispensing fortune and jewels and wealth,
he is a prince upon the path of generosity.
[...]
John's son, vigorous, white-palmed, of numerous hosts,
the flower of valour of every company;
a red tower of gold, of mindful heart,
the mighty generous flower of joyousness.

The surety of the lands that he has harassed,
manly, fierce, of numerous troops;
a white-skinned weaponed moon of prowess,
mighty is the wont of his household companies.

A man of cold blades, without mercy to his enemy,
an omen of plenty in bestowal of gold;
foreigners are short-lived from his slaughter
and from the overthrowing.
                    (In Watson, *Scottish Verse*, pp. 113–19)

Conventional features of this kind of poem are the comparison, setting the human subject beside a figure from heroic antiquity; his genealogy; and the *caithréim* (battle-roll), describing his victories (sometimes proceeding from east to south in the account) over other nobles; accounts of conspicuous gifts he has made, or of his splendid possessions. Because the accounts of feats and gifts also indicate the limits of the hero's achievements, they are sensitive points; their recitation is a reversal of power, because the poet is judging these limits. The language is a feat in conforming to difficult metrical rules; it involves a wealth of archaic words, which link the hero to the world of myth; it is rich in allusions to other stories, and in fixed periphrases; it is ornate in the same way that a ceremonial gift is; it ignores the rules of coherence and word order in speech. This is startlingly similar to Welsh praise-poems of about the same time, which we know to go back in an unbroken line to the sixth century and sub-Roman times. So I think these features do define a common, and 'Celtic', culture of the 'Irish Sea province' in early modern times. We would be surprised, if we visited the courts of La Tène and Hallstatt chiefs, not to hear similar poems being recited by their *bardoi*. The preoccupation with praise, fame, generosity, personal adornment, prowess in war, prestige objects, genealogy and lavish consumption presumably reflects what the nobles admired, and also the traits which led the people to support them as rulers. As we know, the arrival of a literate plebeian mass audience provided a new source of income; but there was a significant pause while waiting for this to arrive. When it did arrive, it was an audience speaking and reading English; and the old genres of praise-poems and raid-poems were obsolete. Only in Wales was a broad reading audience found.

Let's just ask if it matters what order the epithets come in. I don't think it does: the poem is static; every line repeats the same situation like spokes coming out of a stopped hub.

There is a Celtic trait of using a noun qualified by a noun in the genitive where other European languages like to use a clause or a noun plus adjective; in older Irish *fer legind*, lit. 'man of reading', translated 'scholar'; in modern Scottish Gaelic, *luchd-turais*, 'company of travelling' for 'tourists', *fear togail fhuinn*, lit. 'man of raising of tune' for 'precentor'.[6] In fact clauses without a finite verb seem to be quite common in Irish (and in Welsh poetry, I think). 'Three signs of ill-breeding: a long visit, staring, constant questioning.' A feature of Celtic syntax is the ejection of the subject from the main clause, so that 'It is a fine farmer that Michael was' is the typical construction. I would suggest that the non-subordinating, cataloguing, construction ('Three signs of ill-breeding: 1, 2, 3') is an expansion of this. Imitators in English can easily forget that the weight of ornament in this poetry goes along with its shortness of breath. Such constructions are, because verbless, without tense. This is useful in panegyric, where objects and events are reduced to possessions, trophies, ornaments, of the chief being praised. (The mode of panegyric can also be applied to the praise of God.) The validity of proverbial truths is also not confined in time, and they consequently exist in a special gnomic present; this style is common in folk poetry, supplying portable and reusable lines of the 'It's a long, long road that has no turning' type. These are certainly a threat to modern poetry. The inflexibility of proverbs goes along with static conventional contrasts and comparisons, a lexicon of frozen values. Thinking in stanzas and sentences, as we shall see, goes along with using vocabulary in an original, colourful, and eventually personal way.

A feature of Celtic speech (i.e. Irish and Welsh) is verbless noun clauses, which combine with the rule, discussed above, that every line of verse has to be closed and self-contained, to give a characteristic movement of language. This is a link, not just between Welsh and Gaelic (Scottish and Irish), but also between classical poetry and the language of today. It makes hypotaxis difficult, while simple sentences are broken up into separate clauses ('It was a young man who reaped the field', rather than 'A young man...'), and complements precede the headword ('Young was the man...'). 'Men came to Catterick, bright was their host', not 'whose host...'; the Welsh text has a relative particle before 'was', *a oedd fraeth eu lu*. These patterns can get pretty irritating when retained as picturesque touches in bad translations into English.

This panegyric poetry was doomed when the local landowners faded away as the economic sustenance of poetry and began to exercise political power through papers and attorneys rather than face to face. Hyperbolic and hierarchical, valuing eloquence more than truth, it is ill-suited to modern and empirical people. It was sustained by a whole way of thinking about politics and authority:

> Manifest was the displeasure of God, and misfortune to the Irish of fine Fodhla [...] Immense and countless was the loss in that place; for the prowess and valour, prosperity and affluence, nobleness and chivalry, dignity and renown, bravery and protection, devotion and pure religion, of the Island, were lost in this engagement.[7]

This is how the Irish Annals describe the Battle of Kinsale of 1601, where Mountjoy defeated O'Neill and sealed the fate of Gaelic Ulster. (Fodhla is Ireland.) The contrast between this vague and vatic diction and the businesslike discourse of the colonising London Companies seems to straddle a couple of millennia. A fine string of nouns, again.

A minor theme of this work will be the contrast or succession between the wasteful, flamboyant, competitive, showy pride of Celtic tradition, and the sombre-suited, sober, egalitarian prose restraint of the Nonconformist Protestant preacher, the 'organic intellectual' of Celtic society as it presented itself at the dawn of the twentieth century. The one was expressed by eulogy, war poetry, catalogues of possessions; the other by sermons, reverent biographies of holy men, and hymns, but also by journalism about the affairs of the day and even by radical politics. The birth of peripheral nationalism is tangled up with Dissent. Both could command soaring eloquence.

Peripheral Modernism: Joseph G. Macleod (1903–84)

on things that move where they stop,
on oscillations that are echoes before they are sounds,
reminders to those gone deaf,
to eyes born weak
revelations.

Joseph Macleod also published as Adam Drinan. His published books of poetry are *The Ecliptic* (1930), *The Cove* (1940), *The Men of the Rocks* (1942), *Women of the Happy Island* (1944), *The Passage of the Torch* (1951), *Script from Norway* (1953), and *An Old Olive Tree* (1971). The first of these is a book in the High Modernist style of the 1920s, emphatically London in setting, zodiacal in structure, related to such writers as Edith Sitwell and Wyndham Lewis, and to the dialogue in Aldous Huxley's novels. It is an extraordinary book. Macleod was an actor, and ran the Festival Theatre in Cambridge (Barnwell) from 1933 to 1936, with an experimental and left-wing bias; later, he was a BBC newsreader and is mentioned as such in Graham Greene's novel *The Ministry of Fear*. He interests us here because of his later work, written when he was living in the Hebrides in the 1940s. It makes a decisive transition from esoteric modernism to realism, mixed with Gaelic myth; no discussion of poetry about the Clearances would be complete without reference to his *Men of the Rocks*. This phantasmagoric narrative describes a Western Scotland. It opens with a description of a glass boat, containing the souls of dead men; the boat dissolves and they turn into seals. A series of poems then evokes the past of the region. Most of the usual themes of the Clearances appear: dying in a ditch after being evicted, having the house burnt over you, the treachery of the lairds, anti-clericalism, exile, starvation and so on:

Night of the next moon. Beached and landed.
Oats, and cattle, and a strath once shaggy;
tales ran warm here; women sang
when the furrowed world was young.

What will we gather in the time of hairst
if it will not be bracken and heather?
Who from the hill will answer, other,
lonelier, than the pipe of plover?
What has he got that seized and feued it?
Dead birds and solitudes!

(from Poem I)

More recent problems are treated, too, such as steam trawlers catching all the herring, shortage of land, soil depletion. Poem IX describes a rebellious Highland intellectual, probably Donald MacLeod: 'They kept me poor and cast me out // I felt the power of laird and Lord / and feared the very lies I scorned / but held my study like a fort.' This poem is written in assonating stanzas. Poem XIII evokes a waterfall:

> The falls sound: and the sound is a shape
> [...]
>
> the force of the people
> the voice of the people
>
> where water breeds no slavery of fish
> where earth jumps beyond service of writs
> where gravity wrests itself from the rich.
>
> In the song of its freedom I heard the oppressed could sing
> in the roar of its power the friendship of fine machines
> in its orchestration a joy that will never finish.

This is about Tom Johnston's hydro-electric scheme for the north of Scotland, one of the most admired of state initiatives; the poem is a Celtic Romantic Socialist Technical Progress Praise-song, and something of a collector's item. Note the fish/writs/rich assonance, using consonants in the same articulatory class, as in ancient Gaelic poetry. Macleod gives us the material basis for thinking about history; his success is in finding visual and sensuous equivalents for the economic processes that underlie society. Poetry had at that time the potential for expanding, via documentary and drama, into showing the life of a society rather than of an individual or a pair of lovers; Macleod was clearly influenced by documentary cinema. But he and Charles Madge were edged off-camera. Perhaps he is too firm in describing behaviour through economics only. In Poem XV, he is shown squinting through a pebble with a hole in it to 'see' visions, a method used by ancient Irish bards. At the end, the tone moves shockingly into that of a wartime thriller film: the Home Guard or Territorials are overcome by nameless invaders, presumably the Germans; the laird is revealed as a Fifth Columnist, a Fascist; the narrator is killed by a tripwire which intercepts his motor-bicycle as he rides for help. At this point, he turns into a seal and joins the other dead of his community. The eerie, romantic tone reminds one of contemporary works such as Powell and Pressburger's *A Matter of Life and Death* and *A Canterbury Tale*, and

'Murdock' (by Francis Berry), and perhaps *The Ministry of Fear*. The theme of class conflict and reincarnation reminds me of *The Man in Grey* (directed by Leslie Arliss, 1943), a tale of nineteenth-century lovers cheated by class, which is framed with two 1943 sequences in which the descendants of the baulked lovers are together and clearly everything is going to be all right. At the time, class society had just about reached the end of its lease, and was engaging in spirit-rapping to see what would happen next.

Macleod's work of the forties is fey and uses word repetition to create a songlike effect, dulling the intelligence which keeps showing itself in his line. But his view, like that of other Highland poets, is sombre, protesting, and politically radical:

> Granite steps and granite stiles
> field-walls of granite cubes
> bond of subinfeudated land
> lips of prehistoric pots
> megalith ports of colony springs
> rocks that lift from tufted turf
> toes from blankets, single stones
> planted in the centred fields
> for sheep to scratch; pillars of rock
> rollers only a horse can shift
> granite posts with sockets drilled
> iron-plugged; crosses carved –
> > rock too hard for norman's tool
> he had to fetch across his own
> his stone his titles and his fiefs.

This passage, with its string of verbless clauses, is from *The Cove*, which I believe to be about Cornwall; the historical revisionism of decayed western shorelines is the same. Chronicling the way in which private property in land was signed by demarcations which became the most visible feature of the landscape, Macleod bitterly connects it to the demarcating and ordering function of language:

> Labels on every enclosure
> for noises of beast and bird, and
> nouns, verbs, adjectives for every sound we make,
> > On the vocal island
> no island label;
> no word for the sound of the sea.

By now the whole landscape is a text whose utterance he is trying to contest, a lying geology of property-marks. Vexed and weary, he imagines a time Before:

> Cormorant colony spreading wings heraldic
> from days when patterns encouraged wills to work
> prehistoric town of pyramid homes
> governed by no governor, lacking class and cloth,
> where back came only fisherfolk
> regular at sunset with their fish inside them.

Here on an Atlantic shore, he is explicit about worldwide connections:

> Thrift covers worn steps, feverfew the twisted rods, and at one end
> where electric cables branch from an unbotanic root
> wrenched off thumb-thick, put in your vasculum
> this grey corolla segment of a graduated compo disc.
> [...]
> Already these superannuated miracles
> have been dismantled. Still they stick up from the cliff
> in hewn granite for ever. But no memorial as yet
> rises up out of the grass, of lies, horror, mess of
> imperial mischief, of furtive wealth,
> of slavery retransmitted by discovery.

The equipment was installed by Marconi for experiments in cross-Atlantic radio. It is a relief to find someone stubborn and clear-headed enough to write explicitly socialist verse. This was as rare in the 1940s as it was in the 1970s. It is distressing to note that the sense of Atlantic decline is the same in 1994 as it was in 1940; will things be much different in 2040?

George Campbell Hay (1915–84)

George Campbell Hay deserves mention for a tiny streak of success, principally a single poem about a boat. His career is a good illustration of the sputtering nature of Scottish poetry: scattered, fickle, inconsistent, ambition followed by self-neglect, research mixed with pastiche. The nationalist proposal is that cultural independence would bring this to an end. This episodic quality makes it hard to be sure that one has seen everything of his work that counts; faced with his books, one always has the sense of something missing. Hay wrote in Scots, Gaelic and English as a literary-political gesture; to write a body of great poetry is the only gesture that could make his cause win. His only book in Anglo-Saxon (Scots and English) is *The Wind on Loch Fyne* (1948); he wrote mainly in Gaelic, which he learnt in his teens. The translations I have seen of his Gaelic poetry show a regressive medievalism, applied to sentimental nationalism – costume poetry. Other Scots poems have been published in magazines. The 1948 volume contains one excellent poem, 'Seeker, Reaper', about a boat, which is based on early medieval Norse poetry, eccentrically written with two litany-like stanzas in Gaelic and Norse, indebted to a cerebral point about the contacts between Gaelic and Norse poetry (the attack on the centrality of the Paris–London route again), but reaches a genuine shaping power in which language is radically stressed to imitate the motions of the sea and of sailing ships:

> She's a glint, she's a glimmer, she's a glimpse, she's a fleeter,
> she's an overhauler, leave-astern, a hale-fleet-beater;
> she's a kyle-coulter, knot-reeler, thrang-speed spinner,
> her mood is moulded on her and the mind that made her is in her.
> She's a wake-plough, foam-plough, spray-hammer, roarer,
> she's a wind-anvil, crest-batterer, deep-trough-soarer,
> she's a dance-step turner, she's a broad-wake-scorer,
> She's a sound-threider, bight-stringer, her hert runs oot afore her.
> When the big strong seas come on like walls, cold-white-heided,
> she doesna flinch a point for them. Straight her wake is threaded.
>
> (From 'Seeker, Reaper')

In this noun-string, Hay was thinking, not only of the splendid seventeenth-century Gaelic poem 'The Birlinn of Clan Ranald', which describes a war-galley, but of Viking poems such as the one by Thjodolfr Arnorsson in which he compares a bank of oars, imagined from below, to the motion of an eagle's wing in flight. Hay was the son of J. MacDougall Hay, the author of the classic novel *Gillespie*, which has dialogue in Scots.

Iain Crichton Smith (1928–99)

Iain Crichton Smith, from the island of Lewis (which 'faces Greenland', as they say), began writing in Gaelic and switched to English. He was a writer of great fluency in his second language: the Preface to his *Selected Poems* (1981) refers to twelve books of verse, and many uncollected poems. The question is why someone so fluent and so adroit has made so little impression.

The poems on pages 117 and 187 give a clue: they are virtually identical. Why didn't the editor notice this? Could it be because Smith, while invariably smooth and appealing, never pushes the definition of his forms to the point at which they are unique and therefore memorable? Indeed, there is nothing that is specific to Smith. He sometimes reminds me of Ritsos:

> It seemed that there were masts. It seemed that men
> buzzed in the water around them. It seemed that fire
> shone in the water which was thin and white
> unravelling towards the shore. It seemed that I
> touched my fixed hat which seemed to float and then
> the sun illumined fish and naval caps,
> names of the vanished ships. In sloppy waves,
> in the fat of water, they came floating home
> bruising against their island.
>   (from 'The Iolaire')

> The coloured windows give way to plain.
> The horsemen crossing the moor are comrades
> going the other way into the country
> of the undisciplined and free.
> Here there is the Land of the Straight Lines
> with a banner black and silent,
> a black mirror
> with the image of an old rose.
>   (from 'If You Are About to Die Now')

The fact that one can extract brilliant stretches from Smith's work emphasises his failure, how he has consistently padded out his poems with sentiment and explanations. I think there is a nucleus of excellent work (perhaps 40 pages, perhaps even 80), but it needs to be separated out from reaches of undistinguished casual chat.

Smith is fond of noun clauses:

> And the cows with their helmets and the great horns tasting grass that was cleansed by them and each skull quite under the plough gently fertilising the earth far from heaven.
>   ('The Poppy', p. 69; trans. from Gaelic)

> O melodeon of my tears, the new music is shining over the ripening moon of the barley, the golden moon of the long night, the moon of boys, the moon of Lewis, the moon of the shoes of the new fashion.
>   ('The Melodeon of the Spirit', p. 67, trans. from Gaelic)

This is distinctively un-English – or perhaps I should say un-Scottish. Notice the repeat-word 'moon'.

Forever
this sharp scale in our poems,
as also the waste music of the sea.
('The Clearances', p. 34)

Notes that are sent about thunder,
cards about lightning,
chairs that tower like skeletons out of the storm.
('In the Middle', p. 223)

island, what shall I say of you, your peat bogs, your lochs, your moors and berries?
the cry of your birds in the fading evening.
Your flowers in summer glowing brightly where there are no thoroughfares.
The perpetual sound of the sea.
The spongy moss on which feet imprint themselves.
The mountains which darken and brighten like ideas in the mind.
The owl with its big glasses that perches on a late tree listening.
The mussels clamped to the rocks, the fool's gold, the tidal pools filling and
    emptying.
The corn that turns from pale green to yellow, my scarecrow rattling in the wind.
The smoke that arises from my fire.
(from 'From the Notebooks of Robinson Crusoe', p. 211)

Smith is so smooth a stylist that these Gaelic quirks do not make his verse awkward. I am not saying that it reads like a translation; nor am I saying that noun clauses, and catalogues of noun clauses, are a good thing because they are ancient and Celtic. What I am saying is that the term 'Celticity' might be located by these material, objective traces. When I say that this construction is un-Anglo-Saxon, there may well be regions, especially those of formerly Celtic speech, where it is quite common in spoken English or Scots; but certainly it isn't mainstream Anglo-Scots. As for the appearance of verbless clauses in English and American poetry, that is a specialised phenomenon which is probably quite unrelated to Celtic language structures; similar clauses are found in twentieth-century German and French poetry.

Smith's poetry is limited by his weakness at dramatising political and social issues. He continually fields such themes as: the British Empire smashed the Highlanders in 1715 and 1745 only to recruit them as soldiers to fight its wars; the Clearances stole the land from the people; Calvinism leads to sexual repression; I feel sad when I go back to the island where I was born from my life in Glasgow; the sea brings fishermen their livelihood while swallowing them and taking their lives in return – but his recognition of their importance in the social thought, and also the experience, of north-western Scots is accompanied by an unwillingness to stage them artistically. I'm not saying that the underlying truth can't fuel works of art, just that the artist needs cunning to tap this energy. Smith's relationship to these themes is floating: he is not an unsubtle man. But, even if he is not taken in by these sentimental themes, he has not developed a mythology of his own as an alternative. Further, he's too respectful of the ordinary people to whom these myths are precious to be intelligent and sceptical by mocking them. So altogether he appears to be uncommitted to his own poetry.

The Clearances happened between 1780 and 1840: why is Smith not writing about the 1960s, or 1970s, when he is living through them? It is true that, in an exclusively agricultural community, the distribution of land ownership and use determines everything, and points back into the past; it is quite reasonable to link the emigration of a young man in 1950 to a lack of land that dates from a Clearance in, say, 1830; the impregnable rights of the landowners are even older. Surely a poet of real magnanimity and vision would take on the whole 150 years in one complex vision, however much that demanded? Nor am I very clear exactly what Smith wants. Does he want the land law of Scotland changed? A shift in the price structure benefiting herrings and potatoes? The abolition of deer parks? The reliance on the Clearances theme comes about partly because every-one agrees on the meaning of those events, and partly because they are remote and unthreatening.

Smith, coming to write in English, adopted the English style of the period; since this was the early fifties, it was the Movement that influ-enced him, limiting his scope and impact. The historical decline of the Gaidhealtacht has given him a theme suitable for, almost demanding, writing at the highest pitch, while in a sense depriving him of the possibility of doing so. This emotion expressed itself in a sour, and Larkin-like, mocking at the vulgarity of modern Scottish life. The potential of this attack by poetry on the culture of ice-cream parlours is unrealised. Smith never articulates his disgust, or examines the ideals (presumably, of the vanished Highland past) that Scottish tourist towns fail to live up to. I cannot read his Gaelic; but his English style is featureless and almost passive. The theme would require, first, a comprehensive historical analysis (I will come to this in a moment); second, a definite attitude towards present-day politics which would give the feelings a focus. Without this, piteous pictures of the past are likely to strike one as lacking in intelligence. One has to bear in mind that these themes were handled, not only by Joseph Macleod and Sorley MacLean (the latter a great writer) in the 1940s, but also by Gaelic poets such as Mary MacPherson at the time they were happening, and in the aftermath.

Smith has said, in an interview:

> There was a period when I was writing my poetry when I felt [...] a kind of blackness... that you are shouting into a room which echoes back to you... It's a hollow echo, there's nothing there... Well, no, not just that there's no audience. There are no ideas, nothing that can allow you to write poetry.[8]

He relates this to the intellectual condition of Scotland. It is to Smith's credit that he has identified this hollow: every Scottish poet has to face it, and it is the quality of their response to it by which we judge them, as brave men behave bravely in captivity. It would seem that fluency, populism, modernist formal intransigence, and extremist political or linguistic positions are just ways of evading the basic misery.

The hole is partly, of course, a 'God-shaped hole'. Smith criticises Presbyterianism in poem after poem. By attacking this, you attack the unifying ideology of the old Hebridean society – the thing that most people believed in most intensively. An atheist could only be an outcast in the Islands. Judith Ennew describes Lewis as an island gripped by the Free Church, where individuals are perplexed by a tri-cultural conflict of values, driven into anomie by 'the contradictory norms of three value systems, Gaelic, Puritan, and English'.[9] The Presbyterian clergy were also the ones who decided to equip the children of the Gaidhealtacht to face a hostile world by teaching them English. They took this decision in their role as organic intellectuals, as the socially responsible group in a society that largely consisted of one class and had been abandoned by 'their' aristocracy, by now of alien culture and residence. An intellectual writing in Gaelic would have to take a conservative stance on language and a social stance which denied the authority of the church. This is a hard double to pull off. Perhaps modern artists have to go through this outcast experience; perhaps Smith failed by refusing to go through it. His attack on the church is muffled because he does not want to criticise people from Lewis, people he knows personally. Perhaps he is not only fluent but also socially skilled, papering over differences to avoid conflict. If you look at his poetry from this angle, it's very successful; but perhaps less successful as art.

Derick Thomson (1921–)

Smith's childhood friend Derick Thomson is a professor of Celtic Studies who has written only in Gaelic and whose poems, consequently, I have only read in translation. *Creachadh na Clarsaich* (*Plundering the Harp: Poems 1940–80*) is replete with noun clauses. Gairm have refused me permission to quote from (the English translations of) Thomson's poems; the first excerpt I had chosen was a seven-line sentence with no verb, although with five verb-nouns, and with no run-on of sense between lines, although there is parallelism. The second extract, from the same poem, was an eleven-line sentence with no verb, although with five verb-nouns, and with no run-on of sense across line-breaks. The third extract was a seven-line sentence with no verbs and no verb-nouns, with a repeat-word which occurs four times, and with no run-on of sense across line-breaks. The reproduction of Gaelic phrase structure does not make for the most natural kind of English. We are left wondering whether this distaste for finite verbs, tense, and syntactic movement derives from features of Gaelic speech contemporary with the poem (i.e. the speech of the 1950s and 1960s), or from features of Gaelic literary composition, deriving from a remote and rich Irish past, and 'contemporary' to the sixteenth or some other century. Again, some of Thomson's poems, separated out from the whole, would adorn anthologies; but the whole is tedious and under-developed. Thomson is a much more limited poet than Smith. Perhaps the quotations would not have borne this out; perhaps they would. His poems shed some light on Smith's: for example, it is useful to know that the *Iolaire* (Gaelic for 'eagle') was a ship that sank off Stornoway, drowning many homecoming servicemen from Lewis, at the end of the First World War.

Some areas of Scotland may formerly have been places where everyone voted the same way (David McCrone quotes Victorian elections in which 87 per cent of the Scottish vote was Liberal[10]); but present-day Scotland is just not like that. Even the ignored Conservatives clocked up 24 per cent of the vote in the 1987 general election. There is no consensus position, so political positions have to be argued. Thomson takes the whole nationalist position for granted and does not dramatise, or argue through, the issues. The presentation of politics in allegory freezes the material and makes it inert, like a sentence without a verb; Thomson's mind is completely made up. The apparent radicalism of being against the constitution of the land in its present form does not go so far as thinking about nationalism.

Thomson's poetry cannot attain a meaning unless it is attached to a vision of the future of the Highlands and Islands. The concerns of politics may well seem unpoetic if they are all about the price of beef cattle, the financing of roads and bridges, the siting of quarries, and the development of tourism – but this is precisely why political poetry is hard to write. Politics without hard-headedness is just slogans.

Thomson's weakness of analysis is derived from an excessively organic theory of politics and community, where dissent is impossible without being an alien. Aesthetic refinement of style is limited by an attempt to appeal to the whole community, if only *in absentia*. Thomson lacks confidence in the autonomy of art because he is afraid of appealing to a splinter group of an audience already far too small. His polarisation seems to produce a potent surplus of unambiguity about his partisan beliefs, but actually causes a deficit of meaning, as the materials of argument are not supplied.

Sorley MacLean (1911–96)

The task of writing about a national disaster such as the Clearances asks for a poet who has a political philosophy that offers an alternative solution; someone of intellectual and moral integrity, so that the overall logical construction of the poem does not contain jarring inconsistencies, pushed out of the text only by tricky and unsuccessful subterfuge; someone of erudition, so that what they say is true, which also demands of them the common touch, the ability to write about ordinary people without becoming prosaic or clumsy; and someone with immense powers of rhetoric, so that the dimensions of the event, both moral and geographical, do not shatter the puny boundary structures of the poem. Scotland is fortunate that all these qualities were combined in one man, Sorley MacLean, who has written about the Clearances in such poems as 'Screapadal', 'Two MacDonalds', and Part 6 of *The Cuillin*. MacLean's family background included not only superlative bearers of the Gaelic folk tradition of song, music and oral history, but also earnest and God-fearing adherents of religion. Their church, the Free Church, was implacably opposed to secular culture, including dancing, singing and music. MacLean has recorded how he gave up Calvinism for socialism at the age of twelve; nonetheless the spiritual discipline and high moral standards of Calvinism have been decisive for his work. He has often made moral reproaches, in the face of the Clearances, the rise of Fascism, and the militarisation of the Cold War era; such talk would have no substance if it came from someone without moral standards. Indeed, it is hard for someone imbued with a hedonistic and secular ethos to write about politics except by satire. The earliest political activists in the Highlands had been early nineteenth-century evangelists, and these militated against authority, if only because authority was against them. The early nineteenth century saw the arrival of printed Gaelic Bibles and to some extent of Gaelic literacy, and Bible-reading undermined religious authority and led to ardent Protestantism perhaps for the first time in those parts. The defeat in the 1840s of the attempt by the landlords to impose their choice of pastor on the congregation, and to persecute other pastors (the Free Church) out of existence, was the first victory of the people in the Highlands over their lords, and was the model for the Land Wars of the 1880s. The quality of earnestness is also decisive for MacLean's love poetry; if he were dealing in transient sexual liaisons, it would not have a thousandth of the impact. This moral integrity does not come from simplifying the poem, or from regressing into the styles of a simpler age, as so many think; but from the highest spiritual aspirations. Self-questioning does not lead to emotional fragmentation, except in the case of those who lack belief in themselves; for someone pure of heart it leads to greater unity and integrity. Because it involves the compression of much (future) time, by the powers of the intellect, into an instant of the present, it resembles memorisation, something important in a Bible-reading and an oral culture.

MacLean's poetry is the answer to a riddle, namely, 'What happens to aristocratic poetry when the aristocracy change their language and absent themselves from the scene?' The English thought everything could be bought and sold, because the institution of the nuclear family had created a market in land, unhindered by the belief in family continuity expressed in land tenure. If the answer was 'private property', the question was the destruction of kinship. It was the English preoccupation with other people's land that made modern history turn out the way it did. The Celtic societies neighbouring the English really didn't understand possessive individualism; it was like a sound they couldn't pronounce. The old 'object poems' were really about status; their occasions were the death of a lord (with a major shift of status for the heirs) and the rewarding (or purchase) of fealty, bringing an individual into a definite relationship with the gift-giver.

MacLean was raised in two factions of the Free Church, and one of the founding events in the history of the Free Church was the Disruption of

1843. This was a response to a piece of Westminster legislation which granted the right to appoint the pastor of a parish to the landowner of the place, as in England. In Scotland, the pastor was elected by the congregation – which could not be said of the English legislators. The law turned the office of spiritual adviser into a piece of property, which could be bought, sold, or inherited. Spiritual welfare was, like the inhabitable land, to be the property of a few – the English arrangement. At the Church of Scotland's Synod of 1843, the majority of the delegates walked out and formed a new church, in defiance of the government and its bad laws. This meant losing their homes and their incomes. The translation of spiritual power into property, the rejection of property in favour of the spirit, are significant for MacLean, because he took the forms of a poetry which had been preoccupied with prestige possessions and directed them at spiritual virtues. We could say that the Disruption, seeing the symbolic expulsion of the landowning class from their claims to leadership, made it possible to take the old aristocratic praise forms and give them a new content.

Later, after various reunions, the Free Church (the non-reunited remnant of the new church created in 1843) was especially strong in the Highlands. The issue was indirectly that of possessive individualism. It was quite a regular thing for troops of cavalry to break up the Free Church congregations as they prayed. This meant that hanging on to proper Calvinism was a sign of having won a fight. This fitted into ancient Celtic concepts of contests, with the poem as obligation to the hero; the kirk became not just a precious possession, but the prize of heroes. The Gaelic poetry of the nineteenth century took on both the Free Church and the struggle of tenants with Anglicised landlords, and MacLean's praise of socialist heroes is not a complete break with either theme.

Something I remember dimly from early childhood is stories about services being held in boats on a lake or on the foreshore by the edge of the sea. These strange non-places sound like the answer to a riddle, but really they were responses to the right of landowners to forbid gatherings on their land; the Free Church had to meet on land that was not owned by anyone. MacLean is not much interested by objects, but the land itself plays a leading role in his poems: it is an object of fascination because it was the source of frustration and longing for so many years. It has replaced the horses, swords, cloaks, cups and so on of the old praise poems.

Gaelic experts assure us that the dialectic between folk and classical forms is important for MacLean's poetry. Watson's introduction to the

1918 anthology *Bàrdachd Ghàidhlig* (from which MacLean recalls reading many poems in class as a schoolboy) states that the classical poetry comes to an end around 1730, while the rise of modern poetry (i.e. folk poetry in accentual metres) is around 1600 (or it first appears in manuscripts then), and its most fruitful period is about 1640 to 1830.[11] The modern manner emerges at much the same time in Ireland. The old poetry was 'not very intelligible to the people generally', although the ruling families understood the old words. The modern poetry most values race, physical beauty, manly accomplishment, free-handed generosity, and wisdom in council.

Critics able to read the evidence say that Gaelic poetry was in a low condition in the 1930s, after fifty years of mediocrity. Sermons and folk-song were intact sources of moral and aesthetic energy, of passionate language; MacLean was exceptionally blessed in being able to draw on these. The economic circumstances of the 1930s pointed every Western European poet at moral relations and at the need to speak with the voice of the people: the times recommended the resources that Gaelic by chance, after misfortune, had in store. Lacking Gaelic, I can only report what John MacInnes says on MacLean's style and diction: 'In contrast [to the translations] the original Gaelic exhibits virtually an entire spectrum of language. Transparent simplicity is found side by side with a formidable density of verbal texture [...] practically all the available registers of Gaelic, ranging in quality from the demotic to the arcane, are included at some point or other.'[12] MacInnes quotes MacLean on early modern Gaelic songs: 'Technically they are simple but adequate, their metrical structure being the old syllabic structure modified by speech stress [...] I think that is the most permanently satisfying basis for Gaelic metrics'.[13] Gaelic is a 'stress-timed' language, like English, so that the count of unstressed syllables is not very important; we are to understand that syllabic metre is a subtle effect in Gaelic, because it is a rule which, while consistent and easy to hear, goes against the spirit of the language. It would, following Thurneysen and Wilhelm Meyer, have been borrowed from Latin, which is not a stress-timed language; Thurneysen quotes early medieval Irish texts which define syllabic metres as learned (*rhythmus artificialis*), stress metres as unlearned (*rhythmus vulgaris*).[14] So we have the tantalising suggestion that syllabic verse is a subtlety of the bardic schools, and of Irish learning, which was an object of fascination, and part of the glamour and puzzle of poetry, for Hebridean folk-singers.

At any rate, it seems that MacLean's verse is an interference pattern, or shimmer, between two metrical models; and sounds, to a learned reader, like folk-song. 'MacGill-Eain employs the traditional Gaelic system of internal as well as final rhyme very freely';[15] this means the syllables halfway through the line in consecutive lines rhyming. MacInnes points out that 'Gaelic poetry, in which the oral element is so strong, frequently displays the paratactic style associated with oral poetry throughout the world. The stanza, or even the line, is usually self-contained, in sense as in syntax. In MacGill-Eain's work in general what we find is the normal thematic development of literary poetry.'[16] The tight association of line-break with sense unit might be found in English poetry, or especially in songs before poetry stood by itself; enjambement and a greater breadth of verse movement can be associated with the late sixteenth century, a time of revolutionary change in poetry, and MacLean represents the same kind of liberation in Gaelic poetry; he writes poems, not songs. Unsurprisingly, his choice of vocabulary is also distinctive and unconventional: 'The context of his poetry gives the common currency of Gaelic, as well as the antique and unusual words, the quality of newly-minted coin. Recurrent words – among them words that express degrees of brightness, unrest, unattainableness, transience, suffering, pride – form his unmistakable signature.'[17] His vocabulary is far greater than the everyday language: 'the linguistic authority and arbiter of usage that MacGill-Eain constantly cites is the Church – in his case the Free Presbyterian Church, of which his family were adherents'.[18] Douglas Sealy cites an example of MacLean's closeness to folk-song tradition. An old song runs:

> I will not be striving with the tree that will not bend for me
> though apples should grow on the tip of each branch;
> if you have left me I bid you farewell,
> there was never an ebb that was not followed by flood[19]

which MacLean adapted as

> I am not striving with the tree that will not bend for me
> and the apples will not grow on any of the branches;
> I do not bid you farewell, you did not leave me:
> it is the ebb of death that no flood follows
>
> (from 'Ebb')

As a thirties poet using folk forms, Lorca would be the name most readily cited; I would prefer to mention Idris Davies and Glyn Jones.

The long poem published in *Chapman* in the 1980s, *The Cuillin*, had in fact been written in 1939, under the direct influence of *A Drunk Man Looks at a Thistle*: MacLean became radically dissatisfied with it and gave it up, at much the same time that MacDiarmid, overreaching himself with the gigantic poem, originally called 'Cornish Heroic Song for Valda Trevlyn', burnt out and lost his ability to compose poetry.[20] The sense that civilisation was on the edge of the abyss no doubt incited people to compose *summae*.

MacLean remarks, of the artistic repertoire of Gaelic verse:

> I ought to put every effect
> that Norway and Ireland
> and old Scotland gave to my people
> together in mellowness
> and to offer them to the wonder
> that is fair and shapely in your face.
> (from 'The Sunny Fold')

The vista this opens up is of a north-western European world of forms and symbolic arrays, with Skye as a centre whose periphery, scattered in an archipelago linked by flocks of galleys, would include Dublin, Munster, Iceland, Oslo, Bergen, Riga, Novgorod, and the landfalls of Wales. The notion of Norse influence on Gaelic verse and folk culture is attractive, because it would only have taken one bilingual person, any time between the ninth and the sixteenth centuries, for this influence to materialise. It is reasonably certain that families such as the MacLeods originally paid for Norse panegyrics, before adapting to a Gaelic milieu. If Gaelic poetry has absorbed this Norseness, it is no longer palaeo-Celtic, but the outcome can be a new and cumulative Celticity. Transmission of narratives is certain; the more supernatural elements in Icelandic narrative are frequently linked by scholars to Irish influences. Literal translation of a bardic poem in either direction is hardly thinkable, because of the elaborate technique of the verse; translation of the simpler forms of folk-songs would have been much more feasible. Oral literature is based on generative mnemonic frames which *are* susceptible to re-use in a different language. The Gaelic world did not know Roman rule, the Dark Ages, the twelfth-century renaissance, the Renaissance, as other European peoples did; to assess the flow of its history we need other languages, cultural worlds, chronologies, rhythms of flourishing and withering, anxieties, objects of prestige, acquisitiveness, entry ports, notions of routes and contiguity. This world had no city, but rather an ocean.

Genealogy is a branch of knowledge which has not been taken up by science: there are no professors of it. Hebridean or Eskimo experts can't market their wares. Yet the detailed knowledge of individuals which it carries with it is superior to the aggregative, statistical methods of the Enlightenment's social sciences. The most famous trend in twentieth-century English history-writing is Namierisation, the reduction in political history of simple, elevated, opposing principles to the multiple contest of groups of individuals linked by opportunism, advantage, alliance and kinship. By reduction I mean adding of detail! Such was the structure of British parliamentary politics at the accession of George III in 1760; it is frequently said that the Age of Principle is now over, as politicians see themselves purely as managers and facilitators. MacLean's account of society equally lacks a gap between abstract principles and the everyday action of individuals; it is based on a knowledge of old-style Highland politics, where loyalty and kinship counted for everything. His primary feat is the almost bardic task of knowing everything possible about genealogy and about the history of individuals, living or dead; the gap between the personal and the political never opens up in his poetry. This is possible, I think, because his emotional territory, Skye and Raasay, is not a mass society. The crisis of modern poetry is partly a crisis of knowledge: not of wrong theories about society and psychology, but of inadequate nutrition with social fact for demonstrating them. It takes a vast store of knowledge to follow the individuals within a social system, as Lewis Namier did, and as oral history in a society such as that of the Hebrides does. I spoke of principle, which in fact came to the Hebrides with the evangelical movement, and then produced radical politics; the accepted wisdom is that close acquaintance with society and economy makes one less idealistic, less committed to ethical principles, but my experience tells me the reverse. MacLean's store of knowledge doesn't make him doubt that high principles are needed in personal relations, in work and contracts, in thought, and in art.

Scientific sociology and psychology start with an assumed ignorance, and incur expense which limits their progress towards their goals; the hope is that the uncovering of principles or laws will translate back down into the practical reason which, within the arms of state or corporations, judges concrete living individuals, and will qualify the decisions made by face-to-face knowledge. Decisions such as who to appoint as a head teacher, or whose exam paper to give a high mark to, are local and empirical; they concern individuals. We could perhaps think of society, not as a structure, but as an array of discriminations, or classifications. This would resemble, not a language, but the cognitive matrix of oppositions that underlies and remodels a language. Judging character is difficult; 'scientific racism' and class prejudice are merely two premature attempts to reduce subjective, highly skilled decisions to a system. Part of the pressure shaping a Scottish writer's description of Scottish society is the power relationship, i.e. the fact that the discriminations which organise Scottish society are being made from outside, by Westminster or by English capitalism. Just as the Gaelic, Scots and English languages mix in Scotland, so also different ideas of what society is and who the individual is compete to be the cognitive array that a particular brain brings to bear at a given moment.

Genealogy is closer to literature, to the knowledge that poets, playwrights and novelists use, than social science is. There is a historical fault line between Derick Thomson or Iain Crichton Smith and the legendary past: but MacLean, happy to use by-words from Gaelic tradition, straddles it. There is a story by the Central Labour College teacher D. J. Williams (in *Storïau'r tir coch*) which opens with an account of a great rural storyteller, speaking a strong dialect, who comes from a family that has been in the neighbourhood for a very long time, so that he knows all the possible stories, and all the parts of them, their antecedents and their ends.[21] This is Atlantic cultural conservatism: a beach where strange artefacts fetch up from around the world and are not again lost, obstinate accumulation as the stock of an artist, the seduction of a storyteller who never reaches the edge of language, where things become dark and the story breaks off. MacLean has the same breadth of knowledge:

> The snow serenity of sunlit mountains
> and the white Whiteness that was in the longing
> of O'Rathaille in his sadness
> a straying wanderer on the mountain.
>
> Maol Donn in the Big Music of MacCrimmon
> and the Echo that came unasked
> to Blind Ruairi stirred and stung
> with the hauteur of humiliation.
>
> Homer in the death of valiant Hector
> and Helen, fairest of the fair,
> and poor Priam prostrating himself
> in the tears of him who killed his dear one.
>
> High-headed Deirdre mourning as she was leaving
> Alba and the glens she loved so greatly;
> acute Shakespeare struggling in the strife of his nature,
> heaping thoughts about his anguish.

Blok as he saw coming
the thing thought not to be reached,
the great Red Revolution of man,
the wandering light that was long sought.
                    (from 'The Tree of Strings')

MacLean's knowledge of oral legend enables him constantly to suggest a whole world, beyond and around the poetry, however little he reveals of it. Something about his poetry suggests that it goes on for ever. The passage just quoted is organised in four-line blocks which, in the Gaelic, I guess to represent *ceathramhs*, the four-line units composing perfectly complete units of sense, which MacNeill (quoted above) describes for Irish poems of the thirteenth century. This completeness and definiteness leaves a space at the end of a quatrain which is pivotal for the poem – either a disaster or a new start which bestows definition and variety together. If the stanza is complete, it leaves no run-on to float the next one; which, if it benefits from this unstopped impulse, is not complete in its own compass. The use of four-line stanzas in a traditional metre resembles what Idris Davies was doing, in the same years, for South Wales; the stanzas of his poems are based on hymn metres, as Anthony Conran points out in his edition of *The Angry Summer*.[22] Glyn Jones tried, at the same time, an English adaptation of the folk-form of the *pennill*, also four lines long. The impersonality of the form allows it to speak for common experience, where a more modern and subjective form could only look on from outside. Davies's work deals with social conditions, during a big strike and during the Depression, more massively, more obstinately, more inflexibly, than MacLean; but lacks the latter's capacity for introspection and for large-scale intellectual movement. I would hazard that MacLean's ability to construct an argument in verse, subsuming the tight quatrains and riding them on its deeper underlying energy, comes from the big arguments of Calvinist preaching. I don't find it in the bardic poetry. But after all, he could have learnt this mastery of logic from philosophy, especially from Hegel, Marx, or any Marxist of high calibre; except that he absorbed the theological arguments in Gaelic, and his vocabulary seems to go back to Presbyterianism (and so to Calvin's remarkable Latin) rather than to German and the nineteenth century.

Egan O'Rahilly, Homer, Blind Ruairi, the composer of 'Maol Donn', Deirdre (from 'The Exile of the Sons of Uisliu', *Longes Mac-n-uislenn*), Shakespeare; you don't absolutely need to know who these people are, they are self-describing, like figures in some medieval painting. MacLean likes to use by-words, *aretai* as we might call them, named individuals proverbial for their virtues, because he is interested in excelling in courage, devotion, selflessness, and so on. One could write the history of twentieth-century poetry in terms of the disuse of *aretai* – and the appalling struggle to find new mediations, where the new theories of history and society and psychology fall down and we are increasingly faced with experience that can't be verbalised or related to the experience of others.

Perhaps Blok is cited as a Symbolist, rather than because of his failure, for a few months, to see through the cruelty of the Bolsheviks. MacLean confesses to Symbolist principles; his use of objects is wholly unlike the dead and deaf objects of poems of the regionalist ideology. It is tempting to link the 'white Whiteness' of the first stanza quoted to Andrey Bely (the 'white'), and the Russian Symbolist use of whiteness; although it is also the title of an allegorical poem by O'Rahilly (c. 1670–1726), which strangely anticipates Solovyev and Blok in its central image.

A key word in MacLean's poetry is 'pride', or 'hauteur'; translating, in the Gaelic, words with the root *ard*, which means both height and pride. (This so far as I can pick out from the Gaelic and from Gaelic dictionaries.) 'Hauteur' combines the literal and psychological senses. The Church Latin word *superbia*, from *super*, also does this. It is not quite coincidental that MacLean writes about mountains: they are the highest things in the Celtic world, and function within the poems not merely as objects, but as *ard*, peaks, objective correlatives for exaltation, for dizzying far sights, for the self-admiration of making such climbs; and for the possibility of falling. It is, it seems, precisely in this word 'pride' (*ardan*) that the dramatic confrontation between the bloody and glamorous glorification of the old Gaelic poetry, and of its secular rulers, and the democratic Puritanism of the nineteenth century is held and brought out – destabilising everything else, throwing it into incessantly new patterns. For pride was a central concept for the Puritans, as little else than the impulse that made men run upon their damnation. *Ard* can mean the peak of anything, as in the title of the Irish High King, or the Irish president today; MacLean writes constantly about people who were the peak of some quality, and this splendid and far-sighted recitation of excellences, of the prides of the Gaelic world, would vex a religious person by its temptations to vanity and self-will. It is not impossible that MacLean, writing most of his poetry in a few years around 1938, fascinated by events in Spain, was influenced by the notorious Spanish pride, incarnated then as the courage of workers in Madrid and the Asturias.

The Fife (communist-nationalist) poet and engineer T. S. Law (1918–98) uses, in his 1948 pamphlet *Whit Time in the Day*, the word *heech* (high) for a similar quality to MacLean's *ard* words, of hauteur, obstinacy, excitement and defiance; it comes four times in his poem 'The Clenched Fist'. Perhaps we have here a semantic crossover between the two major languages of Scotland. Law had a strange non-career in which his class and politics told against him for those who equate assertiveness with lack of intelligence. He was a *heech* writer, and acquiescence is not proof of sensitivity.

The function of these by-words for excellence seems to me archaic: that is, the sight of each excellence, graded according to its kind, inspires in us the longing to achieve perfection, an act of imitation delivering itself in conjectures of kinds not described by the poem, whose impacting edge bursts in us as ideas breaking up, or being formed, in profusion and instability. This poetry cannot be read as autobiography, a self-confirming story that is completed, and dies, in its own compass; but only as a means of searching our own souls, lured out of their investments by wonderful feats on the edge of visibility and comprehensibility. MacLean deals with the fundamental Celtic problems, the political weakness of the Atlantic societies and the uncertainty of their future, not by blank, conservative denial, as an R. S. Thomas might do, but by building the uncertainty and risk into the poem in the form of conjecture and of forming ideals. At this point humility, the strength of the Presbyterians, and pride, the strength of the Gaelic warriors, are combined in one swoop. Frequently, he seems to be observing, or expecting, failure, but uses this as a measure for imagining and desiring higher achievements. Three times, in *From Wood to Ridge*, he refers to pride in the context of the Battle of Inverkeithing, where the clan MacLean lost most of their adult males, and their land, and won a fine reputation.

MacLean never joined the Communist Party, or accepted the Marxist philosophy, but his commitments lay in that direction, and Ross and Hendry quote letters in which he says that he intended to follow a much more purist and pro-Russian line, poetically, after the war. The timing is important for assessing the spiritual qualities of the communists MacLean wanted to join; they were living in a dream world, but they weren't power-worshippers or position-seekers. In 1944, when he was living in Edinburgh, MacLean was converted away from this pro-Soviet position by a long series of conversations with Sydney Goodsir Smith, who dwelt particularly on the Soviet betrayal of the Warsaw Rising. We know now that Goodsir Smith was right a thousand times over. I think it's fair to say that Western communism deteriorated in the following years, as those who were not credulous and self-righteous took in the facts about what was happening to democracy in Eastern Europe. In 1944, believers in Stalin weren't a group self-selected for their inability to think. However, MacLean had become detached from his previous work, and his increased political maturity also deprived him of his agenda for the future.

It's in keeping with MacLean's ideals that hard work as a schoolteacher, both for the children in his care and for the cause of Gaelic in schools, reduced him almost to poetic silence for thirty years, between 1943 and 1972. MacLean has in fact written some poetry of great importance since his retirement in 1972, as well as publishing the abandoned long poem of 1939, *The Cuillin*. The decline of Gaelic, in these years and throughout MacLean's life, has left his poetry, in its original language, high and dry. Of 140,000 Scottish Gaelic speakers in 1941, the majority were unable to read Gaelic, after English-medium schooling; of the rest, only a fraction were interested in reading books, and modern poetry probably came low down the list.

MacLean's poetry absorbs the past and has a vision of the future, however much at risk; this mastery of time derives from profound introspection clarifying the self, which is presumably the Calvinist heritage of soul-searching; and from passing the tests imposed on the self by excelling and being true. The notable feats that he carries out are acts of moral resolution; the quality of his love and of his commitment to the future of his people are the subject matter of the poetry, even though neither the love (for Eimhir, in the poems to her) nor the political schemes came to fruition. It's inevitable that we admire this resolution above all other qualities. MacLean's words carry the weight of truth because he demonstrates the continuity of the self, or of principles, across the devouring, information-eating, effacing flux of time. Socialism is no good without emotional commitment; it cannot be devolved to laws that sit on paper and not in the hearts of men. A writer can't analyse social relations without dealing with the bonds of obligation and solidarity; slippery individualists can't write about mutual dependence. Great political poetry cannot be based on scepticism. The relationship between this triumph over Time and the other one, the preservation of the past by cultural accumulation, is clear in poetic terms and may exist in psychological terms too. The fearful cost of the constant self-testing is apparent in a number of poems, of which 'The Knife' is the most dramatic. It is in 'Honeysuckle', a poem of the 1970s, that we find the clearest use of Calvinist psychology: MacLean says it was 'long, long, before I understood / that love is so selfish / that it will blind the eyes of the spirit / with the joy of the eye of the flesh'. This must refer to what Calvinist speech more usually calls the carnal eye, which can only see the *created* world, in opposition to the eye of the spirit, which is directly visited by the Holy Ghost; 'carnal' is often collocated with 'pride'. Here MacLean reproaches himself for creating an illusion as the object over which his emotions wandered; he was only able to write great love poems because of his furiously high spiritual standards, which themselves came from his religious upbringing. 'How will I stand up against their cavalry / since my heart is but half flayed?' ('Prayer'). When he speaks of 'flaying', this simultaneously means torture and the sloughing of an earthly envelope which was clogging the eye of the spirit. At the most intense moments his whole work resonates as if something mighty were trying to find a weak spot; but such is its quality that he can, without blaspheming, use of a mortal woman the words coined for describing the opening of the human soul to God. The poem says at the end that 'heart love has / a transitory victory over the condition of the flesh'.

MacLean makes many claims which make us as readers put counter-pressure on the fabric of what he says to reassure ourselves: the better the news he has to tell us about the powers of the human spirit, the more fearful the hammer-blows we swing at his verse to see if it has any weakness in it. If something carries you up fifty feet in the air, you do wonder about its solidity. One of his figures is the real and allegorical object, where the feat of memory that he carries out is a feat, almost of wooing, which does away with our doubts; at the same time, the effort of visualisation for us is a source of pride, and lets us escape into the aesthetic. I find these objects also in bardic verse:

> Here was the Cétach made a spoil: beautiful was the godly garment, Crimthann's mantle, a hundred cumals' worth, a gaudy treasure of fine tassels. Thrice fifty tassels, I trow, round its border, it is recorded: none of them scanted in value, each with its several apple of red gold.[23]

Here is a power object, in modern terms, which it tests the mind to visualise and know: when you imagine the cloak, how many tassels can you see? The demands of eulogy meant that the bards excelled at such descriptions, since the nobility delighted in such artefacts, the high-performance cars of the day, and didn't want generalities in the descriptions. The art of oral poetry is all to do with the strengths and weaknesses

of the memory, and so is the art of abstract thought, which mixes the
stereotyped and the intact and puzzling. This figure also appears in the
Bible, for example in Ezekiel, chapter 1: the prophet organises his trance
vision as an allegorical object, which can more easily be memorised and
shared. I feel that MacLean's intrication of the allegorical and the concrete
comes from both traditions. *Thou also, son of man, take thee a tile, and lay
it before thee, and pourtray upon it the city, even Jerusalem*: he has astutely
turned the difficulty of imagining society, the inadequacy of all attempts
to carve it on a tile, into the aesthetic sense of heroism and transcendence
which draws us out into the sublime, where our faculties are exceeded.

MacLean was writing, at his moment of greatest productivity, about
the most pressing problems of European politics: Spain, the rise of
Fascism, the decay of capitalism; he is a contemporary of his contemporaries, his sensibility blocked by no armour. However, his language seems
to have absorbed, in its restless fluency and variety, many structures from
an older Gaelic tradition, whether bardic or folk-song. For example, when
we read Watson's translation, 'Gone is the glory of Innse Gall, a cause of
woe is haunting it; sickness and affliction without hiding is the great
conspicuous injury' (elegy for Norman MacLeod, 1705), we can guess that
the sense of devastation, which the bard had to develop for the funereal
elegy (*marbhnadh*), one of his main sources of revenue, was transformed,
via the nineteenth-century political poems against the clearing landlords,
and reinforced by the lamentations of the Old Testament prophets, into
MacLean's pessimistic vision of the decline of the Gael and of European
democracy. When he rhetorically repeats a word,

> I saw the *tree* rising,
> in its branches the jewelled music,
> my own fair love moving strings:
> the image of joy blossoming.
> I saw the *tree* in a distant land
> and its far sad music sore for me,
> my own fair love with her fingers on harp strings,
> restless the gold voice of their crying speech.
> Going from my sight the longed-for *tree* […]
> (from 'The Tree of Strings')

we can wonder whether this derives from the cumulative praise of an
object, as it might appear in a bardic poem celebrating prestige objects, or
whether it is like a preacher who picks a single word from a text and uses it
to highlight a theological concept in an exegetic sermon. Both destroy the

texture of everyday language, to make something greater and more con-
templative, by slowing down its flow, forcing the attention to find new
distinctions. Time becomes saturated and no longer flows. We find the
same device[24] in the poetry of Joseph Macleod, and in poems by Iain
Crichton Smith and Derick Thomson quoted above. The repetition of a
key image in the first line of successive stanzas serves to bind them
together. I find that these tone-giving words are nuclear forms of
allegorical landscapes, memorisable forms that serve to hold the attention
and to make palpable complex propositions about theology or history.
MacLean's landscapes are never there merely as beauty spots.

A glance at the poems of Taliesin (said to be late sixth century) shows
repeat-words to be quite common:

> *Gweleis* i rac neb nym gweles
> pop annwyl. ef diwyl y neges.
> *Gweleis* i pasc am leu am lys.
> *Gweleis* i diel o dyuyn adowys.
> *Gweleis* i keig kyhafal y blodeu.
> Neur *weleis* vd haelhaf y dedeu.
> *Gweleis* i lyw katraeth tra maeu
> bit vy nar nwy hachar kymryeu.
> (from *Poems of Taliesin*)[25]

The repeated word means 'I saw'. Almost all the genuine poems of
Taliesin share the same feature. This link between the last great poet of the
Celtic languages and the first is puzzling. The results of a hasty survey of
the field are now sketched. The use of repeat-words is common in the
oldest Celtic poetry, and is found sporadically throughout the historical
sequence. It has associations with the lower forms of poetry, since sophisticated poets tend to avoid it; and with spells and incantations, where the
repetitive naming of the object of the spell is vital to the result. It is
extraordinarily common in the Scottish folk-charms of the *Carmina
Gadelica*, and almost absent from Scottish bardic poetry. MacLean uses
the thematic word in a Symbolist way, as the key in which the associ-
ational complex of the poem is set, allowing freedom and firmness. Such a
means of binding is found already in a poem in Murphy's *Early Irish
Lyrics*, dated by him to AD 800, which is sustained throughout by an image
of a woman's life as the daily cycle of the sea, which floods and ebbs: either
'ebb' or 'flood' appears in 10 of the 35 stanzas. The value of repetition may
be related to a song style in which each line is an autonomous aesthetic
unit, and the alternative use of summarising sentence structure (with

pronouns, relative pronouns and conjunctions), with its semantic carry-over, is frowned upon.

An early MacLean poem, 'Kinloch Ainort', is a run of praise-epithets, cumulative but almost static:

> A cavalry of mountains, horse-riding summits,
> a steaming headlong haste of foam,
> a slipperiness of smooth flat rocks, small-bellied bare summits,
> flat-rock snoring of high mountains.

We see the same device in the boat-poem of George Campbell Hay quoted above. This is one of the devices of Gaelic poetry most tempting to a poet from a different culture; it is also flashy, I suppose, and loads itself up until it can't go very fast. At any rate, MacLean only used it in this one poem. It resembles, perhaps, the catalogues of 'On a Raised Beach'.

MacLean uses 'the eye of the flesh' to signify dullness, self-seeking, blindness; he is far away from the regionalist poets who write about objects in the belief that objects cannot lie and so are better poetic subjects than ideas or feelings. He uses objects and landscape primarily as mnemonic shapes to guide the attention to the abstract idea he wants us to comprehend. The association of these thought-forms with longing (*fad*, distant or far, is a favourite repeated word), conjecture, aspiration and testing suggests that they have no poetic role outside human intentionality – as indeed objects do not possess intentions or display behaviour. The flourishing of spades, potatoes, farmhouses and so forth in regionalist poems represents a fear of feeling and reason, an anxiety about the merely human.

In 'For a Hundred Years of the Gaelic Society of Inverness', MacLean suggests that being on the heights simultaneously permits unique encompassing glimpses and brings problems of visibility; defects of perception is one of his favourite themes. If we connect this to the problem of perceiving Gaelic society, a task at which politicians and civil servants so often fail, it describes the periphery's case against the metropolis in general. Regionalist poets fail because they think social reality is openly visible and transparent in straightforward realist accounts, concentrating on animals and objects; whereas it is the difficulties of understanding that brought about regional resentment in the first place.

In MacLean's work the task of imagining a better future, tangled up as always with the imagining of a future personal and romantic happiness, takes place in the same space of words as the imagining of the poem, and the painstaking and precise finding and placing of words for the local task makes the Utopian enterprise lose its fog of vagueness, boundlessness and arbitrariness. The concreteness at the non-ideal level in MacLean's writing does not disguise his rarefied intents, but transforms and partially realises them. His objects are simultaneously sensuous and abstract; thinking without a vocabulary derived from sensations seems as difficult as writing poetry that piles up objects (stones, spades, potatoes and so on) without any kind of pattern-making or intentionality animating them.

After *Dain do Eimhir* (1943), MacLean published no new books. It was not until Iain Crichton Smith's version of the *Dain* came out in 1971 that more than a few scattered translations of MacLean's work became available in English (or Scots). *Springtime and Neap-tide* (1977), selected poems including MacLean's own translations into English, was a landmark in Scottish literary history, even if, one would say, thirty-five years late. *From Wood to Ridge*, the collected poems, with English translations by the author throughout, came out in 1989.

It is frustrating to be writing a survey of modern British poetry and hit the fact that the greatest contemporary British poet (in the estimation of some, including myself) is inaccessible to formal reflection because of my total ignorance of the language he writes in and its literary traditions. I stand gazing at a centre hidden by a gleam, and I do not understand what of it I can see. Scots Gaelic was itself a periphery attached to the poetic centre in Ireland, where the expensive Scottish poets used to go for training. Essays in Ross and Hendry's book make it clear that Irish Gaelic speakers can read MacLean's work without too much difficulty. The Irish dialects closest to Scotland, and to Skye, were in Ulster, and were destroyed by armed action in the years after 1610, under circumstances we all know about – history into linguistic geography. The poet's brother, Calum MacLean, did fieldwork in Western Ireland, and perhaps his native Gaelic wasn't too far from what they spoke there. Had Sorley MacLean read Classical Irish literature? Had he read the vernacular poetry, much closer to folklore, which followed the decline of the bardic tradition? The folk-songs that MacLean heard sung as a child are independent of the elaborate, aristocratic, Classical Irish tradition; but this folk tradition could be seen as a type of underdevelopment. Without the knowledge of Scottish and Irish Gaelic, one can barely even frame these questions.

Notes

1   Fionn Mac Colla, *And the Cock Crew* (London: Souvenir Press, 1977).
2   J. F. Campbell, *Popular Tales of the West Highlands*, IV (Edinburgh: Edmonston and Douglas, 1862), p. 152.
3   Eoin MacNeill, 'Introduction' to *Duanaire Finn* (Dublin: Irish Texts Society, 1908), p. xxiii.
4   The repeat-word translated as 'race' is *clann*.
5   Trans. William J. Watson, in *Scottish Verse from The Book of the Dean of Lismore* (Edinburgh: Scottish Gaelic Text Society, 1937), pp. 91, 93.
6   The Swiss scholar Heinrich Wagner wrote on this in an essay which I can no longer find. See Boyd Robertson and Iain Taylor, *Teach Yourself Gaelic* (London: Hodder and Stoughton, 1993).
7   From the *Annals of the Four Masters*, cited in J. Bardon, *A History of Ulster* (Belfast: Blackstaff, 1992).
8   Christopher Carrell (ed.), *Seven Poets* (Glasgow: Third Eye Centre, 1981), p. 47
9   Judith Ennew, *The Western Isles Today* (Cambridge: Cambridge University Press, 1980), p. 110.
10 David McCrone, *Understanding Scottish Society* (London: Routledge, 1992).
11 William J. Watson, 'Introduction', in *Bàrdachd Ghàidhlig* (Inverness: Northern Counties Publishing Company, 1918).
12 MacInnes in Raymond J. Ross and Joy Hendry (eds), *Sorley MacLean: Critical Essays* (Edinburgh: Scottish Academic Press, 1986), p. 138.
13 MacInnes in Ross and Hendry (eds), *Sorley MacLean*, p. 140.
14 Rudolf Thurneysen, *Gesammelte Schriften*, II (Tübingen: Max Niemeyer, 1991), pp. 60–98.
15 MacInnes, in Ross and Hendry (eds), *Sorley MacLean*, p. 142, using the Gaelic spelling of the poet's name.
16 MacInnes, in Ross and Hendry (eds), *Sorley MacLean*, p. 144.
17 MacInnes, in Ross and Hendry (eds), *Sorley MacLean*, p. 146.
18 MacInnes, in Ross and Hendry (eds), *Sorley MacLean*, p. 147.
19 MacInnes, in Ross and Hendry (eds), *Sorley MacLean*, p. 67.
20 Alan Bold, *MacDiarmid* (London: John Murray, 1983), pp. 345–51.
21 D. J. Williams, *Storïau'r tir coch* (Llandysul: Gwasg Aberystwyth, 1941).
22 Idris Davies, *The Angry Summer*, ed. Anthony Conran (Cardiff: University of Wales Press, 1993).
23 J. Carmichael Watson (ed.), *Mesca Ulad* (Dublin: The Stationery Office, 1941), p. 49.
24 It is visible on pp. 65, 83, 95, 97, 103, 109, 111–17, 127, 129–31, 135–37, 139, 171, 173, 175, 177, 179, 205, 245, 273 and 285 of the paperback edition of *From Wood to Ridge*.
25 Ifor Williams (ed.), *The Poems of Taliesin* (Dublin: The Dublin Institute for Advanced Studies, 1975), p. 9.

7

Putting a People in its Place:
Anglo-Welsh Poetry 1937–1979

It is extraordinary how many modern Welsh writers have been political activists. This is a quite different pattern from England. It is Atlantic radicalism, on a West coast suffering long-term economic decline and feeling itself remote from the outlook of the government in London. The regionally polarised patterns of electoral geography will presumably be reflected in poetry taking an increasingly regionalist and politically radical view. However, in the realm of the media and the powers that be (not of Welsh public opinion), these attitudes are dangerous, semi-legal, excluded from a voice in decisions. The Welsh have been frustrated and radicalised since the 1920s; as exponents of decentralisation, Welsh poets are thirty years ahead of English ones. Loyalty is given to another social system, the Utopian one, which is simultaneously boundless and too small to sustain a whole poem. The knowledge which knows of it is simultaneously crotchety and pedantic, and shapeless and tenuous like the wind.

Extremism may be a sober and thoughtful response to the extreme experiences that Wales has been through in the twentieth century. But political extremism puts wrecking stresses on the artist's sociological intelligence and political analysis; and makes the work of art hostage to issues which, decades later, may look utterly different to how the artist first saw them. But anyone who doesn't want a revolution in Wales has a lot of tangible truths to write off as accidents.

As commodities, the publications of Anglo-Welsh poetry are all very clearly identified as Welsh, and this labelling of the event precedes and controls what can happen inside the poems. This publishing enterprise came into being in a retail set-up dominated by the Anglo-American big names, and frantically sells its difference from those in order to preserve market share. Because Welsh people do not identify Wales with innovation, intelligence or aestheticism, the managers have rejected poetry displaying these characteristics as failing to hold the Welsh brand image, and so the history of Welsh poetry over the past thirty years has not seen, as in northern

England, a breakthrough into artistic autonomy. When the word 'Welsh' on the cover of a book arouses a wave of identification and possessiveness in the consumer, this practice traps them inside predefined limits, where they can prevent experiences from reaching them. This separates them from the practice I would recognise, where one only cares for the capture spiral within the poems and not for the signals on the cover. These practices are as different from each other as poetic activities founded on prayer, contemplation, trance or drugged states are from either one.

Anglo-Welsh poetry offers, then, some difficulty to the exporter; but I can recommend (apart from Dylan Thomas!) anything by David Jones; *The Angry Summer* by Idris Davies; *Collected Poems* by Alun Lewis; *Poems* and *Gods with Stainless Ears* by Lynette Roberts; *The Four-Walled Dream* by Nigel Heseltine; *Modern Welsh Poetry*, edited by Keidrych Rhys; *Selected Poems* by Glyn Jones; anything by John James; Emyr Humphreys's sequence *Ancestor Worship*; a few poems by Raymond Garlick; *Burning Brambles* by Roland Mathias; *The Lilting House*, edited by John Stuart Williams and Meic Stephens; the modern part of *The Oxford Book of Welsh Verse in English*, edited by Gwyn Jones. This poetry, still in the shadow of poetry in Welsh, which commands more loyalty whatever its literary merits, emerged as a self-consciously regional school with the magazine *Wales*, edited by Keidrych Rhys and Nigel Heseltine and published from 1937 to 1939 and then again from 1943 to 1949. The magazine was edited from London, which was also where the poets tended to meet. Poets who began publishing in the thirties include Dylan Thomas, Glyn Jones, Gwyn Jones, Idris Davies and David Jones; nothing on the same scale had preceded this. Welsh origin could be claimed for the dominant English style of the forties, since Henry Treece and Dylan Thomas had helped to shape it; that decade saw the flowering of the poets of Wales, and new poets of the time include Lynette Roberts and Alun Lewis. Rhys's *Modern Welsh Poetry*, published by Faber in 1944, is a fascinating and exotic object full of brilliant poems which have never been republished.

Lynette Roberts (1909–95)

Lynette Roberts published two volumes with Faber, *Poems* (1944) and *Gods with Stainless Ears* (1951, but written in 1943). A third book was turned down. She also published a pamphlet of short stories, *Village Dialect*, with an eccentric introduction about folk-speech. Any definitive analysis of

Roberts's work is held back by the existence of much unpublished poetry, for example the epic poem *El Dorado*, which was broadcast on the radio. (Some details of this are given in a fascinating issue of *Poetry Wales* from 1983, dedicated to Roberts. This includes extracts from her unpublished letters and autobiography.) John Pikoulis has been preparing a collected edition. Roberts gave up writing after a religious conversion in 1952, and so far as I know never returned to it; the texts in question date from the years between 1944 and 1952. Roberts was born in Argentina, since her father was a railway engineer (the British-owned Argentine railways were nationalised by Peron in 1947). The majority of her available poems refer to South America, although this includes places in Brazil and Mexico as well as Argentina. She came to London to attend the Central School of Arts and Crafts, and later worked as a florist. A first poem was published in *Wales* in 1939. She went to Wales on getting married, in 1940, to Keidrych Rhys. The story told in *Gods* is about her living in Plasnewydd, a Carmarthenshire village, during the war, and worrying about Rhys, who was serving in the anti-aircraft artillery. She then had a liaison with the poet Victor Musgrave, about whom I know nothing (except Seymour-Smith's anecdote that Musgrave went to Brighton and became a psychotherapist by the simple gesture of putting up a brass plate saying 'Psychotherapist').[1] Roberts's accounts of village life are vivid partly because it was totally unfamiliar to her; she was obviously nostalgic for South America, which is why she writes about it so much. The last thing in *Poems* is a seven-page extract from *Gods with Stainless Ears*, which was already complete by this time (and known as *Cwmcelyn*).

Gods deals with love in the form of separation: the narrator is living in poverty in a Welsh cottage while her loved one faces death from above in the army. It is about the fate of a woman in wartime; there is no action. However, there is an account of one of the great air-raids on Swansea. The air-raid on Swansea is counterbalanced by the conjecture of a great development of air transport, of geopolitical scope. This is from the part first published in *Poems* (1944):

> Air white with cold. Cycloid wind prevails.
> On ichnolithic plain where no print runs
> And winter hardens into plate of ice;
> Shoots an anthracite glitter of death
> From their eyes – these men shine darkly.
>
> With stiff betrayal, dark suns on pillow
> Of snow; but not eclipsed, for out of cauterised

Craters, a conclave of Architects with
Ichnographic plans, shall bridge stronger
Ventricles of faith. They know also

Etonic vows: the abstractions which may arise:
That magnates out of pre-fabricated
Glass, may build Chromium Cenotaphs –
Work and pay for all! Contract aerodromes
To lift planes where ships once crawled, over

Baleful continents to the Caribbean Crane.
Down, to the Southern Christ of Palms
Back on red competitive lines: chaining
Chinese fields of tungsten: above pack-ice
Snapping like wolves on Siberian shores.

In this dream documentary, pioneers die exploring pack-ice where a future set of air communications, with installations, will serve South America, spanning the Pacific and the Antarctic. I suppose the reference is to the Welsh colony in Patagonia, with no road transport to the exterior. I suppose tungsten was a raw material cut off from its markets by transport costs. 'Ichnolithology' is the study of fossil footprints, and the sense is that no-one had ever crossed those plains at ground level. 'Ichnographic' has to do with drawing up ground plans. I don't know what 'Etonic' is. This poetry is very difficult at phrasal level. Take the phrase 'Gods with stainless ears'. I am baffled by its sense, since Celtic Otherworld dogs did not have white ears: 'But of all the hounds of the world that he had seen before, he had never seen one of the same colour as them. This is the colour they had, white so bright it gleamed, with their ears of red. And as much as the whiteness of the hounds gleamed, so gleamed the redness of the ears.'[2] However, I suppose that if they shone this implies that they were without stain. Given the colour white here, it is tempting to make a link with the quotation from Revelation heading Part Five of the poem: *A gynau gwynion a roed i bob un o honynt,* 'and white gowns were given to each one of them'. (The red might be supplied from higher up: *nad ydwyt yn barnu ac yn dial ein gwaed ni,* 'are you not judging and avenging our blood?') But I think the dogs in question are in reality aeroplanes.

I take Roberts as, with Alun Lewis, the most significant new poet of the forties; and I take it that she disappeared because she was written off in bulk along with the New Romantics (including her husband and his friends), in a great error of perspective: her sense is hard to grasp, but she was a very accurate writer. The more you look at it, the more sense it makes. Take this passage about sewing a shirt for a soldier husband:

> In
> Sandals and sunsuit lungs naked to the light,
> Sitting on chair of glass with no fixed frame
> Leaned to the swift machine threading over twill:
> 'Singer's' perfect model scrolled with gold,
>
> Chromium wheel and black structure firm on
> Mahogany plinth... nails varnished with
> Chanel shocking! ears jewelled: light hand
> Tipped with dorcas silver thimble, tracing thin
> Aertex edge: slim needle and strong sharp
>
> Thread – Coats' cotton 48 – trimmings, and metal
> Buttons stitched by hand: excelling always as
> Soldier shirt finished floated down to earth.
>   (from *Gods with Stainless Ears*)

Close examination reveals a realistic description of startling precision and carefulness. Coats was a Paisley thread-maker; old Singers had curved black bodies with a gilt scroll pattern on them. Sunsuits were presumably rather simple and revealing garments.

One of the main profiles in Roberts's poetry is religiosity. It's disappointing that she should have become so very religious and yet given up poetry at the same time. Religion, the main component of popular culture and belief, represents the legitimacy of modern Anglo-Welsh poetry, and also its acceptance of a popular role. Roberts's full-page quotations from the Welsh Bible seem to fit in with this; but I'm not at all sure that her case resembles the others, given that she grew up outside Wales and was living in Sussex at the time of her conversion.

The second profile is Roberts's strong visual sensibility. Clearly her style starts from a sophisticated awareness of modern art (i.e. up to the thirties) and of the difficulty of representing anything without breaking all bounds of convention.

The Latin American profile involved chiefly wild and colourful vegetation and a sense of great distances. Writing a long poem about a possible airline seems eccentric, but is not so odd for the daughter of a railway engineer; the issues of remoteness and development are of burning interest in a country such as Argentina, most of which is still underdeveloped and remote. Taking Argentine–Australian commerce by the shortest route, over Antarctica, is a seductive idea. Although Roberts quotes at great length from the Welsh Bible (in *Gods*), she can't have been familiar with this in childhood, when in fact she attended a school run by nuns. Although she was fascinated with Wales (and, I believe, spent most of her life there), it might be more interesting to treat her as the first inrush of Latin American literature into the British world; Wilson Harris's novels of the 1940s are perhaps the most direct comparison to *Poems* and *Gods with Stainless Ears*.

The fourth profile is concern with reproducing folk speech, and realistic treatment of life in a Welsh cottage, in wartime, without much money. Again, Roberts's principal concern was with realism: describing the visible world without intrusive preconceptions, and striking off South Welsh village speech to the life.

> 'WAR. There's no sense in it.
> For us simple people
> We all get on so well.
> Hal-e-bant.
> The cows are on the move.
> I must be off on the run:
> Hal-e-bant. *pussy drwg*.
> Hal-e-bant Fan Fach.
> Hal-e-bant for the day is long
> We must strengthen it
> *Ourselves*:
> To the cows
> Fetch them in.'

I believe the Welsh dialect phrase means 'drive away', or 'drive it away' (*hal ef i bant*). Fan Fach would be the cat's name (Little Patch, addressed in the vocative?). I suppose the villages on the coast still had a few Welsh phrases scattered in their speech. What Roberts says in the introduction to *Village Dialect* is that there is a universal speech of pastoral peoples, which is very direct and concrete and rhythmic, and is the universal basis for poetry; a nonsense theory, I'm afraid. It sheds light on her creative difficulties, as someone who was both very direct and very hard to understand. She probably felt guilt at not being lyrical enough. It's common for poets who develop a very personal rhythm to bring out meretricious theories explaining that it's universal.

Roberts's husband gets mentioned in the critical histories (he liked beer and figured in the anecdotes), but she remains invisible to the whole fabric of anecdote and secondary literature. She has been unacceptable to the literary culture, whether Welsh or English.

The 1950s

Roberts was a unique writer, but some kind of context is visible in the 1944 anthology: a brilliant school of poets who vanished from sight in the post-war era. I would guess that the pressure to show communal solidarity repressed the development of style. In 1953, Dylan Thomas died; Idris Davies suffered a crisis of political beliefs and in his relationship to his own community, and died in 1953; Lynette Roberts stopped writing poetry; Glyn Jones branched out, but continued to write some poetry, which is the best of the past forty years. Many of those active in Welsh poetry fell silent for want of outlets. However, in this underground state, a stylistic purge was taking place; Apocalyptics cut their poems to the bone. Anthony Conran, in the most substantial account of Anglo-Welsh poetry yet to appear, identifies the fifties as a poor decade:

> Apart from R.S. Thomas, and the continuing work of Vernon Watkins, Anglo-Welsh poetry seemed to disappear off the face of the earth! [...] poets who had been younger contributors to *Wales* [...] stopped writing verse about this time [...] Emyr Humphreys turned to prose, and Davies Aberpennar to Welsh. My guess is that it was ultimately the change of the tide in Wales itself that prompted this silence on the part of the Anglo-Welsh. [...] The sense of stasis was overwhelming, after the excitement and dynamism of the 'thirties and 'forties. After this numbness what emerged was a poetry of exile.[3]

What we find in print is dull testimonies to friendship and parenthood.

The expectation of all English readers of Anglo-Welsh poetry is that they will find lots of poetry like Dylan Thomas's. I have to disappoint the reader; Thomas was very Welsh, but other Welsh poets can't write like Dylan Thomas. (There are certain exceptions to this.) Possibly Vernon Watkins (1906–67) put paid to writing bardically in English. No-one has imitated him despite the praise expressed for him (the title-page of *The Lilting House* calls him *y mwyaf yn ein mysg*, 'the greatest among us'). Nobody should imitate him; he was a terrible poet. Perhaps people thought his windiness was the genuine voice of the Welsh bard, and this mistake pushed a whole generation towards plainness of style. I have the impression that the bardic style became, in 1950s Wales, identified as 'high', which induced most poets to plump for 'low', for sociological reasons.

Henry Treece went right on publishing with Faber, five volumes in all, but has been quietly forgotten by general consent. R. S. Thomas (1913–2000) possesses authority without appeal, and has towered over other Welsh poets; a survivor and senior figure at a time of boom, he supplied the whole tone for poets born between approximately 1915 and 1930. He enjoys a great reputation, although I must admit that I don't like any of his work, and the prospect of reading all of it filled me with fear and despair. He was the parson of a series of remote rural parishes: to live where no educated people live suggests someone whose respect for his own intelligence knows no bounds, even as he loses the ability to argue. His work, if highly controlled, is undistinguished in style. Behind it, there are assumptions and unconscious emotions which are of iconographic interest.

He published his first volume in 1946, at the Christian end of the Apocalyptic style. Twenty or so more have followed. The story goes about Thomas – who knows if it's true? – that although an English speaker, he refuses to speak English to any visitors, or to his parishioners. Certainly he stood up at a National Eisteddfod and said that anyone who didn't try to speak Welsh was an un-person in Welsh terms. Words such as 'self-righteous', 'rigid', 'vindictive', 'tyrannical', 'nationalistic' and 'punitive' spring to mind. Thomas remarks in his autobiography, *Neb*, that he wanted to live in a rural parish because his aim was to expound the Gospel, and the symbolic language of the Gospel was brought to life in the natural furnishings of such a place, which had, for example, sheep everywhere. The landscape is not there for itself, but to illustrate truths of which he is already certain: this strains the relationship between poet and reader, who, if no new information is on offer, is only present as either a dutiful pupil or a recalcitrant one. His poems are compact: there is a line of sensibility to be drawn between those who think the apodictic is bad, and those who think that explaining arguments and qualifying statements is bad, because it wastes time.

Neb shows Thomas's four great political preoccupations: the problem of poverty, anti-Englishness, the wrongness of war, and the need to preserve nature from humankind. As he remarks, remoteness from population centres, lack of time to study public affairs, obedience to his ecclesiastical superiors, and a decision to concentrate on pastoral duties and on poetry prevented him from involvement in politics. His poetry is all moulded by political beliefs, which show the outlines of communitarianism, and even its prehistory in thirties pacifism; but it shows no political thought. He was totally unused to meetings, to argument, to the exchange of ideas, to questioning or expounding his own ideas.

The parish clergyman is liable to become either a radical or a snob, and for Thomas it was the former. He is not a smooth and urban character, and *really* dislikes the middle class and the English. His thorough dislike of anyone above the lower class explains his anti-Englishness: since he lived in Wales all his life, he never learnt anything at all about the English, except for the English-speakers in his parish, who were genealogically Welsh, and were the landowners. You can't hate a lot of people you've never met; or, if you do, your feelings have a vacant quality – which is the main flavour of Thomas's poetry. He blames war on English militarism; but very few historians believe that England arranged the wars of 1914 or 1939. This belief is popular, it seems, among clergy and other educated people in Ireland, Scotland and Wales. Thomas's poetry says nothing about a social ideal, because it almost always deals with solitary humans, as an upland and pastoral landscape indeed supplies; dialogue is very rare in it. If Thomas seems not to be on intimate terms with the reader, this is partly because only middle-class people read poetry, and he hates them. He rejects the refinement and qualification of argument in poetry partly because he rejects the refinement of social standing and discrimination which a vicar comes up against every day. As he says, 'little things plain and without show appealed to him', just after using the same word (*rhodres*) to say that he hates cathedrals, full of 'show and banners of war'. This takes us back to the cult of littleness of the Georgian poets, from whom he got his stylistic start.

Thomas rejects, in Christian exposition, the intellectual and dialectical works that followed the New Testament, and the metaphysical style which was the greatest achievement of Anglican poetry. Thomas never uses paradox, because things seem straightforward to him. He has said that when he moved to Aberdaron, in Llŷn (in about 1970, I think) his themes changed from man to 'the question of the soul, the nature and existence of God, and the problem of time in the universe',[4] topics which someone might well have written about in AD 200. His staging of the philosophical movement of doubt, speculation, competition between alternatives, revelation and so on is elaborate but not quite intelligent enough. When he argues with God, it is too hard to tell which voice is which. He is vastly more intellectual than any other Anglo-Welsh poets, Roland Mathias excepted. His late poems have a puzzled, dogged and non-angry tone, obstinately searching for a God who clearly isn't there.

His typical rants against the machine are dissolved here by a fascination with astronomy, seen as a way of finding God coded in the starlight (as the wise men from the East did in Matthew chapter 2). Thomas's gales of disapproval assume authority; in fact he seems like the last of a breed of patriarchs, the boundaries of his moral and political decrees the more sharply defined and brusquely uttered because most of the people around him see them as unreal distinctions. His concern with boundaries seems, today, like a paranoid territoriality, dialogue and social imagination crushed by an excess of testosterone. If poets should show a mix of beauty and moral authority, Thomas's mix has one ingredient almost absent. Yet he is very popular. That gruff, grumpy, comminatory, patriarchal tone is a flavour people want to consume.

Conran states that the 'interregnum' of 1953–65 ended with the first number of *Poetry Wales*, if not with the start of Triskel Press in 1963.[5] This magazine was edited from Merthyr Tydfil: the institutional base has shifted away from London, there is a new graduate audience in Wales, and from 1967 the era of regional Arts Councils is upon us. Here is the start of the movement that should interest us most: here also is where Conran's book ends. Conran refers to these poets as the Second Flowering, the first having been the poets who published in *Wales*, and we would include Emyr Humphreys (b. 1919), Leslie Norris (b. 1921), John Ormond (b. 1923), Raymond Garlick (b. 1926), John Tripp (b. 1927), Anthony Conran (b. 1931), Brenda Chamberlain (b. 1912), Harri Webb (b. 1920) and T. Harri Jones (b. 1921) – largely, the generation born in the 1920s. The 1969 anthology *The Lilting House*[6] collects their best poems, and is recommended. Ormond, Mathias and Humphreys were in the 1944 anthology; others had begun publishing in the fifties, but had met with many frustrations and, so to speak, missed their entrance. They don't show any resemblances to the radical English poets who emerged from about 1964 onwards; they were not students in 1963. (Welsh student radicalism was Nationalist.) The two staples were Georgian poetry and the academic poetic variant of Christian moralising which had then seized universities all over the Western world; easy of access, and codified notably in the Australian Vincent Buckley's *Poetry and Morality*. The theology of the fifties – Sartre, Kierkegaard, Buber, and perhaps Jacques Maritain and Gabriel Marcel – called for moral agonising. Personalism was important – a withdrawal from the state articulated by Bonhoeffer's 'religionless Christianity', elaborated by Albrecht Ritschl in the nineteenth century, and presumably the parent of communitarianism. A preoccupation with personal witness against the wicked and mighty followed the compliance of the Catholic and official Lutheran churches with the demands of Hitler, and the communist attack on the weak social commitment of the churches. When Raymond Garlick witnessed police mistreatment of nationalist protesters in the late 1960s, he had been waiting for the sight for twenty years; scene and observer exactly matched, and these are important poems.

Anglo-Welsh Poetry and the Regionalist Ideology

Even as someone suspicious of Saxons and the South, I have to admit that poems by individual Anglo-Welsh authors resemble each other, and poems by different authors resemble each other even more, if possible. There is a Standard Anglo-Welsh Poem, whose set terms are fields, stones, old houses, cemeteries, ancestors, old legends, manual work, village characters, family members, guilt, memory. Quite probably such themes reflect common Welsh experience, frustrations and sensibility, repeated because they are true, and would instantly appeal to Welsh people without any literary education. This standard poem uses the word 'roots' because it is stylistically afraid of the word 'morals'; it exhibits the regionalist ideology, as I have described it: blood, sod, spades, God. Everything is a projection of family values: relations to ancestors are simply relations to parents in a different form. This is the pivotal substitution in political symbolism: family relations, showing equality, repression and solidarity, scaling up to a view of how the land should be governed. The talk is all of obligations and respect. But the poetry is unable to portray family life, especially to portray a vision of a happy family.

We read that Maurice Barrès wrote a daily article on the war throughout the First World War; Welsh nationalism does not have this broad narrative stock in trade, but is frequently Christian, pacifist, anti-imperialist, and decentralising. Instead of raids and conquests, we have the *ecclesia*, with particularism as the wall that protects it. The main policy of the Plaid was defending the Welsh language: *Achub y Gymraeg, achub Cymru* (save Welsh, save Wales), as Ambrose Bebb put it in an article in the twenties.[7] The census figures for people able to speak Welsh have steadily dropped, from 54.4 per cent of the population of Wales in 1891, to 43.5 per cent in 1921, 36.8 per cent in 1931, 26 per cent in 1961, 20.8 per cent in 1971, 18.9 per cent in 1981 and 18.6 per cent in 1991. Although the quantitative decline has stabilised in recent years, replaced by qualitative decline, the Plaid seems to have lost this cause. I don't see how it can continue as a party now this issue is closed; I don't see how a nationalist party can confine itself to the 20 per cent of the population that speaks Welsh. Emyr Humphreys dances around this question without admitting it is there. How can you define Welshness if it's not by language? What objective are you fighting for? This rigidification of views, ignoring of evidence, sense of dread before the unknown, is not wholly atypical of the Anglo-Welsh poets.

The plan for protecting Welsh was immobility and autarky. Local communities were to be self-sufficient and no outsiders were to have power within them. Land, for example, was to stay with Welsh people and not to be alienated to the highest bidder, who could force the people from their own soil. In this way every threat could be averted. This was not a perfectly clear policy, so we need not explore its every implication. It is quite against everything being property that can be bought, so that loose masses of money have all the social power. The two are not incompatible: I mean that society could operate with a private sector run by capital, and a government whose laws modify that power and offer protection to the poor. Local government is quite capable of influencing a town away from supermarkets (which are typically owned by large corporations) and towards small shops which are locally owned. The shopkeepers might also be Welsh-speaking; the removal of all influences more distant than a few miles was a way of protecting Welsh – which was threatened by migration, trade, transport, and broadcasting, among other things. Broad horizons actually did mean English horizons.

The case for devolution is that the British civil servants don't have the local expertise that Welsh ones would have. So reciting local knowledge in vast detail, with repeated and sentimentally dramatised scenes showing the ignorance of the English, is one poetic form of arguing for nationalism; but how unappealing must be, to anyone outside, the constant imputation that not knowing who Mrs Huws's second cousins are disqualifies you from being intelligent or having an opinion.

Three everyday forms of knowledge are topology (the distribution of objects in space), genealogy (as an extension of relationships within the household), and work skills. All of these are attractive to a nationalist poet, as defining the life of the community, which must be protected from change; we can imagine a poem about an old sampler (manual skills) handed down from a great-grandmother (genealogy) who lived at a particular farmhouse (locality). But these forms of knowledge are also all intensely boring, and in fact the first imperative of literature must have been to get away from this kind of information and to find something else to fill its columns with. Knowledge of other human beings (recognition, retention of their kinships and alliances, knowledge of their standing in the social hierarchy) is basic to our psychic structure, and goes back to pre-human social apes; but that knowledge must be transformed to be available to poetry. In preparing this chapter, I have come across a certain number of Welsh names, and I hope I can remember the separate identity of most of them; there are two Gwyn Williamses, two Gwyn Thomases, but Tony Conran is Anthony Conran and Ormond Thomas is John Ormond; this is knowledge, but not in the same way that a line of poetry is knowledge. Wales is a small country; I was struck to find out that Emrys ap Iwan was the teacher of T. Gwynn Jones, but the prospect of all those names, all those places, all those jobs, is utterly dispiriting: information without higher pattern knocks you out.

I didn't really understand the Anglo-Welsh poem until I read *Yn chwech ar hugain oed*, by D. J. Williams, and *Cwm Eithin*, by Hugh Evans. These are classical works on which the poems are dependent. The Georgian poets were similarly overshadowed by the prose works of Richard Jefferies – which at their best resemble D. J. Williams. The argument around Anglo-Welsh poetry has been blocked by mutual incomprehension: the aesthetic ideal behind the poetry exists in verbal form, but in the form of great prose works of an older generation. Attacking the ideal was, really, misguided; but the poems had a structural weakness, as this sort of aesthetic is not really suited to the short poem. The Anglo-Welsh poem knows more than it is telling. There are two great modern poets in Welsh: Waldo Williams and Euros Bowen.

The depiction of the human figure is a great point of weakness in this poetry: occupying so much of the surface area, but so compromised by the initial Christian presuppositions. In this area we find the claims to authenticity, made in the prose that advocates the poetry, making it superior to art poetry; and the awkward discrepancies that prevent the poetry from fulfilling the charming ideals of the prose. The unrespectable characters of the Georgian model were eliminated from the copy, which, with its stress on morality, had no sympathy to spare for sinners. The central heroic figure is the virtuous man (who is also Welsh nationalist, cultured, politically sincere, selfless, and so on); the prodigal son cannot edge on stage even to show repentance. The resultant style has already been described. A reminiscence of pastoral care is the belief that unrelenting attention to the fabric of people's lives is seriousness and authenticity; so that prolonged descriptions of someone knitting or digging potatoes, or of the garments they knitted and the potatoes they dug, are the practice of virtue. Even a small dose of this is enough to prevent you writing an interesting poem ever again. The *locus classicus* for this is Gillian Clarke's 'The Far Country', a poem unexcelled in its direction.

The genre of *cof* (also *cofiant, cofadwriaeth*) is one of the more important genres in Welsh-language tradition. Literally it means memory, but by extension it means biography, and in particular the kind of laudatory, pious biography put together and read by loyal pupils, sons and disciples. The possibilities in describing the life of a nineteenth-century clergyman are rather restricted. This genre has profoundly influenced the presentation of the human subject in Anglo-Welsh poetry; no tradition of reportage has existed in Wales to supply a more sceptical and informative model of describing character. In daily life, there is gossip, something astutely used by certain writers, but unfortunately *cof* is more prestigious. Indeed the whole Second Flowering way of writing about Wales is *cof*-like, reverential, stiff and banal. Not much attempt is made to interest the reader. Because the subject is being praised for being Welsh and for exemplifying Welsh social values, and inevitably resembles the composer of the *cof*, the tone is always close to self-praise.

Self-esteem is a factor too often neglected in literary criticism, but this kind of exchange of honorifics is of little interest to the reader. These social relationships can perhaps only be made writable through stories. The assignment of social status by poetry is closely related to the function of shame. Many people are ashamed of the sound of their own voice: this is context-conditioned, and the printed page is one of the most unnerving and shaming contexts. The solidarity exhibited in so much Welsh poetry aims to establish that the poetry is a sympathetic, non-shaming context. Poetry is naive in its identification of the poem with the personality; the sound of someone's voice conveys almost too much information about their age, sex, size, social origins and emotional stability, and the poem is a projection of the voice. This tying of the voice to social presentation and standing makes the rules of narcissism the rules of the poem.

Character is poorly evoked when an individual has no choice between different ways of behaving, and the literary context lacks other characters making real the choices and their consequences. Recent Welsh literature has a dreadful inhibition on satire, a shortcoming we notice all the more when we place it against Welsh conversation, in which gossip and humour play vital roles, and the older religious prose, which can go deep into psychology while drawing the line between right and wrong. Patriotism has prevented Welsh writers from a calm depiction of social forces in conflict. If we put together the elements of fearfulness about the future, distaste for everyday life, a strong sense of norms, a sense of mission, a frustrated wish to exercise power, a feeling of defeat, psychological blocks shutting out much of contemporary reality, and conservative and religious values, we can see why the literature of the Second Flowering was mainly thorns. It retreats into honorific eulogies to Good Men and into inhuman evocations of stones and tombs. Welsh people usually appear either as symbols (of authenticity) or as victims. The motif of the hermit in Humphreys's poems represents authenticity, tied to a place and not compromising, but he has abandoned life.

Another form of knowledge is topography. Owen M. Edwards writes:

> *Mae'r oll yn gysegredig…* It is all sacred. Every hill and every valley. Our land is a living thing, not a dead grave. Every hill has its history, every locality its own romance. Every vale is new, every region has its own glory. And to a Welshman, no other country can be like this. A Welshman feels that the struggles of his forefathers have sanctified every field, and the genius of his country has consecrated every mountain. And feeling like this makes him a true citizen.[8]

So the evocation of hills and fields comes to take on a momentum which has nothing to do with pictorial values. Place is also the parish, the deserted site where the community used to reside. The educated man of an earlier time possessed authority by virtue of holding office in a parish, and as a result of the abandonment of the central ceremonial space learned speech has been reduced to a commodity. The tension is between social control and aesthetic appeal. Underlying the sense of desolation and irrecoverable damage, which is present in quite a few poems by committed nationalists, is an archaic physical identification: attribution of moral virtues, or pain and wrongs, to the land; the run-down state of the countryside in certain of R. S. Thomas's poems is the projection of a psycho-physical state. By this paranoia the image of some malign central force, an Influencing Machine, acquires body, so that the literary argument is 'these fields would be more fertile if not for the English'. This projection was so over-used in the 1940s that it fell out of favour. 'Welsh Bastard', a poem by T. H. Jones, says that his father died at the battle of Camlann (fifth century), and his father at the battle of Catraeth (late sixth century), and so on. This transcendence of individual identity is an extension of family values to nationalism; the more generations you go back, the more people are related to you, and at some point you reach a horizon where all Wales is one super-family – a liminal zone where divisions vanish and the personality is either effaced or universal.

This sense of consecration (we may recognise this Latin word in *cysegredig*) gives rise to a punitive and pernickety bearing. Lived life has been reduced to the act of paying respect – something unreasonable to request of the reader. Where does it leave beauty, the imagination, pleasure? No doubt hostility to strangers is a deep human instinct; the topographical poem is exclusive and possessive. The poem has to attract people to come in, and tolerate them when they have come in. It's uncomfortable being in a poem where you feel the writer is watching you like a hawk, indignation at the ready, in case you show that you lack respect for their great-grand-mother, and that they're ready to glow with vindictive triumph if it turns out that you *don't* know how far Mynachlog is from Llynachmog. Welsh people do spend a certain amount of time making fun of the English; but they want to spend almost all their time making fun of people from other parts of Wales. Somehow this local rivalry doesn't appear in the poetry – perhaps one reason why it lacks the movement and vivacity of conversation.

Another strand is the sanctity of labour. This can as well be socialist as nationalist. The Scandinavian kind of study of folk life pioneered by Iorwerth Peate at the Welsh National Museum in Cardiff, and in his books such as *Diwylliant gwerin Cymru* (*Welsh Folk Culture*, 1942), is almost entirely about material culture, for example the house, the hearth, furniture, clothes, carts, farm implements. Peate remarks that there is no place for a study of the fine arts in Wales, since there are few traces of them and those there are are not peculiarly Welsh. The study of material culture was most attractive to small countries in which high culture was exiguous and mainly imported. Peate notes that the Folk Culture section of the Welsh National Museum, founded in 1936, was the first of its kind in the Empire. Farm implements and household goods do offer the possibility of studying the life of the people as a whole, and not just the aristocracy. Peate's book is fascinating; when he shows a photograph of a horse harnessed to a sled (*car llusg*), one instantly realises the difficulty of working a farm where the slopes, the rain, and the lack of paved surfaces made wheeled transport impossible, how hard it was to make any money on such hills. But what of a poet who thinks that piling up endless stocklists of pitchforks and kitchen ranges represents poetic quality or vividness?

Another interpretation has to do with the insecurities of middle-class employees in the caring professions; because they rise economically by exhibiting a form of attention which involves both compassion and supervision, any moment of selfishness makes them anxious. Contemporary British poetry in general is written and read by teachers, and tends to be tediously under-motivated for non-teachers. This supervisory and competitive care makes it impossible either to construct interesting characters or to write exciting poetry in the first person. But by now reading tedious poetry has become a demonstration of fitness.

Not facts, but the overall behavioural regimes within which facts are manipulated, must draw our attention; there is a split between levels of education in ways of dealing with facts, and this has a class implication because those who reach the higher levels are few. Jackson and Marsden, in *Education and the Working Class*, remark that there is a shift between schools and universities, but already felt during A-levels, from memorisation to asking why.[9] Welsh nationalist poetry has the overall pattern of argument pre-set, and so marshals the variable details. The rejection of conceptual thought in favour of concrete detail sets the poetry at a low position on the class scale, i.e. corresponding to secondary education. The appetite of poetry readers, including me, for ideas is influenced by the allure of secondary education, but is mighty when frustrated. This low tone either builds a constituency by appealing to a broad spectrum, or puts the cap on oppression by withdrawing the privilege of the oppressed, which is to think and speculate.

Both socialist and nationalist writers are so emotionally committed to collectivism, radicalism and distaste for the English that they can use the same imagery. As Jeremy Hooker points out, there is a convenient presentation of the two opposite sides in Humphreys's *The Taliesin Tradition* and *When was Wales?* by the Marxist Gwyn A. Williams.[10] Humphreys's account of recent Welsh history is alarmingly inadequate. It is based on wrong or dubious notions about national and personal identity. Something else very disappointing is that there is almost no consideration of Anglo-Welsh literature. The explanation for both of these aspects, as well as for the paranoia and visions of doom that Humphreys supplies in such generous measure, is that he has been a Welsh Nationalist Party member since 1939, and sees Welsh politics through the single issue of the preservation of the language. English-speaking Welshmen are either kept off stage or turned into demons. *The Taliesin Tradition* is actually a pseudo-political book written at the mythical level; it is not really about culture (as works) or about history in the quantitative, analytical sense. Humphreys's view of his own lifetime is unconvincing because he's committed to a party, which was also a losing one, and to a cause, a lost one. His denunciations of Labour and Anglophones are indirect, launched without fire, slippery: not an overt attack, just undermining and pitying.

The Old Testament Strain

Humphreys paints a picture of the annihilation of Wales, planned in the 1950s by faceless bureaucrats. This is simple paranoia and he makes no attempt to provide any sources or proof for his fantasies. There is no central power in Britain able to do such things, least of all under a Conservative government as in the 1950s. This is merely the infantile image of desolation. The inability to contemplate certain possibilities leads to their becoming psychic voids and images of disaster. Humphreys shares these blind spots with his characters. In his sequence *Ancestor Worship* (published 1970), Poem IX shows someone retiring to lead the life of a hermit, after a massacre that has traumatised him (this is based on a medieval poem, no. 19 in the *Oxford Book of Welsh Verse*). Humphreys seems unable to associate this hermit fantasy with the alienation which urban people feel, and which he imagines a close community can stave off: experiences similar at the biochemical level are disconnected by him, and interpreted in opposite ways. The Second Flowering offers not the absence of alienation, but its presence dressed up in affabulations drawn from Christian myth. In fact, it does not offer the experience of integration: as they were writing, these poets were a political minority in Wales, and the situation of the Welsh language got worse every year.

Humphreys reiterates that Anglicisation means indifference and paralysis and alienation: it is not just the means of political defeats, but is a defeat in itself. He uses the word 'identity' but has no theory to back it up; his criteria for judging history are not made clear. He writes off every Anglicising move in tones of gloom and horror, but never tries to prove that Anglicisation is a bad idea. It's a circular argument: everyone who stops speaking Welsh is a traitor and therefore to stop speaking Welsh is bad, because it is the action of evil men. 'Show me a man who disowns his own language and I will show you a man who will renounce his Christ when the time comes for equally sordid reasons', as Emrys ap Iwan wrote in the 1870s, right at the beginning of Welsh nationalism. But by now

Wales is 80 per cent English-speaking: are 80 per cent of Welsh people Judases? The vexation besetting Anglo-Welsh poets is not the attitude of the English, but the Old Testament execrations to which they are subject from Welsh nationalists. Our poets use the rebuking tone of the Old Testament, both of its historical books and of its prophets. Indeed, the whole of the Old Testament can be seen as a compilation of conservative Jewish nationalists filled with fury against other Jews who adopted the more appealing customs of modern times and neighbouring nations. This model had already been adopted by Gildas, the first known Welsh writer, in the fifth century; it was a favourite of the Puritan classics, and even of such an Anglican prose writer as Theophilus Evans; it hangs over the Anglo-Welsh poets, or at least Humphreys, R. S. Thomas and Raymond Garlick. The Old Testament priests had a way of speaking to the nation. The poets face a crisis of authority: they aren't ordained or called by a congregation, so they must agitate within the texts to impute that there is a code of laws and that they are fit to be judges of it.

Humphreys cannot deal with modern history because he refuses to countenance the possibility that English-speaking people are more than ghosts, delinquents, moral wrecks. He is not assessing events in terms of economics or literary achievement, things subject to inspectable evidence, but in terms of identity, an impalpable stage property which wiggles around like ectoplasm. I found Humphreys's sense of nothingness interesting: if you leave the room where we are all together, you will cease to exist. While I admit that the Apocalypse has struck in many parts of Wales during the twentieth century, his analysis ignores economics and even leaves out politics in the usual sense: it is only about language and solidarity with tradition. This fear of the dark is one of the results of strong group feeling. It is difficult in this atmosphere for an artist to achieve solitude, to achieve any autonomy from total community. It is difficult to think abstractly. Humphreys does not ask where alienation is found, but merely decides that it is found wherever English is spoken, and expects us not to notice him doing this. This question is too important to be left to patriarchal revelators.

A concealed agenda has hindered the logical structure of Humphreys's book: it is not history, merely a string of splendidly told historical vignettes with some solemn moralising to give it weight. It gives memorable pen portraits of a number of people you need to know about in order to follow arguments about Wales; but you already need to know quite a lot in order to unstitch the careful calumnies and suppressions of facts in Humphreys's suspiciously integrated narrative. The myth of closeness, usually measured by knowledge of Welsh, holds that everyone is equally close while simultaneously giving a firm yardstick, since not everyone speaks Welsh, for stating that some are closer than others. The Welsh-speaking community, whose few thousand members are held to represent Wales, and which is seen to imply both knowledge and sympathy, is a model for what the Anglo-Welsh book offers: insiderness. The poetry offers exercises in being Welsh, practice hours in the sense that a learner of Welsh needs hours of conversation practice in a Welsh-speaking environment. The writer's knowledge claim that 'I'm more like you than you are' also claims that 'I can make you become more like you than you are'.

Nationalist discourse insists on the myth of identity, a concept I have tried to throw out. If identity exists, it is an asset to the Welsh nationalists, because the English-speaking Welsh have less identity, even if they are perfectly happy and prosperous. But only about 11 per cent of the Welsh population ever votes for Plaid Cymru. People want gratification; more abstractly, they want wealth, power, standing. Can we imagine someone who has wealth, power, health and standing, and who is still unhappy? It's convenient for parties who are permanently out of power to invent imaginary problems: the government can't solve them, but is unable to accuse the minority party of similarly failing.

Bobi Jones published in 1986 a 21,000-line poem, *Hunllef Arthur*, which is a mythical account of Welsh history, similar in plan to *The Taliesin Tradition*. Jones, brought up an English speaker, missed being an Anglo-Welsh poet by learning Welsh in his teens. Closeness is applied to history by flattening out any differences between eras: everybody talks like a fervently Christian Anglo-Welsh poet of the 1950s. Arthur tells his men that they are fighting to avoid being a 'psychological colony' (*trefedigaeth seicolegol*). Change and conflict are excluded from history, which becomes a simultaneous realisation of a timeless, crystalline structure of Christian community, strained and blurred only by oppression from outside (from a *dark land to the east*). Just as the Nonconformist world set its face, from 1840 or so, against the advance of Bible criticism, and so against modernity, so nationalism, while claiming to be a conversion experience in which the truth is revealed, is not compatible with the study of history from the sources. *Hunllef Arthur* is a large-scale poem, and probably a fuller realisation of the ideals of the Second Flowering than anything in English.

There are perhaps 48 million English people just next door, able to read Anglo-Welsh poetry; but the attack on educated English people makes it rather difficult to promote the poetry in England. When the nationalist philosopher J. R. Jones refers angrily to 'the negative and submissive craving for "dialogue" and "tolerance"',[11] you get the feeling that those men out digging in the potato-field aren't looking for their roots, but making a grave for Englishmen caught by nightfall. The English tourist in Anglo-Welsh literature has the rare opportunity of discovering an alien society without learning a new language. However, if the imagination has a definite form, given by social experience, the literature will remain inaccessible to foreigners, because of its way of seeing the world. But in fact the successive styles of English poetry – neo-Romantic, Movement, Existentialist, pop – show an overwhelming *similarity* to contemporary Welsh styles. It isn't as if Nonconformism, mining, manufacturing, the family, unemployment, sheep, hills, rain, the sea, were unknown quantities in England (and English poetry). The common run of English poetry is regionally based, full of concrete things, moralising, preoccupied with family responsibilities and a nebulous sense of the past, foggy with guilt, just like Welsh poetry. Possibly, being so slighted by the English reading public arouses dark thoughts about prejudice and low status and not being taken seriously. Jeremy Hooker seems to be driven more by a sense of obligation than by aesthetic delight. An Englishman surrounded by hostile Welsh will express devout respect for tribal sacred objects. The poets, annoyed by being the object of tourism, may be perfectly happy to irritate readers from 'outside'. But how can you be a writer read outside your own region without being effectively a tourist attraction? Can reading be so different from tourism? By sourness, refusal to cooperate, outbursts of scorn for what is precious to other people, you threaten the reader who does not ascribe to you the status you wish. Under pressure both from England and from Welsh Wales, these writers mostly perceive themselves as an out-group, and their poetry is furrowed by an angry search for defensible assets ('identity').

The Spread of English

The exhortation to lead a more Welsh way of life is tautologous as a social reform. To break out of the self-referential loop, we ought to go back to the nineteenth century and a self-confident Welsh community: there are indications that the clergy of that time saw Welsh ignorance of English as a way of preserving the flock from modern and subversive ideas, as did, analogously, the clergy of Brittany and Flanders. The excessive touchiness about sticking to one language rather than another may connect with a desire to preserve a rigidly ordered society and to prevent the arrival of a loose, typically twentieth-century society, in which leisure activities can unfold without constant moral policing. This looseness applies to morals but also to challenging the authority of social superiors – something Methodism has always been down on. The nationalist vision of a dis-ordered society may turn out to be socialist South Wales.

In Islwyn Ffowc Elis's *Cysgod y cryman*, an attack on proletarian con-sumerist behaviour, not atypical of the period (the 1940s), is signalled by the character in question using a remarkable number of English words in his Welsh. The landowning family on whom the novelist's interest centres, however, speaks a Welsh with no Anglicisms whatsoever. Cymric purity is thus a signal not only of bilingualism and social connections outside the parish (they can recognise Anglicisms because they have such a good command of English), but also of moral integrity and an intent to preserve things as they are.

The drift of the Welsh people away from Welsh has been one of their most marked behaviour patterns, along with the drift away from the churches, which it closely resembles. Welsh writers, outside the socialist culture of the south-east, have indignantly rejected both attractions. They disapprove of the Welsh people. The appeal of English was partly practical, to do with passing exams and getting jobs, and partly very light and subjective: people became fluent in English partly because they were attracted to magazines, films and radio programmes in English, or because using English words had snob appeal, which using English altogether exerted more encompassingly. In the world of small towns and rural settlements, people who have seen a wider world are respected as more intelligent and better informed: of course knowing English, a little or a lot, was a sign of this in the rural world of Welsh Wales. No-one wants to appear ignorant, so people ornamented their speech with snatches of English. This snatching up of what glitters and fascinates and attracts must be one of the principles underlying literary appeal; compare the import of French words into English. Stopping this kind of flow is like stopping people from reading magazines or eating sweet things: you can manage it, but it goes against the grain. Even if the purists hiss like kettles, the acquisition of English is a natural process in which ordinary people follow their inclinations. If they regret it in moments of retrospect, it's like someone regretting eating biscuits: if I hadn't eaten all those biscuits, I wouldn't be fat. But at the time you wanted to eat them, and they were very pleasant. So which is your real self? Anglicisation has been the product of thousands of unconscious decisions, the result of consumer choice. Of course, it has also been more drastic in the case of people migrating to an English-speaking area, or marrying someone who doesn't speak Welsh.

We can characterise the urge to learn Welsh, on the other hand, in terms of middle-class respect for education and diligence: you go to the evening class instead of going down the pub. The poetry of the 1950s made much of the opposition between mass consumer behaviour (ice-creams and supermarkets are often mentioned) and authentic behaviour, which is tangled up with education and diligence. But there is another interpretation of the Welsh intellectuals' notion of identity, namely that it aims for a vast increase in social control, that it seeks to displace central government and commodity capitalism in order to hand power over to an educated minority, a 'moral elite' of local residence, and that it represents social values which matter very little to most people. The oscillation we have to keep in mind is that between 'the values of society' and 'the way people like to behave'; if someone doesn't observe certain values, in what sense do those values belong to them?

To grasp the sense of frustration of the educated and nationalist Welsh, we have to go back to history. The social order in many parts of Wales at the beginning of the twentieth century was the rule of the Nonconformist chapels, exercising a grip on the individual consciences of the people, and less creditably wielding the force of ostracism and contempt. This network was overwhelmingly local and face to face; it was justified in front of everyone's eyes by the verbal magic of preaching, by which the pastors demonstrated their fitness to lead, and where the congregation experienced not only inner emotion but also intense togetherness. The driving force of the conversion waves (*diwygiad*) was the visible energy and faith of the newly converted. Failures – to take over the whole country, to bring about the kingdom of God, to achieve total happiness – could also be blamed on the *godly's* lack of faith. This atmosphere of frenzy and guilt soaked its way into Anglo-Welsh poetry. Poets seem to be accepting the blame for the failure of the Welsh language to take over the whole of Wales, as the nationalists exhorted. The Methodists (in particular) went in for introspection and psychological analysis, with a favoured set of inner events to which the godly wished to conform (or to which they were expected to conform) in their upward path. However, the poetry is notably weak on psychological analysis. So far as I can see, this is true of modern Welsh fiction too: stress is laid on concrete details.

The chapel was institutionally linked, via shared local leaders, with the Liberal Party, which was electorally dominant in Wales from the late nineteenth century, but was also, periodically, in power at Westminster and hence ruler of the whole British Empire – an ally not to be ignored. The chapels were almost entirely Welsh-speaking. Their clergy were the Welsh intelligentsia, writing many of the books and determining which books could be read; their deacons and men of influence were local notables, lawyers, shopkeepers, well-off farmers, powerful but still part of the community. This monopoly, over four or five decades, of public authority was the reward for winning a struggle against the Welsh Tory Party, for centuries disposing of seats as the apanage of the landowners, but fatally handicapped, after the arrival of the secret ballot, by the association with this tiny minority of Anglican gentry and clergy. This made for a single-party country. Even the trade union leaders were tightly linked to the Liberal and Nonconformist establishment. The big estates were largely broken up and sold in the aftermath of this political revolution; the Church was disestablished and lost its tithes; the long-distance power links vanished, replaced by short-distance links. Wales was controlled by a network of local religious authorities, running community life, and allied both to business and to the government. They effectively were the government of Wales. Devolution would be a return to this state of affairs.

This monopoly was shattered in the elections of 1922 and 1923, when Labour came to hold the majority of Welsh seats. This was a change of sweeping importance. It seems that the power of the chapel in Wales had been exaggerated: a very large proportion of the population were not religious at all, and with adult male suffrage arriving in 1918, they now had the vote. Dissent had always been a middle-class movement, albeit upwardly mobile and resentful of the squires. It was centred on social control: presumably a large part of the society being controlled resisted this grip. Other factors were the over-enthusiastic commitment of the chapel (carried away by adulation of Lloyd George) to the World War, the rise of mass trade unions replacing the old narrow-based craft ones, the collapse of the Welsh language in the south-east, the industrial conflicts of the Edwardian era, with their sequel in the involvement of the unions in the counsels of government as a concession to maintain war production, and even the arrival of cinema replacing pulpit oratory as a form of popular entertainment. The Liberals retained electoral support, but the chapels were on the wane. This was the moment which allowed a new Welsh Nationalist Party to emerge, in 1925. The absence of the Liberals from modern literature is puzzling, but is partly explained by the fact that Plaid Cymru adopted their philosophy and even their social base among the clergy of Welsh Wales. More important, throughout, was the rise of the Labour movement and its Marxist rivals. Meurig Walter's splendid 'Seminary' speaks for many:

Here there are men who vomit words
and make an art of bumping heads
against the Citadel of God,
and bump the bruise to numb the pain.

Obese with thought, they sprawl and watch
God bubbling in the mind's retort,
and check their graphs by tests supplied
by Brunner, Berdyaev and Barth.

They thumb the leaves of yellow books.
Their backs crook with the sack of thoughts
they pilfer from the bins of men
who kept an open house for God.
(quoted from *Modern Welsh Poetry*)

Gwyn Jones, in the earliest definition of the Anglo-Welsh scene, described it as a revolt against Nonconformism;[12] but even as he wrote this, it was becoming a flight back into Nonconformism. The nationalists are not a creative and modernising and self-conscious formation: they are a disenfranchised former ruling class. The Liberal Party had swept the board, in the 1880s, by redefining the Welsh ruling class, the old families in the halls, as English; the Nonconformist conscience was wholly committed to small communities, which could be morally policed, and where shame was a mighty force. The Plaid's distrust of the London government drew on historical suspicions of the Church of England and of the wars started by the mighty British state. The power taken away from London was to be taken on by men of local influence and standing – in practice, perhaps the pastors and the deacons of the chapel.

The modern period is marked by the struggle of two intelligentsias: the nationalist one, consisting of clergymen, teachers, civil servants, journalists and university staff; and the Socialist one, often working in just such jobs, but also in trade unions and in the Labour Party. There is also to some extent a geographical split, between industrial Wales and the more traditional north and west. The Plaid's visions of social collapse have the ring of revivalist meetings, it has stuck to a notion of extreme social control, and its literati have rotated around this rather than around aesthetics. The socialists had an equivalent commitment to revolution. Plaid Cymru was electorally quite unimportant until the 1960s, but was already strong among writers, especially Welsh-language writers, in the 1930s: a social vision without a people.

The Theology of Alienation

Anyone deafened by the constant talk about continuity and tradition will notice eventually that Anglo-Welsh poems belong to the 1950s, and that the hymn form, the staple of Welsh poetry for three centuries, has been abandoned. The mystery of the 1950s is less the literary revival of Christianity than the sudden inability of Christian writers to use the 'timeless forms'. The problem is how to achieve the same communal tone, the same ring and sweep, in modern poems; the last forty years have been bad ones for Christian poetry. Modernisation in British poetry, and possibly American poetry too, has been carried out at the expense of a reading public. The poets of the Second Flowering did not want the benefits of intellectual and stylistic freedom that modernity can bring. They have the problem of defining, so that they can anathematise deviations from it, what the Welsh way of life is; it eludes their description and narration, where a lack of persuasive narrative goes along with an excessive sense of outrage and of ethical commitment. How can you take as a presupposition something that isn't there? Because a modern society is so complex, it's hard to marshal the data and describe the sorts of people. Welsh society is changing very quickly and has done over the past century or two; whatever a poet of the 1970s yearns back to itself replaced a previous social order, and not very long ago. The level of understanding of the employees of local government, to which group most Anglo-Welsh poets and their audience belong, is more or less non-technical sociology, an all-purpose tool of considerable power, acceptable to the new products of the universities, and taking over, to a remarkable extent, the discourse of churchmen. This offered a way of thinking about Welsh society, but triumphed in extension, whereas deep rules say that a poem is short. The problem of poetry was how to persuade its readers to give up the accuracy possessed by administrators and the quality newspapers, in order to go back inside the poem – which became not only less precise but also more rigid and moralised.

The advantage of poetry over sociology is the personal viewpoint, but the style of the 1950s was based on self-denial, on moral self-control; in parallel, the poetic advantage of high-flown language was thrown away in favour of severity. The advantage of moral education was held to be steadiness in love, which unfortunately did away with anything so flighty as love poetry. Competing with urban sophisticates held to be rootless, the moral poet gets so snarled up in a close community that he merges with the ground: poems about landscape are really signals of stability, that is fidelity, that is enduring love.

The absence of the English from the stage is startling: no-one seems to have the literary scope to portray Welsh and English people striving against each other, interacting. Perhaps they aren't striving against each other, and this is all literary pretence. But literature cannot have nationalism as a theme unless it takes on its central tenet, the supposed English yoke. No, nationalism presents itself in the poems as a pervasive state of bad temper. I believe there is no good Welsh nationalist poetry, and this is because of the falseness of the political analysis offered: none of the real social problems of Wales can be ascribed to the English. The exception is language change, but since no-one is without a language in the upshot, the victims appear to be Welsh writers losing their market – a kind of grocer's grievance. The interest of Welsh poetry of the sixties and seventies is that the sophistication of the poets led them away from crude nationalist positions, which they consciously held. Roland Mathias (b. 1913) has apparently not been a nationalist, even though every one of his poems is either about Wales or about Brittany. He is not committed because his poems are dialectical: a constant questioning and shifting of viewpoint takes on the complexity of modern thinking about perception, identification and interpretation, simultaneously with a modern poetic – which the Anglo-Welsh sensibility seems to have disliked. The shimmer of these poems embodies, as much as anything can, the depth of history, its resistance to grand ideas and even to solutions. This confounding of partisanship offers the possibility of really convincing political poetry in the future.

The Socialist Culture of Wales

But now in the winter dusk
I go to Dowlais Top
[...]
And see the rigid phrases of Marx
Bold and black against the steel-grey west,
Riveted along the sullen skies.
        (Idris Davies, from 'I was Born in Rhymney')

The main event of modern Welsh history was the industrialisation of the south-east (that is, Monmouthshire, Glamorgan, and part of Carmarthen), and the creation of a new society. The real boom began in the 1840s and didn't slow down until after the big orders time of the First World War. Gwyn A. Williams says that as a result of the Industrial Revolution, four fifths of the people of Wales came to live in the industrialising south-east. The 1911 census figures show a million people living in Glamorgan. Protest against Anglicisation is also a rejection of this new Welsh world. Important strata of the older, smaller Wales were against this new society; for them it is an unpleasant, unsightly area whose dialect is of low prestige – much as Birmingham is regarded by the makers of taste in England. The new Wales is not English, it is South Welsh. Dai Smith has written an indispensable book – which, almost perversely, accompanied a TV series. *Wales! Wales?*[13] is largely a cultural history of the new society which sprang up in Monmouthshire and Glamorgan, in the nineteenth century, around the coalfields. Smith identifies the last quarter of the nineteenth century as the moment when this new culture, whose cities sprang up on sheepwalks, came to recognise itself and to acquire self-confidence. If south-east Wales is a vibrant and artistically productive region, Humphreys's sepulchral and reiterated claim that to lose one's language is to enter a ghostlike state with no culture is merely malicious and tendentious. Gwyn A. Williams has said that '[the] more arrogant, extreme or paranoid exponents of Welshness simply refuse to see any "culture" at all in English-speaking Wales, or else they dismiss it as "British" or even "English". The victims of this response cultivate an equally contemptuous and dismissive response. These attitudes operate within an overall context which is hostile and sometimes actively hostile to any Welshness at all.'[14] Nationalism based entirely on defence of the language may have been a completely wrong reading of the situation, fuelled by guilt and by an inflexible self-esteem. Kenneth O. Morgan has remarked that '[much] of the nationalism of post-1960 seemed in any case peculiarly inbred. It attracted boredom or hostility from the general mass of the Welsh population, especially those in urban and industrial communities in the south-east.'[15]

The end of the revolutionary movement in South Wales followed, at an interval, the end of the revolutionary industrial growth in the region, and took place in two strokes. The region was relatively non-militant even in the 1930s; the state of trade made union campaigns, for anything short of overthrowing the social order, implausible: how can you win a strike when half the workforce is unemployed? In the late 1940s the Attlee government, with Aneurin Bevan as its most romantic figure, realised a great many goals of revolution; from then on, part of the energies of the movement would be bound in loyalty to the existing laws, and part would recognise the further goals as unrealisable. The Red thinkers of the industrial zone may not have walked on water, but the earth seemed to turn to water beneath them. The present became prosperity and the future became uninspiring. The working class evolved into a middle class, the export industries collapsed – a familiar story in the British Isles. The struggles of 1926, before and after the General Strike, and so memorably recorded by Idris Davies in *The Angry Summer*, may already have been the high point and the moment when decline and disillusionment set in:

> But the greatest of our battles
> We lost in '26
> Through treachery and lying
> And Baldwin's box of tricks.
> (Idris Davies, from 'I was Born in Rhymney')

The life of the Red Valleys did not express itself in literature, although some splashes of its vast energy did generate books. There is the moment of Idris Davies, recalling the strike of 1926 ten years later; there are the novels of Lewis Jones, the leader of the unemployed, writing about a community that had neither work nor anything else; there is the life's work of Gwyn Thomas, one of Britain's greatest writers, mainly looking back at a period that he could recognise as having already gone. There does not seem to have been a period of Soviet-style socialist realism. There is the work of Glyn Jones, a populist who was also a socialist, but who chose not to write about politics. Perhaps it's more interesting to be told about South Wales after 1945, with the mines nationalised and life cast in more complex terms; a life we still lead, without necessarily understanding it.

Idris Davies (1905–53)

Davies falls outside our period, but it is important to know about him because he is an example of how questioned traits – political commitment, direct address, the evocation of a community – can produce great poetry. Davies wrote two volume-length poems: *Gwalia Deserta* (1938) and *The Angry Summer* (1943). Both are sequences of short poems evoking characters and scenes, not exactly narratives but tightly concentrated on the economic situation of South Welsh mining communities during political crises. *The Angry Summer* concerns the 1926 miners' strike. Conran helpfully points out that the end of the poem, with the telephone call and the betrayal, does not apply to 1926, but to the strike of 1921, when the other big unions backed out and refused to support the miners, who went ahead anyway.[16] Davies, a miner, was unemployed for three years in the stoppage of trade which followed 1926, but by dint of study became a teacher; to find a job, though, he had to go to England, in 1932.

Davies wrote great poetry embodying an unbearable truth. Modern poetry has favoured the cut, the sudden jump; the method of Davies's poems is persistence until the psychological density becomes quite overwhelming. He relies always on the effect of truth. He moved on artistically, suffering a crisis when in 1947 he moved back to the coalfields after many years in England, and faced the gap that had opened between himself, as a middle-class teacher, and the working class who were his only subject. His best poems are intrinsic to a social situation that the 1945–51 Labour government did away with. Like James Hanley, Lewis Grassic Gibbon and Gwyn Thomas, Davies wrote with artistic success about the 1930s recession when Auden, Spender and the like were failing to because of their narcissism, privileged situations, and attention to style above content.

Davies was not influenced by the various methods of socialist realism which had already evolved on the Continent. It is hard to define the religious elements of Davies's poetry, although the whole tone of his major poems strikes me as deriving from the Prophets, and is one of moral reproach; and his favoured rhymed quatrains resemble hymns, although Housman has been cited as a source. His sly evocations of character remind me of Methodist preachers, so far as I have found these in books. He was unlucky that European cultured taste had by then reacted decisively against biblical language; Davies was a poet of national life in a way that few modern poets have been, yet the precondition of this authenticity (the use of Christian imagery familiar to every Welsh man and woman) ensured that he would not be translated or accepted in France, Germany, Russia, and everywhere else affected by the same Depression. No doubt a similar problem will soon emerge for poets using the socialist language accepted by the majority of the European working class, and terminally unfashionable among the literate audience.

Gwalia Deserta bears a certain resemblance to Edith Sitwell's *Gold Coast Customs*, which concerns the same events, hunger marches and so on. Her remarkably direct social poetry about hunger, cold and despair was not recognised for what it was. Sitwell may have had preconceptions about TB, hunger, rag-pickers, alcoholism and so on derived from nineteenth-century French poetry, but she was lucid enough to look at hunger marchers and write about hunger.

Glyn Jones (1905–95)

Glyn Jones, from the steelmaking town of Merthyr Tydfil in Glamorgan, is a poet 'left over' from the 1940s, first published in 1931 and notably in *Wales* in the late thirties. He published volumes in 1939 and 1954; *Selected Poems* (1975) adds a few more poems; the 1988 volume, also called *Selected Poems*, subtitled *Fragments and Fictions*, adds another 40 pages, the fruit of Jones's retirement. He has also written wonderful novels; but the level of achievement of the *Selected Poems*, especially of certain poems, is quite startling. Look at 'Merthyr', 'The Dream of Jake Hopkins' and 'Profile of Rose', or this for example:

> On cream hills in the sun, leopards and hibiscus
> Burned like bonfires. Her purple shadow with the
> Golden holes lay spread beneath the carob tree,
> Her leaves pushed by the river breeze, and some white
> Epiphany moved exultant in the flamy fields.
> Beside that Tâf, its golden skin twitching
> Under flies, children, we prayed, our sunlit flesh
> Pelted with shadows of white alighting doves;
> While over Jordan, distant in the field, I watched
> The farmer's fire, building from fragile smokes
> Pavilions of blue glass, I heard the cold-maned
> Ponies wild among our windy daffodils;
> And where darkness lay upon the deep, where snow-footed
> To the fishing-boats, the towering Light trod,
> Vestured in torrid purple, like creation,

I rushed my love upon the sea, my foot could not go through.
                    (from 'Images of Light and Darkness')

Lord, when they kill me, let the job be thorough
And carried out behind that county borough
Known as Merthyr, in Glamorganshire.
It would be best if it could happen, Sir,
Upon some great green roof, some Beacon slope
Those monstrous clouds of childhood slid their soap
Snouts over, into the valley. The season
Sir, for shooting, summer; and love the reason.
On that hill, varnished in the glazing tide
Of evening, stand me, with the petrified
Plantations, the long blue spoonful of the lake,
The gold stook-tufted acres without break
Below me, and the distant corduroy
Glass of the river – which, a mitching boy,
I fished –

                                    (from 'Merthyr')

Jones was a schoolteacher most of his life. He was a friend of Dylan Thomas and was impressed by Thomas's poetry when he encountered it in the thirties; this said, his ability to absorb the lessons of Thomas's poetry without producing something quite drunken and half-baked argues high poetic intelligence. His poetry, unlike Thomas's, is perfectly lucid. Anyone who likes Thomas's work should seek out Glyn Jones. He has that flamboyant high style, the poet deliberately showing off and topping bravura effect with effect, like a jazz musician in front of an enthusiastic audience. Of course they're enthusiastic; this is dazzling stuff.

Jones's 'A Sketch of the Author', in his 1939 volume, says a great deal about Welsh socialist poetry:

> My ambition when I began to tire of reproducing endlessly the effects of another man's verse, was to achieve a body of workers' poetry [...] poems which the workers themselves could read, understand and appreciate. [...] My theory was that the true proletarian poetry, the poetry most acceptable to the people, was that which had been written by the people themselves [...] Many of the pieces I wrote at that time arose directly from contact with Welsh folk stanzas [...] I gave up my scheme for the poetisation of the masses because, apart from the inevitable feeling of my own inadequacy, I had no means of reaching them.

The folk stanzas he refers to are *penillion*, four-liners, mostly anonymous and passed around orally.

Jones's most political poem is about the Welsh language, where he warns that its innocence is due to its unimportance:

The Red Dragon triumphs over the silver-backed smokes.
Until the city is a cairn, the language of Llanrhaeadr and Pantycelyn[17]
Shall be used for the utterance of her cruelty, her banalities, her lies.

(from 'Y Ddraig Goch')

Few nationalists have given serious thought to what victory might mean.

Jones also wrote an excellent book – the first – on Anglo-Welsh litera-ture, *The Dragon has Two Tongues*.[18] He edited the Welsh section of the 1949 *New Romantic Anthology*, which also includes Roland Mathias (although, frustratingly, he did not include himself). Aficionados of style history will note that Wales provided a shelter for undaunted adherents of this school: Mathias and Glyn Jones, although not in the public eye, went on writing and refining their style. Presumably London is so pressurised that it crushes unfashionable poets, even though it stimulates new fashions. The poet may thrive better in Merthyr Tydfil.

John James

The name of John James (born in Cardiff in 1939) is never mentioned in lists of Anglo-Welsh poets. Yet he is the most gifted poet using the English language (I can't speak for poets writing in Welsh) to come out of Wales since the Second World War. Despite being exiled in England for a good many years, he affirms clear and jovial adherence to a socialist view of life which could not be more typical of the traditions of the industrial belt. This faith in the people is filtered through a rapid-fire, dodging, almost boxing style, tinged by Apollinaire and Frank O'Hara, which indeed has been the means of its preservation. James's Welshness is seen in the following features: directness of address and closeness to the spoken language; emotional warmth and spontaneity; liking for portraits of friends and conviviality; concreteness; liking for topography; continual cheerful ridiculing of English customs and politicians. His poems belong, for anyone who has heard them read aloud, primarily to oral culture, like so much that is Welsh: nothing more sociable, quick-witted, funny and rapid can be imagined.

The poems I am going to discuss are found in a folder published in 1967; they are called *The Welsh Poems* and there are three of them. (One was reprinted in *A Various Art*.)[19] One is a reminiscence of childhood in Cardiff:

> My father.
> My father runs
> naked across Kingsway, dripping from the canal
> clothes under arm,
> side-stepping drayhorses,
> pursued by an old-time Cardiff cop –
>
> my father hurls stolen eggs at the startled shavees in the
> Hayes Road barber-shop
>
> > (from 'Heredity')

The other two are adaptations of a twelfth-century poem by Hywel ap Owain Gwynedd. We can trace this poem quite satisfyingly: a partial translation exists in a 1948 lecture to the British Academy by John Lloyd-Jones, who divided the original into two; it was also translated by Gwyn Williams and Anthony Conran, the stars in this field. The original is printed in Gwenogvryn Evans's *Poetry by Mediaeval Welsh Bards* (in twelfth-century spelling) and in the *Oxford Book of Welsh Verse* (in twentieth-century spelling), but unfortunately it's too difficult for me to read. The poem is a *gorhoffedd* (rendered as 'exultation' or 'boast'), a variant of the praise poem in which the poet is praising himself. James has seized on the resemblance of this form to the blues: his version is not only a tribute to one of the more dazzling moments of medieval Welsh culture but also a stunning poetic lifting of one of the more flamboyant and braggadocio airs of Muddy Waters or Jimi Hendrix. The poem comes in two parts, the second being a boast about the charms of various maidens who are good friends of Hywel; the first starts with the wave-washed tomb of Rhufawn bebr ('Romanus the brilliant', I suppose), an early Welsh king, on the sea-shore, and becomes an evocation of the beauties of Wales; it is mixed with some mention of his battle feats and diplomatic achievements, and there is a probable comparison of Hywel's own tomb with Rhufawn's – presumably the crowning of a brilliant career. James hasn't really taken to this; he changes it as follows:

> A ton of white rain will overflow my self-shaped sleeping-bag of earth.
> But today I love what is betrayed
> by every indifferent Saesson –
> what will be obliterated
> from the human view –

> the curving horizon breathes
> over the reclined anatomy of the sphere,
> the open lands to the North & West
> still sprawl under the windy skies beyond the cities –
>
> & remote mountain plateaus –
>   Eglwysilan
> where the shepherd raised his eyebrow
> at the question put in English –
> The waters of the Taff shine with the blackness of coal.
> She gushes like piss
> from under a mare's tail
> out of the irregular
> gap in the mountains, through the Vale
> the low parklands barely embank her,
> everywhichway discharging herself in
> deflected forces of current
> over the hidden rocks & the
> spewing over at Blackweir
> with a smell of dead chub & pit effluent.
>
> The waves ceaselessly lay stress on the shore.

Rhufawn has vanished; the boast about battle has vanished; the praise of the beauty of Wales has been relocated to parts familiar to James. Nevertheless the spirit of the original has been brilliantly set down. (*Saesson* is a plural, the singular is *Sais*.) His possessing of Hywel is like Hywel's possession of the long-dead (sub-Roman?) Rhufawn bebr. ('Ton' is a pun on the Welsh original *ton*, meaning wave. In a later line in the poem, 'A ton of wintry rain will overwhelm my lichened bed', 'bed' is a pun on the Welsh *bedd*, meaning grave – which is why it has got lichen on it.)

New Formations

Tentatively, I would identify a new formation of Welsh intellectuals succeeding in higher education since the late 1950s, differing from the earlier blocs of Dissenting clergy, the Welsh-speaking nationalists, and the Central Labour College proletarian thinkers of the South. This new group is far larger than any of the others, is not homogeneous, and imitates each of the other three. It provides both writers and readers for the modern generation of Anglo-Welsh literature. Its members are graduates, they are secular and affluent, they very often have to leave Wales to find jobs sustaining affluence, they regard previous strata of Welsh literati as simplistic and yet heroic. Confusingly, they are often Welsh nationalists and even learn Welsh in furtherance of this. Partly because the exam system and the job market are similar, this group resembles the English equivalent. Resentment of central government and enthusiasm for decentralisation and for regions are fashionable throughout the British Isles today. Anthony Conran has said that

> [the] process [of writing elegies] is in fact a piece of imitative magic, and its compulsive quality is a sign of a class fighting for its very existence. The three components of its power are, first, fear of English domination; second, hatred of the 'narrow' or 'puritanical' or 'parochial' Wales that has been, the peasant or proletarian Wales that is felt as dear and stifling at once [...] and third, career-anxiety, or greed, for the jobs that are opening to the middle class as Wales achieves a measure of autonomy.[20]

This is spectacularly nasty, but clever; Conran's point that writing elegies to lost ways of life is a way of making sure they are dead does ring true. I agree that the relation of the graduate white-collar worker to manual labour is not really nostalgia but fear of slipping back again. What seems to be the new rule is that the life of this new class is seen as quite inauthentic and unsuitable for poetry – the Georgian anxiety. Perhaps reflexivity derives both from the impersonality demanded of public servants such as teachers, and from a sensitivity about assets in an economy of prestige (one is either showing off or failing to compete), as well as from a groundswell of popular hostility to the new middle class. This class avoids appearing centre stage, and writes poems about village types – perhaps to show its own fitness to administer them. The poetry harks back to ancestors, as agricultural labourers or wives or resisters, all the time; distaste for the present needs explaining. The answer may depend on first untangling the new urban society in which the male industrial worker is no longer central, and in which the unemployed, the middle class and the working woman are major players.

I don't think the Second Flowering is of national interest except for a few poems. It does explore the problems of being politically radical and rejecting the centre, which seems to be the condition in which all future poets will write. These poets have been let down by the quality of their ideas, regrettable since after all one would hope that politics would expand the scope of poetry. Virtually all regions outside the Midlands/south-eastern core have gone through economic depressions in the past fifteen years, aligning them with Wales; new poets are radically disengaged and dissociated from the Conservative-capitalist motor which drives the political order. It seems that new English poets are frivolous and lightweight, in contrast to forbidding and serious and moralistic Welsh poets; although both groups have lost faith in the centre. The Welsh group are trying to build an alternative, rather than relapse into private, depressed and disconnected worlds. However, it seems that younger Welsh poets are inclining more towards the apathetic view of politics, and that the radicalism of Wales has passed its zenith; as Dai Smith points out, the Conservatives won thirteen Welsh seats in the 1983 general election, a long way behind Labour but very far ahead of Plaid Cymru (with two seats). A new social order is being built, however distracted we are by our beautiful plans for a more just and less centralised one.

As I have said, the Anglo-Welsh poem had a structural weakness. Since the great let-down of the 1979 referendum on devolution, when the vote in Wales went four to one against, nationalism has receded into the background for poetry. The next generation, born between say 1931 and 1960, is less clearly mapped, and harder for me to judge. However, it seems that the dourness of the sixties has been followed by an era of bright, shallow pop poetry, of little interest to me, although no doubt appealing at convivial readings in bars. The consolidation by an in-group of its grip on the funding bodies and the reviews pages has made nationalism institutional (you can't be a cultural manager in the new world of cultural subsidies unless you believe in Wales above everywhere else), and perhaps impossible to write poems about for that reason; it has been accompanied by a disastrous decline in poetic standards, but the work of Peter Finch and David Greenslade stands out against a cosy beery morass. The Welsh-language poet Bobi Jones put this decline too apocalyptically in his 1992 article (originally 'Tranc yr Eingl-Cymru', 'The Perishing of the Anglo-Welsh'), summing up the process since 1979. The new conventions involve feminism, Green politics, writing for performance in a jovial folk-club atmosphere, Jungian mythiness and 'self-realisation'. A younger generation takes nationalism for granted, but is more cosmopolitan and hedonistic, less enthused by the communalist formula of Christianity, nationalism and existential commitment. Bobi Jones' wish for poetry that was much more committed, nationalistic and Christian, and less artistic, was therefore misguided.[21]

Notes

1 From an unpublished interview with Andrew Duncan, 1993.
2 Ifor Williams (ed.), *Pedeir keinc y Mabinogi* (Cardiff: Gwasg Prfysgol Cymru, 1974), p. 1 footnote.
3 Anthony Conran, *The Cost of Strangeness* (Llandysul: Gomer Press, 1982), p. 266.
4 R. S. Thomas, *Neb* (Caernarvon: Gwasg Gwynedd, 1992), p. 84.
5 Conran, *The Cost of Strangeness*, p. 303.
6 John Stuart Williams and Meic Stephens (eds), *The Lilting House* (London: Dent, 1969).
7 Ambrose Bebb, article in *Y Geninen*, XLI (1923), cited in Heini Gruffudd, *Achub Cymru* (Talybont: Y Lolfa, 1983), p. 60.
8 Cited in Emyr Humphreys, *The Taliesin Tradition* (Bridgend: Seren, 1989), p. 188; the Welsh phrase is a quotation from a poem by Islwyn.
9 Brian Jackson and Dennis Marsden, *Education and the Working Class* (London: Routledge and Kegan Paul, 1962).
10 Jeremy Hooker, *The Presence of the Past* (Bridgend: Poetry Wales Press, 1987); Gwyn A. Williams, *When was Wales?* (London: Black Raven, 1985).
11 J. R. Jones, *Bychanfyd*.
12 Gwyn Jones, *The First Forty Years* (Cardiff: University of Wales Press, 1957), p. 12.
13 Dai Smith, *Wales! Wales?* (London: Allen and Unwin, 1984).
14 Williams, *When was Wales?*, p. 236.
15 Kenneth O. Morgan, *Rebirth of a Nation: Wales 1880–1980* (Oxford: Clarendon Press, 1981), p. 407.
16 See Conran's notes to *The Angry Summer*, p. xxviii.
17 These two names are epithets for, respectively, the translator of the Welsh Bible and the most famous hymn-writer of the eighteenth century.
18 Glyn Jones, *The Dragon has Two Tongues* (London: J. M. Dent and Sons, 1968).
19 Tim Longville and Andrew Crozier (eds), *A Various Art* (Manchester: Carcanet, 1987).
20 *The Cost of Strangeness*, p. 319.
21 See Duncan, *The Failure of Conservatism in Modern British Poetry*, pp. 252–54.

Conclusion
Balkanisation:
The Sound of Confusion

I am still fascinated by Eric Homberger's use of the word 'Balkanisation', which is so evocative of parts of the exploded poetry world since the boom that began around 1959. ('Deregulation' is another term that springs to mind.) But it makes me uneasy, too: does it not refer to a geographical area seamed with subdivisions which are important to events but which we, as Westerners, find too trivial and confusing to be worth remembering? And to a political area populated by factions so polarised against each other, and so intimately intertwined, that no accurate information can be obtained about anything, while on the other hand there are multiple descriptions of every event and every group? I am afraid that this judgment appears to be that of an academic washing his hands of an intractable subject. But what use is a methodology that gives up when there is too much data? What use is a trained intelligence that dislikes problems? The expansion of the field of poetry in Britain (which has also happened in the USA in the same period) is not merely a stagnant bloat, with thousands of people writing the same poem; actually, the new era has seen an unprecedented divergence of mentalities, social opinions and aesthetic systems. A group of poets announce 'We are unconventional and beyond your comprehension'; a professor says this is 'Balkanisation'; these are two descriptions of the same event, which probably, therefore, happened. A tenfold growth of poetic activity meant perhaps a fiftyfold growth in diversity. Things will never be like the fifties again. This is why the old method of taking three poets per decade and proclaiming that they summed up what was going on doesn't work any more.

The way to deal with an excess of data is perhaps to treat it in a sloppy fashion. It's not possible for me to give as firm and accurate a picture of the 1980s as someone could of the 1930s, for example. The gap between precision in treating particular books, and going up a level to the collective landscape, is like the North-West Frontier: you never really establish control of it. *The Sound of Confusion* is the title of a classic album by

Rugby's Spacemen Three. Confusion, of course, is a positive term: it suggests that blurring of the edges of reality, over-excitement, feeling of wildness and unpredictability, to which this band's neo-psychedelic music aspired. I choose it to suggest that a certain loss of control may not be an unpleasant thing.

Nationalism is normally right-wing, authoritarian and conservative, and it is a problem for nationalists in Scotland and Wales, or in English regions, to gain accreditation as radicals and liberals. Recent outbursts of cultural nationalism in Bosnia and Russia, among other places, have made the worship of *ethnos* unfashionable. Information about the resistance of Scots and Welsh to the Empire gives us a model for stating that these nations are not territorially aggressive and do not recognise military struggle as a legitimate political tactic: both Glyn Jones and Norman MacCaig, it emerged from their obituaries, refused to fight in the Second World War because it was a war in defence of the Empire, and both had their careers severely damaged by this record. This area of pacifism, attacking as it does the bases of the modern state, is under-explored; because it involved so many nationalists at the time, it represents a pledge that Wales and Scotland do not believe in the state military complex, and do not wish to oppress other nations. Wasn't Hitler's model of a New Order in Europe just a copy of the British Empire, in which black people had no political rights? Wasn't Hitler astounded when the British said no to his offer of alliance? Wasn't resisting the Empire like resisting the Third Reich? Roland Mathias and Douglas Young went to jail for refusing to fight, Ian Hamilton Finlay was in a Pioneer Corps full, apparently, of pacifist artists; this no-saying was the nucleus of the decentralising radical-ism of the post-war period, whereas the waging of the war represented centralising, technocratic and statist radicalism. (In Australia, the poet Ian Mudie was interned for being anti-British at the wrong moment, i.e. before his government.) More amusingly, recent letters in the *Independent* reveal that the files on 'surveillance on anti-imperialists in the 1930s and 1940s' have still not been released to historians; this would embarrass the Establishment. Some people in those tiny groups of Celtic nationalists were spying on the others on behalf of MI6; presumably the files are being withheld in order to conceal their identities. I suppose someone in Whitehall believed that MacDiarmid and Saunders Lewis really were threats to the Empire. I hope my observation of regional artists has been more sympathetic than that of Special Branch.

This has largely been a history without narrative; I regret not pausing on moments like the 1958 evoked by a copy of *Anglo-Welsh Review* (the first issue, but numbered 23 because it took over from issue 42 of *Dock Leaves*): edited by the Catholic poet Raymond Garlick, blazoned as Festival Edition (the fiesta took place in Bangor), adorned with a dragon and a leek. Inside we find a portrait of Glyn Jones; an essay on nationalism in Welsh music; reviews of books by two of the Powys brothers; a poem ('Above the Glowing Rowan-Trees') by A. G. Prys-Jones (representing continuity, since he edited the first Anglo-Welsh poetry anthology, in 1917); the first ever Anglo-Welsh poem, from the fifteenth century ('O michti ladi, owr leding tw haf / at hefn owr abeiding'); remarks on the lost dialect called Gwenhwyseg; Mathias on the Welsh Saints, revolutionary Puritans of the Civil War era ('a very flamy, fuliginous, set of doctrines'), and other things fitting to be known. The wrapper further lists ten book-shops in Wales that sell it, gives us the phone number (Blaenau Ffestiniog 160), and offers us, from Dock Leaves Press, *The Roses of Tretower*, by Roland Mathias, 66 pp., for 4/10d. Careful study of this, with its long title poem akin to T. F. Powys, and meditative lyrics partly of Cumbrian site, tells me that I could hardly have spent my two half crowns better, if I had had them.

Bibliography

Poetry Collections and Anthologies

Allnutt, Gillian, and Fred D'Aguiar (eds), *the new british poetry* (London: Paladin, 1987)

Anderson, J. Redwood, *The Curlew Cries* (London: Oxford University Press, 1940)

——, *Pillars to Remembrance* (London: Oxford University Press, 1948)

Ashraf, Mary (ed.), *Political Verse and Song from Great Britain and Ireland* (London: Lawrence and Wishart, 1975)

Astley, Neil (ed.), *Poetry with an Edge* (Newcastle upon Tyne: Bloodaxe, 1988)

Bottomley, Gordon, *Gruach and Britain's Daughter* (London: Constable & Co., 1921)

——, *Lyric Plays* (London: Constable & Co., 1932)

——, *Choric Plays and a Comedy* (London: Constable & Co., 1939)

Brown, Fred, *The Muse Went Weaving* (Youlgreave, Derbyshire: Hub Publications, 1972)

Davies, Idris, *Gwalia Deserta* (London: J. M. Dent and Sons, 1938)

——, *The Angry Summer* (London: Faber & Faber, 1943)

——, *The Angry Summer*, with notes and introduction by Anthony Conran (Cardiff: University of Wales Press, 1993)

'E. M.' (ed.), *Georgian Poetry 1913–15* (London: Poetry Bookshop, 1916)

France, Linda (ed.), *Sixty Women Poets* (Newcastle upon Tyne: Bloodaxe, 1988)

Gibson, Wilfrid, *Fires* (London: Elkin Mathews, 1912)

——, *Krindlesyke* (London: Macmillan, 1922)

——, *Kestrel Edge, and Other Plays* (London: Macmillan, 1924)

Halliday, W. J., and A. S. Umpleby (eds), *A White Rose Garland* (London: J. M. Dent and Sons, 1949)

Haslam, Michael, *The Fair Set on the Green* (Bishop's Stortford: Great Works Press, 1975)

——, *Various Ragged Fringes* (Oxford: Turpin, 1975)

——, *Son Son of Mother* (Cambridge: Lobby Press, 1978)

——, *Continual Song* (Hebden Bridge: Open Township, 1986)

——, *Aleethia* (Hebden Bridge: Open Township, 1990)

——, *Four Poems* (Cambridge: Equipage, 1993)

———, *A Whole Bauble* (Manchester: Carcanet, 1995)

Hay, George Campbell, *The Wind on Loch Fyne* (Edinburgh: Oliver and Boyd, 1948)

Heseltine, Nigel, *The Four-Walled Dream* (London: Fortune Press, 1941)

Higgins, Brian, *The Only Need* (London: Abelard-Schuman, 1960)

Humphreys, Emyr, *Ancestor Worship* (Denbigh: Gwasg Gee, 1970)

Jones, Bobi, *Hunllef Arthur* (Cyhoeddiadau Barddas, 1986)

Jones, Glyn, *Poems* (London: Fortune Press, 1939)

———, *Selected Poems* (Llandysul: Gwasg Gomer, 1975)

———, *Selected Poems: Fragments and Fictions* (Ogmore-by-Sea: Poetry Wales, 1988)

Jones, Gwyn (ed.), *The Oxford Book of Welsh Verse in English* (Oxford: Oxford University Press, 1977)

Kirkup, James, *The Submerged Village* (London: Oxford University Press, 1951)

———, *The Descent into the Cave* (London: Oxford University Press, 1957)

Law, T. S., *Whit Tyme in the Day* (Glasgow: Caledonian Press, 1948)

Lewis, Alun, *Collected Poems* (Seren: Bridgend, 1994)

Lloyd, David T. (ed.), *The Urgency of Identity* (Evanston, IL: TriQuarterly Books, 1994)

Longville, Tim, and Andrew Crozier (eds), *A Various Art* (Manchester: Carcanet, 1987)

Loydell, Rupert (ed.), *Ladder to the Next Floor* (Salzburg: University of Salzburg Press, 1993)

MacDiarmid, Hugh, *Albyn* (London: Kegan Paul, 1927)

MacLean, Sorley, *From Wood to Ridge* (Manchester: Carcanet, 1989)

Macleod, Joseph [also published as Adam Drinan], *The Ecliptic* (London: Faber & Faber, 1930)

———, *The Cove* (self-published, 1940)

———, *The Men of the Rocks* (London: Fortune Press, 1942)

———, *Women of the Happy Island* (Glasgow: William MacLellan, 1944)

———, *The Passage of the Torch* (Edinburgh: Oliver and Boyd, 1951)

———, *Script from Norway* (Glasgow: William MacLellan, 1953)

———, *An Old Olive Tree* (Loanhead: M. Macdonald, 1971)

Masefield, John, *The Tragedy of Nan, and Other Plays* (London: Grant Richards, 1909)

———, *The Everlasting Mercy* (London: Sidgwick & Jackson, 1911)

Mathias, Roland, *The Roses of Tretower* (Llandysul: Dock Leaves Press, 1952)

———, *Burning Brambles* (Llandysul: Gomer, 1983)

Matthias, John (ed.), *Contemporary British Poetry*, *TriQuarterly*, 21 (1971)

Morrison, Blake, and Andrew Motion (eds), *The Penguin Book of Contemporary British Poetry* (Harmondsworth: Penguin, 1982)

Murphy, Gerard, *Early Irish Lyrics* (Oxford: Clarendon Press, 1956)

Percy, Bishop, *Reliques of Ancient English Poetry* (London: J. Dodsley, 1765)

Purple and Green (London: Rivelin Grapheme, 1985)

Rhys, Keidrych (ed.), *Modern Welsh Poetry* (London: Faber & Faber, 1944)
Riley, Denise, *Marxism for Infants* (Cambridge: Street Editions, 1977)
——, *No Fee* (Cambridge: Street Editions, 1977)
——, *Dry Air* (London: Virago, 1985)
——, *Mop Mop Georgette* (London: Reality Street, 1993)
Ritson, Joseph, *Northern Garlands* (London: R. Triphook, 1810)
Roberts, Lynette, *Poems* (London: Faber & Faber, 1944)
——, *Gods with Stainless Ears* (London: Faber & Faber, 1951)
Sergeant, Howard (ed.), *Anthology of Contemporary Northern Poetry* (London: George Harrap & Co., 1947)
Schimanski, Stefan, and Henry Treece (eds), *A New Romantic Anthology* (London: Grey Walls Press, 1949)
Simms, Colin, *Rushmore Inhabitation: An Exploration of Borders* (Marvin, South Dakota: Blue Cloud Quarterly, 1976)
——, *No Northwestern Passage: A Long Poem* (London: Writers' Forum, 1976)
——, *Parflèche* (Swansea: Galloping Dog Press, 1977)
——, *A Celebration of the Stones in a Water-Course* (Newcastle upon Tyne: Galloping Dog Press, 1981)
——, *Eyes Own Ideas* (Durham: Pig Press, 1987)
——, *Goshawk Lives* (London: Form Books, 1995)
Sinclair, Ian (ed.), *Conductors of Chaos* (London: Picador, 1996)
Smith, Iain Crichton, *Selected Poems* (Macdonald Publishers, 1981)
Stephens, Meic (ed.), *The Bright Field* (Manchester: Carcanet, 1991)
Thomas, R. S., *Neb* (Caernarvon: Gwasg Gwynedd, 1992)
Thomson, Derick, *Creachadh na Clarsaich (Plundering the Harp: Poems 1940–80)* (Edinburgh: Macdonald, 1982)
Watson, J. Carmichael (ed.), *Mesca Ulad* (Dublin: The Stationery Office, 1941)
Watson, William J. (ed.), *Bàrdachd Ghàidhlig* (Inverness: Northern Counties Publishing Co., 1918)
——, (ed. and trans.), *Scottish Verse from The Book of the Dean of Lismore* (Edinburgh: Scottish Gaelic Text Society, 1937)
Williams, Ifor (ed.), *The Poems of Taliesin* (Dublin: The Dublin Institute for Advanced Studies, 1975)
——, (ed.), *Pedeir keinc y Mabinogi* (Cardiff: Gwasg Prifysgol Cymru, 1974)
Williams, John Stuart, and Meic Stephens (eds), *The Lilting House* (London: Dent, 1969)

Secondary Sources

Bardon, J., *A History of Ulster* (Belfast: Blackstaff, 1992)
Bateson, Gregory, *The Naven* (Cambridge: Cambridge University Press, 1936)

Bebb, Ambrose, article in *Y Geninen*, XLI (1923), cited in Heini Gruffudd, *Achub Cymru* (Talybont: Y Lolfa, 1983)

Bentley, Phyllis, *The English Regional Novel* (London: Allen & Unwin, 1941)

Bergin, Osborn, lecture published in *Irish Bardic Poetry* (Dublin: Dublin Institute for Advanced Studies, 1970)

Bernstein, Basil, *Class, Codes, and Control* (London: Routledge and Kegan Paul, 1971)

Berthoud, Jacques, in Boris Ford (ed.), *The Cambridge Guide to the Arts in Britain*, VIII (Cambridge: Cambridge University Press, 1984)

Beveridge, Craig, and Ronald Turnbull, *The Eclipse of Scottish Culture, or Inferiorism and the Intellectuals* (Edinburgh: Polygon, 1989)

——, *Scotland after Enlightenment* (Edinburgh: Polygon, 1997)

Bezzola, Reto, *Les Origines et la formation de la littérature courtoise en occident, 500–1200* (Paris: Bibliothèque de l'Ecole des Hautes Etudes, 1944–63)

Blake, N. F., *The English Language in Mediaeval Literature* (London: Dent, 1977)

Bold, Alan, *MacDiarmid* (London: John Murray, 1988)

Booth, Martin, *Driving through the Barricades: British Poetry 1964–84* (London: Routledge and Kegan Paul, 1985)

Bott, Elizabeth, *Family and Social Network* (London: Tavistock Publications, 1957)

Cain, P. J., and A. G. Hopkins, *British Imperialism: Crisis and Deconstruction 1914–90* (London: Longman, 1993)

Campbell, J. F., *Popular Tales of the West Highlands*, IV (Edinburgh: Edmonston and Douglas, 1862)

Carrell, Christopher (ed.), *Seven Poets* (Glasgow: Third Eye Centre, 1981)

Chapman, Malcolm, *The Gaelic Vision in Scottish Culture* (London: Croom Helm, 1987)

Childe, V. G., *Prehistoric Migrations in Europe* (Oslo: H. Aschenhoug & Co., 1950)

Chrimes, S. B., C. D. Ross and R. A. Griffiths (eds), *England in the Fifteenth Century, 1399–1509* (Manchester: Manchester University Press, 1972)

Collins, A. S., *The Profession of Letters 1780–1832* (London: G. Routledge and Sons, 1928)

Conran, Anthony, *The Cost of Strangeness* (Llandysul: Gomer Press, 1982)

Cunliffe, Barry, *Greeks, Romans, and Barbarians* (London: Batsford, 1988)

Davies, D. Hywel, *The Welsh Nationalist Party 1925–45* (Cardiff: University of Wales Press, 1983)

Duncan, Andrew, *The Failure of Conservatism in Modern British Poetry* (Cambridge: Salt Publishing, 2003)

——, *Secrets of Nature: Origins of the Underground* (Cambridge: Salt Publishing, 2004)

Easthope, Anthony, *Poetry as Discourse* (London: Methuen, 1983)

Elias, Norbert, and John L. Scotson, *The Established and the Outsiders* (London: Frank Cass, 1965)

Elton, Oliver, *Lascelles Abercrombie, 1881–1938. From the Proceedings of the British Academy* (London: Humphrey Milford, 1939)

Ennew, Judith, *The Western Isles Today* (Cambridge: Cambridge University Press, 1980)

Ensor, R. C. K., *England 1870–1914* (Oxford: Clarendon Press, 1936)

Evans, Gwynfor, *Diwedd Prydeindod* (Talybont: Y Lolfa, 1981)

Finlay, Ian, *Columba* (London: Victor Gollancz, 1979)

Finn, F. E. S. (ed.), *Poets of Our Time* (London: John Murray, 1965)

Fox, Cyril, *The Personality of Britain* (Cardiff: National Museum of Wales, 1932)

Fuller, Peter, *Beyond the Crisis in Art* (London: Writers and Readers, 1980)

——, *Images of God* (London: Hogarth Press, 1990)

Geijer, Erik Gustaf, introduction to Erik Gustaf Geijer and A. A. Afzelius (eds), *Svenska Folkvisor* (Stockholm: Z. Haeggstroms Förlagsexpedition, 1880)

Gerould, G. H., *The Ballad of Tradition* (Oxford: Clarendon Press, 1962)

Grant, I. F., and Hugh Cheape, *Periods in Highland History* (London: Shepheard-Walwyn, 1987)

Green, J. Brazier, *John Wesley and William Law* (London: Epworth Press, 1945)

Gruffudd, Heini, *Achub Cymru* (Talybont: Y Lolfa, 1983)

Halliday, M. A. K, *Language as Social Semiotic* (London: Edward Arnold, 1978)

Harvey, Anthony, 'Some Significant Points of Early Insular Celtic Orthography', in Donnchadh O Croinin (ed.), *Sages, Saints, and Scholars* (Maynooth: An Sagart/St Patrick's College, 1989)

Hawkes, Christopher, 'Cumulative Celticity in Pre-Roman Britain', *Etudes Celtiques*, Vol XIII (1973), pp. 607–27

Heer, Friedrich, *Der Kampf um die österreichische Identität* (Vienna: Böhlau, 1981)

Hey, David, *Yorkshire from AD 1000* (London: Longman, 1986)

Homberger, Eric, *The Art of the Real* (London: Dent, 1977)

Hooker, Jeremy, *The Presence of the Past* (Bridgend: Poetry Wales Press, 1987)

Humphreys, Emyr, *The Taliesin Tradition* (Bridgend: Seren, 1989)

Jackson, Brian, and Dennis Marsden, *Education and the Working Class* (London: Routledge and Kegan Paul, 1962)

James, Mervyn, *Society, Politics, and Culture* (Cambridge: Cambridge University Press, 1986)

Jenkins, Geraint, *The Foundations of Modern Wales 1642–1780* (Oxford: Clarendon Press, 1987).

Jewell, H. M., 'North and South: The Antiquity of the Great Divide', *Northern History* (Leeds), 27 (1991)

John of Salisbury, *Ioannis Saresberiensis, Policratici Libri VIII*, ed. Clement Webb (Oxford: Clarendon Press, 1909)

Jones, Bobi, *Ysbryd y cwlwm* (Cardiff: Gwasg Prifysgol Cymru, 1998)

——, 'Demise of the Anglo-Welsh?', *Poetry Wales*, 28.3 (January 1993), pp. 14–18

Jones, Glyn, *The Dragon has Two Tongues* (London: J. M. Dent and Sons, 1968)

Jones, Gwyn, *The First Forty Years* (Cardiff: University of Wales Press, 1957)

Jones, J. R., *Bychanfyd* (no details available)

Keen, Maurice, *English Society in the Later Middle Ages* (London: Penguin, 1990)

Kirby, D. A., and H. Robinson, *Geography of Britain* (Slough: University Tutorial, 1981)

Klein, Josephine, *Samples from English Cultures* (London: Routledge and Kegan Paul, 1965)

Kohon, Gregorio (ed.), *The Work of André Green* (London and New York: Routledge, 1999)

Laing, R. D., and Aaron Esterson, *Sanity, Madness and the Family* (London: Tavistock Publications, 1964)

Leith, Dick, *A Social History of English* (London: Routledge, 1997)

Littleton, Scott C., *The New Comparative Mythology* (Berkeley and Los Angeles: University of California Press, 1966)

Lloyd, A. L., *Folk-Song in England* (St Albans: Paladin, 1975)

Mac Colla, Fionn, *And the Cock Crew* (London: Souvenir Press, 1977)

McCrone, David, *Understanding Scottish Society* (London: Routledge, 1992)

McCrone, John, *Going Inside* (London: Faber & Faber, 1999)

MacIntyre, Alasdair, *Whose Justice? Which Rationality?* (London: Duckworth, 1988)

MacLean, Sorley, 'Interview', *Chapman*, 66

——, autobiographical statements in Karl Miller (ed.), *Memoirs of a Modern Scotland* (London: Faber & Faber, 1970)

——, autobiographical statements in *Poetry and the Muse*, *Chapman*, 16 (1976)

MacNeill, Eoin, 'Introduction' to *Duanaire Finn* (Dublin: Irish Texts Society, 1908)

Maidment, Brian, 'Class and Cultural Production in the Industrial City', in Alan J. Kidd and K. W. Roberts (eds), *City, Class, and Culture* (Manchester: Manchester University Press, 1985)

——, *The Poorhouse Fugitives* (Manchester: Carcanet, 1992)

Map, Walter, *De Nugis Curialium*, ed. and trans. M. R. James (Oxford: Clarendon Press, 1983)

Mathew, Gervase, *The Court of Richard II* (London: John Murray, 1968)

Messinger, Gary, *Manchester in the Victorian Age: The Half-Known City* (Manchester: Manchester University Press, 1985)

Middlemas, Keith, *Politics in Industrial Society* (London: Deutsch, 1979)

Morgan, Kenneth O., *Rebirth of a Nation: Wales 1880–1980* (Oxford: Clarendon Press, 1981)

Musgrove, Frank, *The North of England* (Oxford: Basil Blackwell, 1990)

O'Driscoll, R. (ed.), *The Celtic Consciousness* (Edinburgh: Canongate, 1982)

Ong, Walter J., *Orality and Literacy* (London: Methuen, 1982)

Peate, Iowerth, *Diwylliant gwerin Cymru* (Liverpool: H. Evans a'i Feibion, 1942)

Potter, Jonathan, Peter Stringer and Margaret Wetherell, *Social Texts and Context: Social Psychology and Literature* (London: Routledge and Kegan Paul, 1984)

Riley, Denise (ed.), *Poets on Writing: Britain 1970–1991* (Basingstoke: Macmillan, 1992)

Robertson, Boyd and Iain Taylor, *Teach Yourself Gaelic* (London: Hodder and Stoughton, 1993)

Robbins, R. H., *Secular Lyrics of the XIV and XV Centuries* (Oxford: Clarendon Press, 1952)

Ross, Raymond J., and Joy Hendry (eds), *Sorley MacLean, Critical Essays* (Edinburgh: Scottish Academic Press, 1986)

Ross, Robert H., *The Georgian Revolt 1910–22* (London: Faber & Faber, 1967)

Seabrook, Jeremy, *City Close-Up* (London: Allen Lane, 1971)

Sheavyn, Phoebe, *The Literary Profession in the Elizabethan Age* (Manchester: Manchester University Press, 1967)

Smith, Dai, *Wales! Wales?* (London: Allen and Unwin, 1984)

—— (ed.), *A People and a Proletariat* (London: Pluto Press, 1980)

Smith, David, *North and South* (London: Penguin, 1989)

Stover, Leon, and B. Kraig, *Stonehenge: The Indo-European Heritage* (Chicago: Nelson-Hall, 1978)

Taylor, Peter J., 'The Changing Electoral Geography', in R. J. Johnston and V. Gardiner (eds), *The Changing Geography of the British Isles* (London: Routledge, 1991)

Thomas, Ned, *The Welsh Extremist* (Talybont: Y Lolfa, 1991)

Thompson, F. M. L. (ed.), *The Cambridge Social History of Britain 1750–1950*, I (Cambridge: Cambridge University Press, 1990)

Thomson, George, *Marxism and Poetry* (London: Lawrence and Wishart, 1945)

Thurneysen, Rudolf, *Gesammelte Schriften*, II (Tübingen: Max Niemeyer, 1991)

Tieghem, Paul van, *L'Ere romantique: Le Romantisme dans la littérature européenne* (Paris, 1948)

Tough, D. L. W., *The Last Years of a Frontier: A History of the Borders during the Reign of Elizabeth I* (Alnwick: Sandhill, 1987)

Turner, Graham, *The North Country* (London: Eyre and Spottiswoode, 1967)

Vinson, James (ed.), *Contemporary Poets (The St James Guide)* (London: St James Press, 1975)

Walker, Patrick, *Biographia Presbyteriana*, I (Edinburgh: D. Speare, 1827)

Waller, Gary, *English Poetry in the Sixteenth Century* (London: Longmans, 1993)

White, Lynn, *Mediaeval Technology and Social Change* (Oxford: Clarendon Press, 1964)

Williams, D. J., *Storiau'r tir coch* (Llandysul: Gwasg Aberystwyth, 1941)

Williams, Gwyn A., *When was Wales?* (London: Black Raven, 1985)

Youings, Joyce, *England in the Sixteenth Century* (Harmondsworth: Penguin, 1984)

Index